Markt- und Unternehmensentwicklung
Markets and Organisations

Change of institutions, technology and competition drives the interplay of markets and organisations. The scientific series 'Markets and Organisations' addresses a magnitude of related questions, presents theoretic and empirical findings and discusses related concepts and models.

More information about this series at http://www.springer.com/series/12561

Jens-Henrik Soeldner

Understanding Social Research Networking Sites

With a foreword by Prof. Dr. Kathrin M. Möslein

Springer Gabler

Jens-Henrik Soeldner
Söldner Consult GmbH
Nürnberg, Germany

Dissertation Friedrich-Alexander-Universität Erlangen-Nürnberg (FAU), 2017

Markt- und Unternehmensentwicklung Markets and Organisations
ISBN 978-3-658-31574-0 ISBN 978-3-658-31575-7 (eBook)
https://doi.org/10.1007/978-3-658-31575-7

This Springer Gabler imprint is published by the registered company Springer Fachmedien Wiesbaden GmbH part of Springer Nature.
The registered company address is: Abraham-Lincoln-Str. 46, 65189 Wiesbaden, Germany

Preface

Research collaboration has played an important role in scientific knowledge production for centuries and is a major enabler for generating new insights that form the basis for innovation. While extremely beneficial, research collaboration carried out in a distributed and geographically dispersed setting poses various challenges. In recent years, advances in collaboration technology have produced new modalities that can help mitigate the inherent costs and challenges associated with research collaboration and help make it more successful. In particular, a new class of social software, termed "social research networking sites", has emerged that offers support for the diverse needs of scientists engaged in collaborative research. However, the mere existence of a technology does not necessarily guarantee its broad adoption and successful use, particularly when several competing platforms are available with similar features. Stakeholders face different challenges: current and potential users need an understanding of the usage potential offered by the various platforms in order to realize the potential and profit in the best possible way; providers can use insights into usage expectations and users' motivations to further improve existing offerings or to create new ones.

Jens-Henrik Söldner addresses these challenges by shedding light on how social research networking sites can be leveraged to make research collaboration in its various aspects more successful. This dissertation takes a comprehensive approach and draws on a rich set of theoretical and methodological perspectives. Jens-Henrik Söldner sheds light on the support capabilities of social research networking sites for enabling collaborative research. His work addresses the following aspects:

- properties, benefits, and challenges associated with research collaboration
- technical aspects of social software, usage potential, and issues associated with adoption and use
- features of social research networking sites and their intended use by their providers
- reasons for adoption and use of social research networking sites within the community of management researchers

- recommendations for the future development of social research networking sites

Overall, the author provides rich insight into how research collaboration in the field of management research can be supported by social research networking sites. His findings can be of benefit to researchers as well as practitioners.

This dissertation not only paves the way for further research, but it also offers new inspiration for researchers from the fields of research collaboration as well as social software. It appeals by its comprehensive approach and relevance for research practice, as well as its direct practical usefulness. It has been accepted as a doctoral dissertation in 2017 by the School of Business and Economics at the Friedrich-Alexander-Universität Erlangen-Nürnberg (FAU).

The book is a highly recommended reading for all those who intend to understand the implications of supporting collaborative research with social software. I wish the book the broad dissemination it deserves.

Prof. Dr. Kathrin M. Möslein

Overview of Contents

Table of Contents

List of Figures

List of Tables

List of Abbreviations

AAAS	American Association for the Advancement of Science
AMCIS	American Conference on Information Systems
API	Application Programming Interface
CMC	Computer-Mediated Communication
CSCW	Computer-Supported Cooperative (Collaborative) Work
ECIS	European Conference on Information Systems
ICIS	International Conference on Information Systems
ICT	Information and Communication Technology
NSF	National Science Foundation
S&E	Science and Engineering
SMEB	Social media engagement behavior
SI	Social Influence
SNS	Social Networking Site (also: Social Networking Service)
SRNS	Social Research Network(ing) Site (also: Social Research Network(ing) Service)
STEM	Science, technology, engineering, and mathematics
UGT	Uses and Gratifications Theory

Part I

Introduction:

Supporting Research Collaboration with Social Software

J.-H. Soeldner, *Understanding Social Research Networking Sites*,
Markt- und Unternehmensentwicklung Markets and Organisations,
https://doi.org/10.1007/978-3-658-31575-7_1

1 Motivation and Relevance

Science and research are critical activities in our today's knowledge and information societies for generating new insights and thus innovations – a task generally regarded to be of the highest importance to any society and the economic development of any country (Drucker, 2012; Ven, 1986). Scientific research itself has become an increasingly distributed task – producing scientific results through collaborative research is a growing trend[1], if not the new normal (Wagner, Park, & Leydesdorff, 2015). The "Science & Engineering Indicators 2016" published by the National Science Board state: "S&E research publications are increasingly collaborative as well as increasingly international in authorship."[2]

This claim is supported by the following recent data published by the NSF[3]:

- *"More than 60% of global S&E publications had multiple authors in 2013, compared with less than half of such publications in 2000."*
- *"Internationally coauthored publications correspondingly grew from 13.2% to 19.2% of all co-authored publications over the same period."*
- *"In the United States, 33% of publications were coauthored with institutions in other countries in 2013, compared with 19% in 2000."*

Science has undeniably become a more and more collaborative and team-based endeavor in recent years (Bozeman & Boardman, 2014; Wagner et al., 2015), embedded within a general transformation of academic knowledge production that is taking place (Möslein, 2005). This development is quite logical since combining the diverse expertise of researchers from different disciplines, institutions, and locations to solve scientific problems provides many advantages (Cummings & Kiesler, 2005).

---

[1] http://www.nsf.gov/statistics/infbrief/nsf12325/, retrieved March 20, 2016

[2] http://www.nsf.gov/statistics/2016/nsb20161/uploads/1/nsb20161.pdf, retrieved March 20, 2016

[3] http://www.nsf.gov/statistics/2016/nsb20161/uploads/1/nsb20161.pdf, retrieved March 20, 2016

On the other hand, setting up research collaborations[4] and carrying out collaborative research also poses many challenges that make effective collaborations difficult to implement. These challenges include deciding how to divide labor between researchers, monitoring and coordinating progress in a potentially distributed and virtual team, dealing with communication issues due to different cultures and languages, and controlling information flow (Walsh & Maloney, 2007). These constitute just a few examples of collaboration, coordination, and communication issues that can arise within collaborative research. If these issues are not controlled sensibly, serious complications in these projects are to be expected that may even threaten the success of these collaborations (Cummings & Kiesler, 2007; Cummings & Kiesler, 2005; Walsh & Maloney, 2007).

Technology that supports communication and collaboration is the natural ally to mitigate the negative effects of distance and non-colocation since advances in these technologies created new opportunities for working together in new ways (Cummings & Kiesler, 2007). Even technologies nowadays considered to be rather basic like email, have been shown to enable and simplify scientific collaboration (Walsh & Maloney, 2007). However, ten years ago from now, technology was not considered good enough yet to support coordinative activities (Cummings & Kiesler, 2007) – not surprisingly, since email is notoriously bad for coordination due to its low media richness and synchronicity (Dennis, Fuller, & Valacich, 2008; Möslein, 1999).

In recent years, collaborative technologies have been further improved, are vastly more capable than email or early CSCW (computer-supported cooperative work) systems and now enable global firms to dynamically organize ad-hoc workgroups with great flexibility leveraging new web-enabled functionality (Munkvold & Zigurs, 2005; Howe, 2006; Turban et al., 2011; Arinze, 2012). The latest evolutionary stage of information and communication tools (ICTs) that support communication, collaboration, and co-creation is called "social software" and encompasses tools like

[4] This thesis is concerned with collaboration in science, which also includes collaboration in the social sciences. In the humanities, collaboration between scholars is a less common phenomenon (Katz & Martin, 1997), so they do not constitute a focal area in the understanding of research collaboration in this thesis

blogs, wikis, and social network sites (van Osch & Steinfield, 2013). Studies of social media use in an organizational context propose that these technologies can improve boundary-spanning activities by allowing and facilitating the identification of and communication and collaboration with external individuals and information (Möslein, 1999). In a business context, these tools are already extensively used and their positive impact on business outcomes is generally widely accepted:

> *"Social software delivers virtual environments in which people can discuss topics and share information. They can interact individually or in groups, teams, communities, and networks. This interaction can be in the context of structured or unstructured business activities. Social software can help users to complete work, handle exceptions, and make decisions. It can even augment physical environments. But organizations will derive optimum value from social software only if IT leaders select the appropriate software for their use case." (Mann, Drakos, & Gotta, 2014, p. 10)*

Figure 1: Gartner's Magic Quadrant for Social Software in the Workplace (as of 2015)

In a business context, selecting the right kind of social software for a given use case is being facilitated by a considerable amount of academic literature (e.g. Richter &

Riemer, 2013) and business consultancy studies like Gartner's (Gotta, Drakos, & Mann, 2015) magic quadrant for social software in the workplace (see figure 1).

For an academic user base, such tools also do exist. In an early categorization of the field, Möslein et al. (2009) identified 24 collaborative social networking services. A tabular depiction of this categorization can be found in figure 2.

Network / Criteria	2collab.com	academia.edu	academici.com	biomedexperts.com	centraldesktop.com	collabrx.com	epws.org	escidoc.org	globaledge.msu.edu	labmeeting.com	laboratree.org	lalisio.com	lumifi.com	mendeley.com	mynetresearch.com	network.nature.com	pingtsta.com	researchgate.net	saba.com	scholarz.net	scilife.net	scispace.net	ssrn.com	thoughtleaders.within3.co
Identity and Network																								
Personal Profile	x	x	x	x	x		x		x	x	x	x	x	x	x	x		x	x	x	x	x	x	
Directory of Profiles	x	x	x	x			x			x	x	x	x	x	x	x		x		x	x			
Search for Profiles	x	x	x	x			x			x	x	x	x	x	x	x		x		x	x			
Interaction and Communication																								
Messages		x	x	x			x		x	x	x	x	x	x	x	x		x		x	x			
Instant Mess. Service						x														x				
Information and Content																								
Wiki			x				x	x							x							x		
Group Editor			x		x															x				
Social Tagging	x		x												x			x			x			
Social Rating																	x	x			x			
Data Upload	x	x	x	x	x		x		x	x	x	x	x	x	x			x	x	x	x	x		
Paper Upload	x	x	x	x			x		x	x	x	x	x	x	x			x	x	x	x	x	x	
Commenting	x		x				x			x			x					x	x	x		x	x	
Topical Focus																								
Generic	x	x	x		x		x	x	x	x	x	x	x	x	x	x		x	x	x	x	x	x	
Specific				x		x											x							x
Degree of Openness																								
Free	x	x	x	x	x		x		x	x	x	x	x	x	x	x		x		x	x	x	x	
Commercial			x		x										x		x							
Open for everyone	x	x	x		x		x		x		x	x	x	x	x	x		x	x	x	x	x	x	
By invitation only				x		x											x					x		x

Figure 2: Categorization of collaborative social networking services (Möslein et al., 2009)

Building on the definition of generic social network sites, such services have been termed *"social research network sites"* (SRNS)[5] and defined as:

"Social research network sites (SRNS) are a web-based service that allows individual researchers to 1) construct a public or semi-public profile within a bounded system (identity), 2) articulate a list of researchers with whom they share a connection and communicate (communication), 3) share information with other researchers within the system (information) and 4) collaborate with other researchers within the system (collaboration)" (Bullinger et al., 2010, p. 3)

Most of these social networking services that were identified at an early stage of their initial emergence by Möslein et al. (2009) are now defunct; three of them, however, have become quite successful and have been able to attract substantial venture capital funding and a user base ranging in the millions, and at least one additional platform has emerged since then. The emergence of additional platforms also leads to increasing confusion in the user base – while existing platforms are still under development, others have been discontinued due to lack of market traction and success and additional platforms have emerged for competition, thus leading to confusion among researchers which platforms to use (He & Jeng, 2016).

Hence, in an academic context, matters are less straightforward than in the corporate world of business organizations. There are a couple of practical and research challenges regarding research collaboration and social software:

1. Computer-supported collaboration is a relatively recent phenomenon in academia (Arinze, 2012) and usage of collaboration tools is not so widespread yet or has been limited to the use of basic collaboration and communication technologies like email (Vasileiadou & Vliegenthart, 2009) with disputed impact on collaboration productivity (Ynalvez & Shrum, 2011).

[5] Social networking sites are often referred to as social networking services – both terms can be used interchangeably. They are also often abbreviated to SNS and are sometimes called more generically 'social media'

2. Even if scholars, e.g. from the Information Systems (IS) field, have studied the impact of these tools in an organizational context, the same scholars have missed out looking at how these technologies may benefit their own practices of doing research, review, and teaching (Kane & Fichman, 2009)
3. Despite a vast literature base on *research collaboration* stretching for more than 30 years and a young, but steadily growing literature base on *social software*, systematic reviews regarding either phenomenon are scarce and practically non-existent regarding *social software for supporting collaborative research*
4. Although early definitions on "*social research network sites*" exist, many academics as potential users of these sites are not aware of the existence of newer, more specialized tools that directly support and enable academic collaboration (Bullinger et al., 2010; Möslein et al., 2009), and little is known about these tools, which use cases they are suitable for, and the motivation of their providers (Renken et al., 2010).

The thesis at hand thus aims to investigate how collaborative research, an important and critical endeavor, can profit from the use of social software. The next two sections will illustrate the research questions leading the inquiry of this thesis as well as the structure of the thesis.

2 The Research Questions of the Thesis

The research context of this thesis is the intersection of *research collaboration* and *social software,* dealing more specifically with the phenomenon of how research collaboration can be supported by recent technological advancements, generally termed social software. It aims to contribute to existing research in these two fields of research collaboration and social software, by answering the following research questions as outlined in table 1:

Table 1: The research questions of this thesis

RQ I:	What is the current state-of-the-literature regarding collaborative research and social software? Are these fields interlinked? What are the research gaps and directions for future research?
RQ II:	What is the current state of technology regarding social software tools specifically relevant to an academic audience? What is their intended use by their providers and can they further be classified according to their functionalities and intended use?
RQ III:	How and why do management researchers use social research networking services?

Answering these research questions is accomplished along a consecutive research process. Every part (apart from part I, the introduction, and part V, the discussion and conclusion) of the thesis represents one step in the research process. Therefore, every part starts off by stating the relevance, purpose, and structure of the respective part, and ends with a brief summary. The overall structure and detailed information on each part are provided in the subsequent section.

3 Structure of this Thesis

This thesis is divided into five parts reflecting the overarching research process that took place in the pursuit of the research goals. Each part constitutes a research step necessary to answer the previously outlined research questions. All parts are laid out in chapters that represent thematic units. To provide further structure, each chapter itself includes sections as well as sub-sections.

Part I is the introduction, which sets the stage for this thesis. This is followed by parts II, III, and IV, which have a modular structure and consist of a systematic literature review and two empirical studies. These parts are mostly self-contained, focus on specific research questions, and can thus be read independently of one another. Part V concludes this thesis by providing a summary of contributions. In addition, it provides implications for practice and research, as well as directions for further research based on the results of parts II, III, and IV. Below, an overview of each of the five parts and how they build upon each other is given. An overview of the thesis is presented in *figure 3*.

Part I – Introduction

This part starts by explaining the rationale and relevance of this dissertation topic. Then the crucial importance of research collaboration for solving scientific problems in today's world is highlighted. In addition, the potential of social software and social networking services as the state-of-the-art technology suitable for supporting scholars engaged in research collaboration is emphasized. The research questions underlying this thesis are presented next. Finally, an overview of the structure of this thesis is provided.

Part II – Systematic Literature Review: Research Collaboration and Social Software

A systematic literature review was essential because the substantial body of literature addressing different aspects of research collaboration is scattered and is split into many different strands due to the complexity and multi-layered nature of the phenomenon. In addition, the literature base on social software was evolving very quickly in recent years due to the newness and importance of the technology, at the same time creating difficulties for researchers striving to get a comprehensive and holistic overview of this emerging topic. Consequently, this part provides a state-of-the-art report on both research collaboration and social software by first systematically identifying and then analyzing 603 publications in the combined field dating from 2000 to 2016. In the process, research from different strands is brought together, analyzed, and classified into four broad categories in the area of research collaboration and into seven areas in the field of social software. Research in each of these categories is summarized and research gaps are identified. This part also provides a discussion and reflects on the findings with respect to the pervasiveness of literature in the field and the research methods used. It concludes by identifying that there is a lack of understanding of how social software applications can contribute to successful collaborative research projects by supporting researchers. It also finds that social networking services, a subclass of social software, are particularly suited to support researchers.

Part III – Empirical study 1: Social Research Networking Sites – Market Overview, Features, and Intended Use

Building on the findings from the literature review that social software and social networking services are particularly suitable to initiate, support, and extend indirect and direct interpersonal interaction and thus enable collaboration, this part aims to establish a deeper understanding of social networking services. To achieve this goal, first, 24 social networking services are identified that address a professional or an academic audience, are open to a broad public, and either represent target audiences from different disciplinary fields or are independent of a particular discipline. Second, using a three-step analysis, the initial sample of 24 social networking services are categorized by their functionalities into five main areas, extending previous categorizations from literature by two additional areas.

As a result, eight social networking services (with six stemming from the initial sample of 24 professional social networking services) were selected for a closer analysis of features and functionalities, since they were purpose-built to support researchers in collaborative settings and other research-related activities. All these eight social networking services for researchers (including the three that have gained significant penetration in the market) are then analyzed within case studies including interviews with their founders and are described in detail. The result of this study is a feature- and affordances-based classification of social networking services that are available in the market and are built for researchers as their intended audience. In addition, a typology of SRNS platforms is derived. This finding can help individual researchers and research organizations to get an overview of what tools are currently available and pick the right tool for their purposes. The study concludes that in order to gain a more holistic understanding of this new class of social software-based tools, actual usage patterns of scholars using these platforms need to be investigated in order to understand how and why do scholars use these services. In the following part, this question is addressed.

I.	**Introduction**
▪	Defines research collaboration
▪	States the relevance of research collaboration to solve today's scientific problems
▪	Highlights the potential of social software to support research collaboration
▪	Presents the research questions underlying this thesis
▪	Provides the structure of the thesis

II.	**Systematic Literature Review: Research Collaboration and Social Software**
▪	Identifies, analyzes and consolidates 603 publications into four categories (for research collaboration) and seven categories respectively (for social software)
▪	Concludes that social software constitutes a suitable technical basis to support researchers in various research-related tasks
▪	Identifies research gaps and directions for future research

III. Empirical Study 1: Social Research Networking Sites - Market Overview, Features, and Intended Use

- Establishes a deeper understanding of social networking services
- Identifies 24 social networking services relevant to a professional or academic audience
- Provides an in-depth analysis of eight social research network services purpose-built to support researchers
- Develops a feature-based classification of social networking services built for researchers and derives a typology of SRNS platforms
- Concludes that actual usage patterns of researchers need to be investigated to understand how and why scholars use these platforms to gain a more holistic understanding of the phenomenon

IV. Empirical Study 2: How and Why Do Management Researchers Use Social Research Networking Sites

- Explores the actual use of social research networking services with a sample of scholars stemming from one academic field by conducting 19 case studies with management researchers
- Investigates the underlying reasons why management researchers use social research networking services drawing on two theoretical frameworks
- Uncovers significant differences in the use of the different platforms depending on the gratifications that can be derived from the use

V. Discussion and Conclusion

- Presents a summary of research conducted
- Describes implications for practice
- Provides directions for future research

Figure 3: Structure of the thesis

Part IV – Empirical Study 2: How and Why Do Management Researchers Use Social Research Networking Sites?

This part counterbalances the findings from part III that were dominated by the perspective of the platform providers. To gain a more holistic view of the phenomenon at hand, the user side is explored by conducting 19 case studies with experienced users of social research networking sites stemming from the field of management research. Motivated by the question 'how and why do management researchers use social research networking site', the case studies encompassing in-depth interviews are analyzed drawing on two well-established theoretical frameworks. The study reveals significant differences in the use of the individual platforms and also helps to explain these differences drawing on the theory. The findings help both the providers of these platforms and their customers (individual researchers and research organizations). Providers can leverage the findings to further sharpen and improve their offerings by better understanding the actual use of their tools and the gratifications that the users derive from the use. In addition, the findings can also help individual researchers and research organizations pick the right tools by better understanding the underlying gratifications that in the end play a crucial role in the adoption and continued use of the tools.

Part V – Discussion and Conclusion

This part concludes this dissertation by providing a summary of contributions. In addition, it provides a comprehensive discussion of the implications for practice and theory as well as directions for future research based on the results of the extensive systematic literature review and the two empirical studies presented in the preceding parts.

Part II

Systematic Literature Review:

Research Collaboration and Social Software

J.-H. Soeldner, *Understanding Social Research Networking Sites*,
Markt- und Unternehmensentwicklung Markets and Organisations,
https://doi.org/10.1007/978-3-658-31575-7_2

1 Research Collaboration: The Need for Technological Support by Social Software[6]

Research collaboration between individuals, institutions, and nations has become a more and more common phenomenon in recent years and is regarded as a major driver for generating scientific insights that form the basis for innovation (Van Rijnsoever & Hessels, 2011; Bercovitz & Feldman, 2011; Heinze et al, 2009). While extremely beneficial, the collaboration part of research collaboration and its distributed and geographically dispersed nature poses various challenges (Walsh & Maloney, 2007), which internet-based means of communication like social software and social networking services have the potential to reduce in part (Vasileiadou & Vliegenthart, 2009; Hoekman et al., 2010).

This chapter first looks at the attributes, benefits, and challenges of research collaboration in detail. Second, it identifies the need for technological support of research collaboration that can help mitigate some of the challenges associated with collaborative and distributed research. Third, it explains why a systematic review of the field is a necessity and constitutes an important contribution. Finally, the aims of this systematic literature review and the research approach and steps used to achieve them are described.

1.1 Attributes, Benefits, and Challenges of Research Collaboration

There is a broad consensus in the scientific world that seminal insights today are typically generated in collaborative research projects (Heinze & Kuhlmann, 2008; Adams et al., 2005; Haeussler & Sauermann, 2013). Among the many drivers and factors that have turned scientific production into a highly social and collaborative

---

[6] This literature review is a vastly expanded version of a previous publication that was presented at the EURAM Annual Conference 2010 in Rome (see Söldner, Bullinger, & Möslein, 2010). Although that publication was co-authored, the research design, the data collection, the analysis of data, and the interpretation of the results are primarily attributable to Jens-Henrik Söldner

activity (Haeussler & Sauermann, 2013) are large resource requirements, the interdisciplinary nature of many research projects, and the increasing specializations of scholars (Katz & Martin, 1997; Laudel, 2002).

1.1.1 Attributes of research collaboration

Research collaboration constitutes a phenomenon that has been systematically studied for many decades. Early studies investigating research collaboration date back to the 1950s and 1960s (e.g. Bush & Hattery, 1956; Smith, 1958; Clarke, 1967; de Solla Price, 1963). Comprehensive papers that provide a broad overview of scientific collaboration have been published by only a handful of authors (e.g. Sonnenwald, 2007; Katz & Martin, 1997; Beaver & Rosen, 1978; Beaver & Rosen, 1979a; Beaver & Rosen, 1979b). Since previous studies of research collaboration have analyzed the phenomenon from a wide variety of different lenses and in very different contexts, a universally agreed-upon definition of the term *'research collaboration'* does not exist (Wray, 2006; Hu & Racherla, 2008). Trying to define research collaboration is thus normally based on the underlying understanding of the term *'collaboration'*, by which a native speaker of English usually understands several individuals, institutions, or even nations working together with a common goal; which is different from cooperation, in which several partners work together with goals of their own. A visualization of cooperation, coordination, and collaboration can be found in figure 4. Table 2 summarizes different definitions of generic collaboration, as found in the literature.

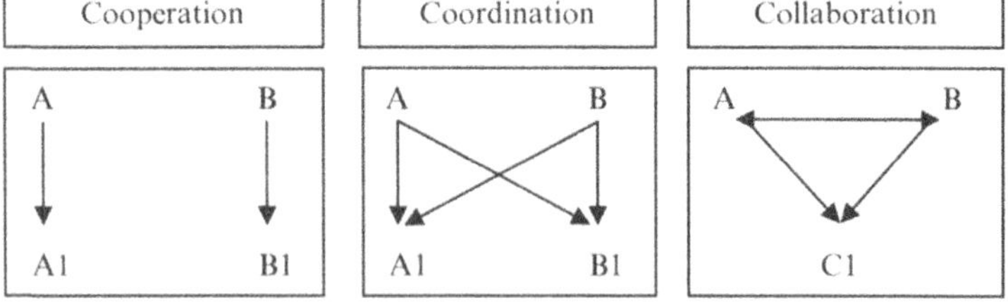

Figure 4: Comparison of outcomes of cooperation, coordination, and collaboration (based on Rogers & Whetten, 1982)

Table 2: Definitions of generic collaboration

Source	**Definition of "collaboration"**
Amabile et al. (2001), p. 419	"individuals who differ in notable ways sharing information and working toward a particular purpose"
Jassawalla and Sashittal (1998), p. 239	"the coming together of different interests and people to achieve a common purpose via interactions, information sharing, and coordination of activities"
Melin and Persson (1996), p. 363	"Collaboration is an intense form of interaction, that allows for effective communication as well as the sharing of competence and other resources."
Sonnenwald (2007), p. 645	"Scientific collaboration can be defined as interaction taking place within a social context among two or more scientists that facilitates the sharing of meaning and completion of tasks with respect to a mutually shared, superordinate goal."
Mattesisch and Monsey (1992), p. 39	"a mutually beneficial relationship entered into by two or more parties to achieve common goals"
Schrage (1995), p. 58	"process of shared creation"

Research collaboration constitutes a more specialized variant of collaboration with the goal of doing (scientific) research[7] together and thus exhibits a number of additional properties. Scientific research is a dynamic process that typically deals with complex questions. The scientists engaged in collaborative research are usually highly specialized in their respective fields (Hara et al., 2003). Research collaboration can take a number of forms, but it usually refers to scholars engaging in collaborative scientific activities, that potentially lead to publications, but do not necessarily have to. Hence, the literature on academic collaboration reflects a wide range of definitions of what research collaboration constitutes. Rhoten and Pfirman (2007, p. 71) describe the phenomenon as follows:

"collaborat[ing] in teams or networks that seek to exchange and/or create new tools, concepts data, methods, or results".

Other authors like Fox and Mohapatra (2007, p. 545) draw a distinction between teamwork and collaboration based on the rank and academic status of those working together:

---

[7] The term 'research collaboration' is normally understood to refer to *scientific* research (Amabile et al., 2001; Katz and Martin, 1997)

"collaboration tends to involve (and refer to) cooperation between scientists who have faculty (or professional) status, whereas teamwork involves (and refers to) cooperation of scientists with students, technicians, and others of both equal and unequal rank".

Other scholars emphasize the importance of the concept of co-authorship (of scientific publications) as a crucial, constituting element of research collaboration (e.g. McDowell et al., 2006). This variety of ambiguous definitions of what really constitutes research collaboration can create problems when trying to actually measure collaboration, because of a lack of an unambiguous, universally accepted definition of research collaboration (Smykla & Zippel, 2010). Apart from challenges in quantitatively studying research collaboration resulting from these disparate definitions (Smykla & Zippel, 2010), research collaboration in its many different forms is unequivocally considered a topic of growing interest and importance.

1.1.2 Motives for and benefits of research collaboration

Apart from being a practical necessity for many researchers, research collaboration is also supposed to exhibit many beneficial effects like having access to a larger array of intellectual resources and expertise through one's network of collaborators. Maintaining a network of (international) collaborators can help enhance productivity and bring improved access to funding (Bozeman & Corley, 2004; Smykla & Zippel, 2010). Other studies point to a strong correlation between collaboration and productivity, both in co-located collaborators and geographically dispersed collaborators, with the correlation being stronger for non-colocated collaborators, i.e. geographically diffused research collaborations (Fox & Mohapatra, 2007). According to Bozeman and Corley (2004), engaging in research collaboration can bring benefits for acquiring tacit knowledge and essential skills, helpful for building a successful career as a researcher (Smykla & Zippel, 2010). Bozeman and Corley (2004, p. 612) sum it up as follows:

"collaboration often has salutary effects with respect to socialization, training, transmission of know-how and just as important, the ability to develop the network ties and contacts so critical to scientists' and engineers' career success"

A summary of the benefits and motives of researchers to engage in collaborative research is listed in table 3.

Table 3: Benefits of and motives for research collaboration

Benefits and motives for research collaboration	Studies
Higher productivity	Beaver, 2001; Lee and Bozeman, 2005; Sooryamoorthy and Shrum, 2007
Improved quality of scientific results	Rigby and Edler, 2005
Access to expertise	Beaver, 2001; Katz and Martin, 1997; Melin, 2000
Access to resources and equipment	Heinze and Kuhlmann, 2008; Sonnenwald, 2007; Melin, 2000; Beaver, 2001
Exchange of ideas (also between scientific disciplines)	Beaver and Rosen 1978, 1979a, 1979b; Katz and Martin, 1997; Melin, 2000; Heinze and Kuhlmann, 2008
Combining and pooling expertise for solving complex problems	Sonnenwald, 2007; Birnholtz, 2007; Beaver, 2001
Keeping one's own activities focused	Heinze and Kuhlmann, 2008
Acquiring new skills	Wagner et al., 2001; Heinze and Kuhlmann, 2008
Improved access to funding	Heinze and Kuhlmann, 2008; Beaver, 2001
Enhanced prestige and reputation	Van Rijnsoever et al., 2008; Beaver and Rosen, 1978, 1979a, 1979b; Katz and Martin, 1997
Political factors	Sonnenwald, 2007
Personal factors	Sonnenwald, 2007
Fun and pleasure	Katz and Martin, 1997; Melin, 2000; Beaver 2001
Mentoring graduate students	Bozeman and Corley, 2004; Beaver, 2001; Beaver and Rosen, 1978, 1979a, 1979b, Melin, 2000
Improved scientific specialization	Sonnenwald, 2007; Melin, 2000

1.1.3 Challenges associated with Research Collaboration

Collaborative research not only creates positive effects, there are also scholars that point out challenges and even adverse effects that can result out of scientific collaboration. Wray (2006) argues that collaborative research can have a negative impact on the motivations of the researchers involved, due to the risk of unfair distribution of scientific credit, the main reward and currency for academic researchers (Heinze & Kuhlmann, 2008) and subsequent tensions and trust issues arising out of that fact (Wray, 2006; Bukvova, 2010). In addition, co-authored publications resulting from collaborative research can result in reduced accountability and potentially to a lowering of the quality of research results (Wray, 2006). While Wray (2006) concludingly states that collaborative research overall benefits science, he brings up a number of valid points that he argues need to be addressed by restructuring and overhauling the scientific reward system as a whole, which has been designed with the single author in mind.

In addition to more general challenges associated with research collaboration that arise out of the current scientific system as a whole, carrying out and performing collaborative research also suffers from more operational challenges and issues due to its distributed and often interdisciplinary nature. According to Walsh and Maloney (2007), these problems can mainly be clustered into two types – (1) problems related to the coordination of collaborative projects and misunderstandings within these projects and (2) challenges associated with culture and (lack of) information security[8]. After an elaborate discussion of these and additional challenges, the authors also point to an area that can help solve some of these challenges involved: collaboration technology (Walsh & Maloney, 2007). At the time of writing of the paper by Walsh and Maloney (2007), collaboration technologies experienced a rapid evolution due to the advent of a class of technologies referred to as Web 2.0 and social software.

1.2 The Need for Technological Support for Research Collaboration

In order to solve the operational challenges associated with activities of coordination, communication, and collaboration to make collaborative research successful, researchers have emphasized that coordination activities are critical to integrating and utilizing expertise coming from non-colocated research collaborators (Cummings & Kiesler, 2007). In addition, they point out that recent advances in collaboration technology can help mitigate the inherent costs and challenges associated with research collaboration and the activities necessary to make it successful (Cummings & Kiesler, 2007; Walsh & Maloney, 2007). The National Science Foundation sums up the challenges of research collaboration and requirements for (technological) support as follows:

---

[8] For a full discussion of these and additional challenges, cf. Walsh and Maloney (2007)

"The very nature of the S&E enterprise is global, often requiring access to geographically dispersed materials, phenomena, and expertise, as well as collaborative logistical support. It also requires open and timely communication, sharing, and validation of findings, data, and data analysis procedures. Projects in areas such as global change, genomics, astronomy, space exploration, and high-energy physics have a global reach and often require expertise and resources that no single country possesses."[9]

The requirements of open and timely communication and sharing of information find their technological counterpart in the affordances[10] of 'social software', a class of new applications perceived to be a successor of computer-supported collaborative work (CSCW) tools (De Wever et al., 2007). Table 3 lists commonly accepted definitions of social software.

Table 4: Selected definitions of social software

Source	Definition of 'social software'
Green and Pearson (2005, p. 1)	"Social software refers to various, loosely connected types of applications that allow individuals to communicate with one another, and to track discussions across the Web as they happen"
Koch and Richter (2009)	Social software refers to applications that support human interaction and are leveraging Web 2.0 technologies in the pursuit of that aim
Drakos & Sussin (2015, p. 3)	"Social software supports physical and virtual environments in which people can find out about each other, have discussions, share information, and generally interact. Interaction occurs at a one-to-one level, or in groups, teams, communities, and networks, and in the context of structured or unstructured business activities. Social software can be used in very purposeful ways to get work done, to handle exceptions, and even to augment physical environments. Business use of social software can improve communication, influence behavior, and extract insights about relationships and specific activities around which social interaction occurs."

Social software as the current successor to CSCW tools thus promises substantial potential to help to reduce the strain and costs of activities of collaboration,

[9] http://www.nsf.gov/nsb/documents/2003/chapter2.htm, retrieved May 12, 2017

[10] The concept of affordances was first introduced by Gibson (1977) as a way to understand what an object can afford, i.e., "what the object is good for."

coordination, and communication, which are so vital to make research collaboration successful (Walsh & Maloney, 2007).

1.3 Why is a Literature Review on Research Collaboration and Social Software needed?

Given the constantly increasing importance of collaborative research over the last few decades, there has been considerable interest from scholars in the phenomenon '*research collaboration*'. However, these scholars come from widely differing disciplines like information systems, management science, sociology, research policy, and philosophy (Sonnenwald, 2007). Not surprisingly, specialized disciplinary communities have formed that study research collaboration in its various aspects and these researchers use different terms and concepts to characterize scientific collaboration and publish in diverse scientific outlets (Sonnenwald, 2007). This has led to many independent research strands, almost comparable to silos and islands, with little interconnections between them.

The potential of social software to help mitigate challenges associated with operational aspects of research collaboration has been noted in some of the more practice-oriented publications in that field (e.g. Walsh and Maloney, 2007). Social software itself is a fairly recent phenomenon that is also being investigated by scholars with different disciplinary perspectives; in addition, little systematic research has been done so far.

This comprehensive, systematic literature review is thus required to paint an overall picture of the fields *research collaboration* and *social software*.

1.4 Goals and Approach

The main goals of this literature review are as follows:

1. To provide a state-of-the-art report on research collaboration and social software including a brief set of current definitions of key concepts
2. To propose a first categorization of these two fields that is derived from the

identified literature and the key concepts underlying the various strands of the literature

3. To pinpoint research gaps and provide directions for potentially valuable future research

In the pursuit of these objectives, this systematic literature review first identifies and analyzes 92 publications in the field of research collaboration and 511 papers in the field of social software. Second, it provides a clustering of the identified papers into four broad categories (for research collaboration) and seven categories (for social software). Lastly, the review discusses the findings with respect to the extensive literature in the two fields, the research method used, and the potential areas for future research.

2 Research Strategy and Analysis

This chapter describes and explains the research strategy that was used to identify the scientific publications that deal with the phenomena '*research collaboration*' and '*social software*'. First, the overall approach of the review is described. Next, details regarding the source selection are elucidated. Then it provides an overview of the analysis process of the review. Finally, occurrences of publications are described by outlet and per year for both phenomena. A summarizing illustration of the overall process including the research strategy and the analysis is depicted in Figure 5.

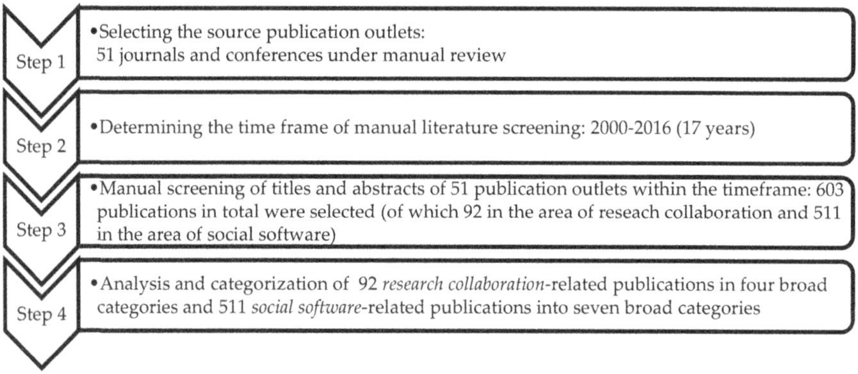

Figure 5: Summary of the research process underlying the systematic literature review

2.1 Review Steps

A methodological examination and analysis of extant literature constitute a crucial step in any academic research project (Levy & Ellis, 2006). In the social sciences, systematic literature reviews can be considered a relatively recent phenomenon (Velamuri, 2013), as traditional narrative reviews were dominating until recently. According to Webster and Watson (2002), a concept-centric approach is more suited to providing an effective and high-quality literature review instead of a chronological or author-centric approach. This approach helps researchers provide well-founded arguments to underline the need for their study and to identify where the literature fits into their own study, in addition to providing further legitimization of research questions and to validating the approach of one's own study (Levy & Ellis, 2006).

Hence, this review follows the concept-centric approach proposed by Webster and Watson (2002) and as a systematic literature review, a clear review protocol is being adhered to and the methods of publication selection and evaluation are stated clearly (Tranfield et al., 2003; Pittaway et al., 2004; Möslein, 2005; Velamuri, 2013).

The concepts or keywords that were used as a filter in surveying the titles and abstracts included search terms derived from the combination "*qualifier + main focus area + additional qualifier*", where qualifier equals *social, online, team, electronic or e-, cyber, collaborative* and *main focus area* equals *research, science, scientific, scholarship, academic,* and additional qualifier equals *collaboration, CSCW, network, networking service, networking site, software, Web 2.0* (and related concepts and technologies like *wikis, blogs, etc.*), *process, structure,* and *support system.*

The literature search was performed *manually* by (a) surveying the titles and (b) subsequent analysis of the abstracts and keywords if the titles looked relevant and promising. Thus, a much more comprehensive was performed than would have been possible by a simple keyword-based automated search. By contrast, a stand-alone keyword search would tend to return far more results with many irrelevant items. The identification of relevant articles followed a three-stage literature selection process: First, the *sources* to be considered in the review were selected (stage 1), then the scope was narrowed down by *temporal* considerations (stage 2), considering scientific publications from 2000 to 2016, a 17-year- period. During step 3, a *manual search* within the relevant set of journals within the timeframe was performed (Webster & Watson, 2002).

2.2 Source Selection

The selection of the sources for this literature review was carried out based on three widely respected rankings:

(1) VHB-Jourqual (version 2)[11]
(2) WKWI ranking ("Wissenschaftliche Kommission Wirtschaftsinformatik")[12], and
(3) AIS ranking ("Association for Information Systems")[13].

Journals and conferences were selected based on the following criteria:

All IS journals that were ranked from A+ to C in the VHB Jourqual list (n_{VHB}=54), all A-rated journals and conferences from "Wissenschaftliche Kommission Wirtschaftsinformatik (WKWI)" (n_{WKWI}=26) and the top 30 rated journals from the AIS ranking (n_{AIS}=30). This led to a total of n_{START}=110 journals and conferences, from which 55 duplicates were removed and 13 journals were excluded that mainly focus on purely technological research issues or were irrelevant due to a specific focus like database design or operations research. In total, n_{IS}=42 relevant publications channels (with n_{ISJ}=39 journals and n_{ISC}=3 conferences) were selected for review.

In addition, five journals from the VHB Jourqual rankings in the areas of *general management, university management, and technology and innovation management* were included since the topic of research collaboration touches academic fields outside of IS, and IS constitutes an interdisciplinary field that touches other disciplines. Furthermore, the proceedings of four additional conferences (Americas Conference on Information Systems, European Conference on Computer-Supported Cooperative Work, ACM CSCW Conference, ACM CHI Conference) were added, since papers dealing with social software and research collaboration were recently published in these conferences, leading to a n_{REVIEW}=51 journals and conferences.

---

[11] http://vhbonline.org/vhb4you/jourqual/vhb-jourqual-archiv/jq2/, retrieved July 3, 2016

[12] http://wi.vhbonline.org/zeitschriftenrankings/, links to the following page where the ranking can be retrieved: http://www.kaifischbach.net/wkwi/orientierungslisten.pdf, retrieved July 3, 2016

[13] https://aisnet.org/?JournalRankings, retrieved July 3, 2016

The large sample has been chosen to include research that is not restricted to specific research methodologies, geographic regions, or restricted types of publications. The final set of publication outlets considered for this systematic literature review is listed in table 5.

Table 5: Journals and conferences integrated into the literature review

Journals identified via VHBjourqual, WKWI and AIS rankings (n_{ISJ}=39)**:** Academy of Management Journal, ACM Computing Surveys, ACM Transactions on Computer Human Interaction, ACM Transactions on Information Systems, Communications of the AIS, Communications of the Association for Computer Machinery, Computer Supported Cooperative Work, Data Base for Advances in Information Systems, Decision Sciences, Decision Support Systems, Electronic Markets, European Journal of Information Systems, Harvard Business Review, Human Computer Interaction, IEEE Software, IEEE Transactions on Engineering Management, Information and Management, Information and Management, Information and Organization, Information Systems Frontiers, Information Systems Journal, Information Systems Research, Informing Science Journal, International Journal of Electronic Commerce, International Journal of Information Management, Journal of Computer-mediated Communication, Journal of Information Technology, Journal of Management Information Systems, Journal of Management Systems, Journal of the AIS, Journal of the ACM, Journal of the Association of Information Systems (JAIS), Management Science, MIS Quarterly, Omega – the International Journal of Management Science, Organization Science, Sloan Management Review, Journal of Strategic Information Systems, Wirtschaftsinformatik
Additional journals (n_{ADDJ}= 5)**:** Academy of Management Review, Administrative Science Quarterly, Management Learning, Management Science, Research Policy
Conferences identified via VHBjourqual, WKWI, and AIS (n_{CONF}=3)**:** European Conference of Information Systems, Int. Conference of Informations Systems, Proceedings of the International Conference on Wirtschaftsinformatik (sic![14])
Additional conference (n_{ADDC}= 4): Americas Conference of Information Systems, European Conference on Computer-Supported Cooperative Work, ACM CSCW Conference, ACM CHI Conference

[14] http://wi2017.ch/en/home, retrieved July 3, 2016

2.3 Analysis of Publications

The literature search as described in the previous chapters resulted in n_{total}=603 publications dealing with the concepts identified by the combination of the keywords, of which n_{collab}=92 are primarily associated with the area of research collaboration, and n_{soso}=511 have their focus in the area of social software. Since a completely manual screening of all publication outlets instead of an automated keyword search via databases was performed, only relevant contributions were taken into account.

All identified articles were each read and extensively reviewed to determine the following information (if applicable): perspectives used in the article, details regarding the sample studied, what methodology and statistical techniques were employed, variables or constructs studied, research questions or hypotheses, tasks involved in the experiment, relevant findings, research gaps and areas for future research.

2.4 Occurrences

The literature review that covered the timeframe from 2000 to 2016 (a 17-year period) resulted in 92 relevant contributions for research collaboration and 511 adequate articles for social software. The distribution of the identified publications in these two areas could not be any more different: while research collaboration-related publications are almost exclusively found in journals, testifying to the maturity of the research subject, the share of journal publications covering the relatively recent phenomenon of social software was very low in the years 2006-2008 and has been on the rise since then, with conference articles still dominating over journal publications. While the total number of publications in social software has peaked in 2013, there seems to be a decline in publications in 2014-2016, possibly indicating that other topics are more fashionable since then. Since the literature review was finally updated in mid-2016, the publication numbers for 2016 reflect an inaccurate picture. Figure 6 depicts the distribution of literature findings for social software by publication type and year with contributions starting to show up in 2006, figure 7 shows the same distribution for research collaboration.

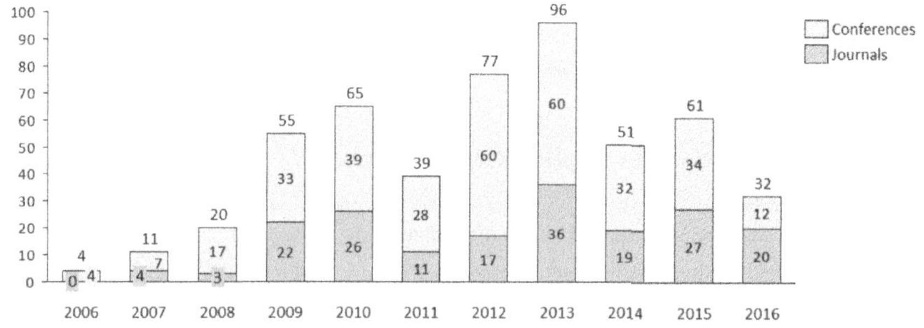

Figure 6: Literature findings for social software by publication type and year

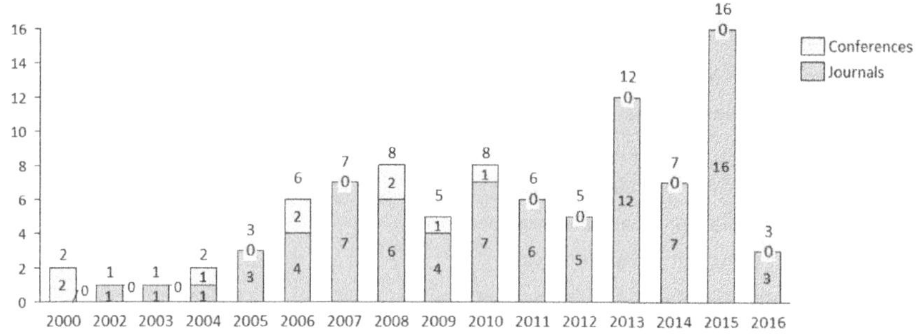

Figure 7: Literature findings for research collaboration by publication type and year

Tables 6 and 7 list the occurrences of publications by outlet for social software and research collaboration.

Table 6: Occurrences of publications in the area of Social Software by outlet

Publication outlet	Journal or conference	Total number of publications
ACM CHI Conference	C	8
ACM Conference on Computer-Supported Collaborative Work and Social Computing	C	10
ACM SIGMIS Data Base Management Information Systems	C	1
ACM Transactions on Computer-Human Interaction	J	2
Americas Conference on Information Systems (AMCIS)	C	145
Communications of the ACM	J	4
Communications of the Association for Information Systems	J	11
Computer Supported Cooperative Work	J	2
Decision Support Systems	J	33
European Conference on Computer Supported Cooperative Work	C	2
European Conference on Information Systems (ECIS)	C	61
Harvard Business Review	J	2
Information Systems Journal	J	7
Information Technlogoy Journal	J	2
International Conference on Information Systems (ICIS)	C	91
International Journal of Electronic Commerce	J	2
International Journal of Information Management	J	4
Internationale Tagung Wirtschaftsinformatik	C	9
Journal of Computer-Mediated Communication	J	28
Journal of Computing and Information Technology	J	2
Journal of Information Science and Technology	J	3
Journal of Information Technology	J	16
Journal of Information, Information Technology, and Organizations	J	1
Journal of Management Information Systems	J	11
Journal of Organizational Computing and Electronic Commerce	J	15
Journal of Strategic Information Systems	J	9
Journal of the Association for Information Systems	J	5
MIS Quarterly	J	10
The DATA BASE for Advances in Information Systems	J	3
Wirtschaftsinformatik	J	11
Total publications in conferences	C	326
Total publications in journals	J	185
Total publications	C + J	511

Table 7: Occurrences of publications in the area of research collaboration by outlet

Publication outlet	**Journal or conference**	**Total number of publications**
Academy of Management Journal	J	1
ACM Transactions on Computer-Human Interaction	J	1
Administrative Science Quarterly	J	1
Americas Conference on Information Systems (AMCIS)	C	3
CHI 2008 Proceedings	C	1
Communications of the Association for Information Systems	J	1
Computer Supported Cooperative Work (Conference)	C	3
Computer Supported Cooperative Work (Journal)	J	5
Decision Support Systems	J	2
European Conference on Information Systems (ECIS)	C	1
International Conference on Information Systems (ICIS)	C	1
Journal of Computer-Mediated Communication	J	7
Journal of Information Technology	J	1
R&D Management	J	1
Research Policy	J	62
The DATA BASE for Advances in Information Systems	J	1
Total publications in conferences	C	9
Total publications in journals	J	83
Total publications	C + J	92

3 Research Collaboration: Research Categories

This chapter presents the categorization of the identified publications in the area of *research collaboration*. First, the approach used to categorize the 92 publications into four broad categories is described. Second, research done in each of the four categories is summarized.

The final selection consisting of 92 publications was first read and categorized based on a full-text analysis. Each publication was tagged with three to four keywords such as research productivity, science policy, university-industry collaboration, international collaboration, e-science, etc.

Then the publications were clustered into sub-groups of four broad categories based on the keyword tags assigned to them. The largest sub-group consists of twelve publications and the smallest of two publications. The categorization into the four broad categories was inspired by extant literature, that was already mentioning the macro-, meso-, and micro-perspective of research collaboration (Hou et al, 2007; Glänzel, 2004), with macro-level there being defined as an analysis of research collaboration on a per-country or international level, meso-level as the institution of the object of analysis, and micro-level focusing on the individual researcher. In this literature review, the macro-level was extended to also encompass publications that focus on changes in the overall research system as a whole and on policy aspects. In addition, a new perspective, the 'technological perspective' was added to take into account publications that focus on newer phenomena like e-science and technological support for research collaboration.

Since formal content-coding was not used for this categorization, these categories should be taken only as an organizing tool, to get a clear overview of published research in the field, and not as a definitive categorization of the body of research.

Table 8 lists the four broad categories with a summary of the topics included and the number of publications for each category.

Table 8: Research categories in the field of research collaboration

Areas	Topics included	No. of publications
Macro-level perspective	International and interdisciplinary research collaboration, policy aspects, and changing modes of knowledge production	15
Meso-level perspective	Research collaboration on the institutional level	23
Micro-level perspective	Research collaboration on the level of individual scientists	32
Technological perspective	Research collaboration in various technological aspects	22
Total number of publications		**92**

Figure 8 depicts the classification framework of the main categories derived from the literature (Hou et al., 2007; Glänzel, 2004) and subsequently modified to include the additional technological perspective including the sub-groups that were identified based on the literature review.

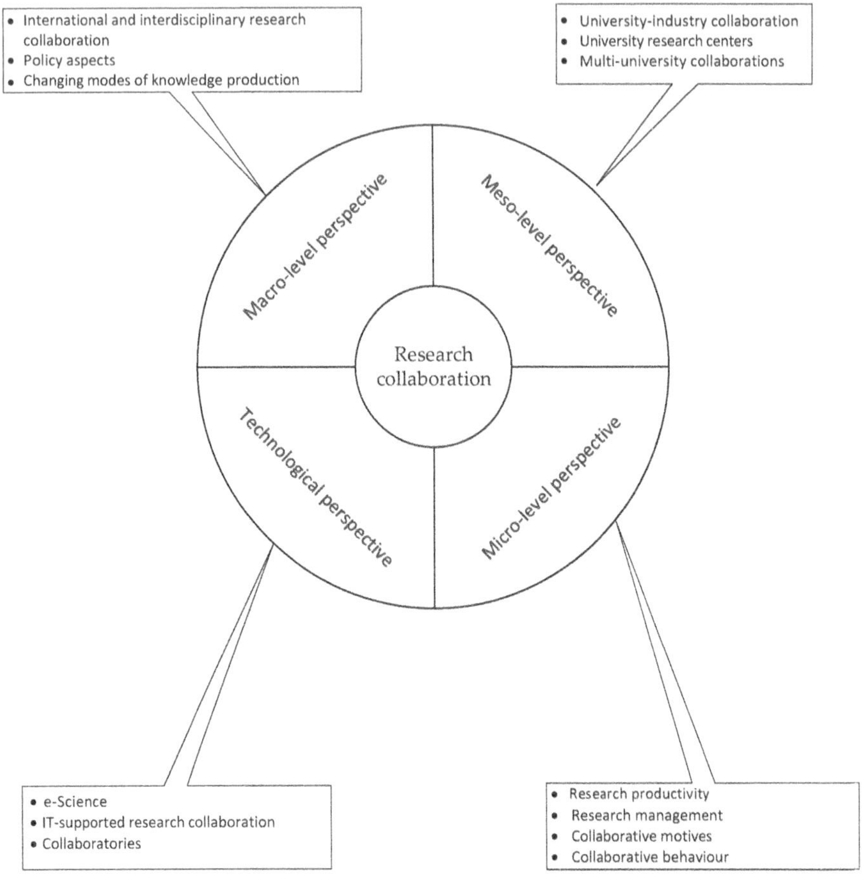

Figure 8: Overview of categories in the area of research collaboration

Below, research from each of the eight categories is summed up in a systematic manner. First, each category is briefly explained and the sub-groups contained are listed. Then research from each sub-group is presented and summarized.

3.1 Macro-Level Perspective

Publications that deal with national and international aspects of research collaboration belong to the macro-level perspective, as suggested by Hou et al. (2007) and Glänzel (2004). In addition, publications that view research collaboration as a phenomenon from a very high level like a political or sociological perspective, where the generic intersection of academia with other social spheres like industry or government is discussed have also been categorized to belong to the macro-level perspective. In total, ten publications have been identified as dealing with these aspects and have been split into three subgroups: '*international and interdisciplinary research collaboration*', '*policy aspects*', and '*changing modes of knowledge production*'.

3.1.1 International and interdisciplinary research collaboration

International and interdisciplinary research collaboration contains publications that investigate patterns of scientific collaborations across countries and disciplines, a topic of interest since internationally co-authored papers are more frequently and highly cited than articles that were produced out of purely domestic collaborations (Narin, 1991; Wagner & Leydesdorff, 2005). Publications pertaining to this cluster deal with questions like 'why is international research collaboration a growing class of research' or 'why does it have a higher impact than publications from a national background', despite the challenges normally associated with collaboration at a distance (Hoekman et al., 2010). Table 9 provides a summary of publications.

Table 9: Research on international and interdisciplinary research collaboration

Study focus	Study	Year	Type
Explaining the rapid growth of international collaboration using international co-authorship and network analysis	Wagner, Leydesdorff	2005	Quantitative
Understanding the effect of distance and borders on the intensity of research collaboration in Europe	Hoekman et al.	2010	Quantitative
Study of the temporal evolution of co-authorship networks in Iberoamerican countries	Lemarchand	2012	Quantitative
Understanding of evolution of interdisciplinary research in new fields using co-authorship and co-citation patterns in the new field of open source innovation	Raasch et al.	2013	Quantitative
Investigation into collaborative interdisciplinary practices in a university setting and the emergence of interdisciplinary communities	Siedlok et al.	2015	Mixed mode

Study focus	Study	Year	Type
Foreign scientists and returning migrant scientists involved in international research collaboration have larger international research networks that non-migrant counterparts	Scellato et al.	2015	Quantitative

3.1.2 Policy aspects

Policy aspects deals with publications that focus on political and policymaking aspects of research. Driven by the notion that research collaboration is beneficial for productivity and various other reasons, research networks sponsored by the European Union require researchers to work together in order to be able to secure funding for their research in the first place (Defazio et al, 2009). Science policy also worked towards shifting academic science to a more entrepreneurial mode with policies designed to foster and increase collaboration between universities and industry (Walsh & Huang, 2014). Authors have contributed by investigating the conditions and mechanisms of science organization (Nedeva, 2013), by analyzing the effectiveness of research collaboration structures in the European Union in the light of funding (Defazio et al, 2009), and by examining the Japanese and US science policies and their impact on publication secrecy and commercialization of science (Walsh & Huang, 2014). Publications belonging to *policy aspects* are summarized in table 10.

Table 10: Research on policy aspects of research collaboration

Study focus	Study	Year	Type
How do funding incentives influence collaborative behaviour and scientific productivity	Defazio et al.	2009	Quantitative
What is the impact of funding on research collaboration	Ubfal, Maffioli	2011	Quantitative
Exploring mechanisms of science organization in Europe	Nedeva	2013	Case study
Examination of impacts of science policies on commercial activities, patenting, and publication secrecy in Japanese and US scientists	Walsh, Huang	2014	Quantiative
Investigation of the public value of science and R&D investments via the UMETRICS infrastructure	Lane et al.	2015	Quantitative

3.1.3 Changing modes of knowledge production

Changing modes of knowledge production encompasses publications that investigate a variety of interrelated and overlapping notions like 'mode 2' knowledge production, 'new production of knowledge' (NPK), 'post-normal science', 'triple helix', or 'finalisation science'. All these notions try to capture and conceptualize undergoing transformations in our scientific world like a more strategic orientation of science systems (Irvine & Martin, 1984) and a focus on the production of relevant knowledge (Gibbons et al, 1994). In particular, the 'mode 2' concept, proposed by Michael Gibbons and his co-authors (Gibbons et al., 1994), a vision of a highly interactive and distributed science system, has gained enormous visibility (Hessels & van Lente, 2008). Table 11 summarizes the research on changing modes of knowledge production.

Table 11: Research on changing modes of knowledge production

Study focus	Study	Year	Type
Comprehensive literature review of new knowledge production concepts	Hessels, van Lente	2008	Literature review
Understanding online communication differences between "Mode 2" and "Mode 1" sciences	Heimeriks et al	2008	Quantitative
A conceptual framework for organizing scientific research in open collaborative projects	Franzoni, Sauermann	2013	Case study
An investigation into increasing bureaucratization of science and its implications for academic labor markets and the scientific credit system	Walsh, Lee	2015	Quantitative

3.2 Meso-Level Perspective

The meso-level perspective encompasses publications that deal with the institutional level of research collaboration (Glänzel, 2004; Hou et al, 2007). In total, 23 publications have been identified that focus primarily on the institutional aspects of scientific collaborations. These publications have been split into three sub-groups: *'university-industry collaboration'*, *'university research centers'*, and *'multi-university collaborations'*. There is considerable overlap between the sub-groups *university-industry collaboration* and *university research centers*, as these topics are closely related. The publications were sorted into the respective subgroup by the dominant focus of the publication under review.

3.2.1 University-industry collaboration

University-industry collaboration contains publications that focus on a phenomenon that is becoming more and more important in the wake of increasingly open and networked innovation processes between academia and commercial, profit-oriented organizations (Hewitt-Dundas, 2012). Publications in that category focus on questions like how to decrease the barriers between academia and business or on understanding socio-technical networks inside of collaborative settings between universities and industry. Table 12 provides a summary of the research on *university-industry collaboration*.

Table 12: Research on university-industry collaboration

Study focus	Study	Year	Type
Understanding socio-technical networks in scientific university-industry collaborations	Davidson, Lamb	2000	Theoretical
How different types of university research centers influence university-industry interactions on an individual level	Boardman	2009	Quantitative
How can barriers in university-industry relations be reduced?	Bruneel et al.	2010	Quantitative
Do differences in universities' research performance influence their knowledge transfer activity?	Hewitt-Dundas.	2012	Quantitative
Comprehensive literature review of 36 publications on the topic of university-industry relations	Perkmann et al.	2013	Literature review
Proposition of a framework to explain how a company's engagement with universities can help increase increase its innovativeness	Jong, Slavova	2014	Quantitative
Investigation into the relationship of academic collaboration with firms' innovation performance in China	Kafouros et al.	2015	Quantitative
Explorative study of how science-intensive companies can overcome issues with 'open data' collaborations with academia	Perkmann, Schildt	2015	Case study
Investigation into gender-related differences in scientists' engagement in university-industry collaboration activities	Tartari, Salter	2015	Quantitative
Analysis of scientists' strategies in dealing with university-industry collaborations	Callaert et al.	2015	Quantitative
Examination of the influence of university-industry collaboration on scientific output	Banal-Estanol et al.	2015	Quantitative
Investigation into the drivers of university-industry collaboration in a low-tech industry	Maietta	2015	Quantitative
Development of a roadmap to strategically plan and enact university-industry collaborations in IS research	Marcolin, Saunders	2015	Conceptual
Assessment of the influence of firms' innovative performance involved in university-industry partnerships	Chai, Shih	2016	Quantitative

3.2.2 University research centers

University research centers captures publications that analyze the influence of the attributes of university research centers on the productivity and collaborative patterns of individual researchers. Since the focus of the studies under scrutiny lies on center-level attributes rather than pertaining to the individual researchers, these publications were categorized as belonging to the meso-level perspective instead of the micro-level perspective of research collaboration. Relevant research is summarized in table 13.

Table 13: Research on university research centers

Study focus	Study	Year	Type
Understanding the influence of research center attributes on research collaboration at the level of individual researchers	Boardman, Corley.	2008	Quantitative
Analysis of the effect of university research centers on collaboration patterns and productivity of university researchers	Ponomariov, Boardman	2010	Quantitative
Investigation into selection dynamics of academic scientists' in their choice to associate with a university research center	Su	2014	Quantitative

3.2.3 Multi-university collaborations

The category *multi-university collaborations* deals with publications that focus on challenges inherent in collaborations between multiple academic institutions and on how favorable institutional conditions can be created to foster effective and efficient scientific research. Another focal area is understanding the role collaboration plays in such settings and its effect on outcome measures like research quality, number of publications, or co-publication frequency. A summary of the publications can be found in table 14.

Table 14: Research on multi-university collaborations

Study focus	Study	Year	Type
Development of a four-fold typology of collaborative projects in the field of physics	Chompalov et al.	2002	Quantitative
Understanding the influence of team size on a variety of output parameters like scientific output and influence	Adams et al	2005	Quantitative
How is collaboration related to the variability of research quality	Rigby, Edler	2005	Quantitative
Analysis of the influence of coordination on project outcomes in multi-university collaborations	Cummings, Kiesler	2007	Quantitative
How do governance structures support or hinder researchers' efforts to engage in scientific collaborations across institutions	Heinze, Kuhlmann	2008	Mixed methods
Influence of organizational and institutional characteristics on creativity in scientific research	Heinze et al.	2009	Case studies

3.3 Micro-Level Perspective

The micro-level perspective of research collaboration focuses on the individual researcher and outcomes and attributes that can be associated with individual scientists like their academic career, academic rank, or research output. This perspective encompasses in total 32 publications, that have been further divided into four subgroups: '*research productivity*', '*research management*', '*collaborative motives*', and '*collaborative behavior*'. As before, there is a considerable overlap between the subcategories, since the topics under investigation are closely related. However, the publications were carefully sorted into the respective subgroup by identifying a dominant focus of the publication under analysis.

3.3.1 Research productivity

Research productivity constitutes the largest sub-category and encompasses publications that focus on questions around productivity in research collaborations, e.g. the relationship of Internet use on collaboration and scientific productivity (Sooryamoorthy & Shrum 2007), the role the scientists' work environment plays on research performance (Ryan & Hurley 2007), or the relationship between scientific collaboration and publication productivity (Ynalvez & Shrum 2011). Table 15 sums up the publications on *research productivity.*

Table 15: Research on research productivity

Study focus	Study	Year	Type
Analysis of relationship between Internet use, research collaboration and research productivity	Sooryamoorthy, Shrum	2007	Quantitative
How do organizational charasteristics influence scientific research effectiveness?	Ryan, Hurley	2007	Quantitative
Longitudinal investigation into the relationship of research collaboration and research output	He et al.	2009	Quantitative
How is Internet use relatied to research productivity?	Vasileiadou, Vliegenthart	2009	Quantitative
Investigation into the relationship of scientific collaboration with publication productivity	Ynalvez, Shrum	2011	Quantitative
How does embeddedness affect research output and impact of scientists?	Gonzalez-Brambila et al.	2013	Quantitative
Analysis of the relation of time spent on research versus on administrative tasks and the impact on research productivity	Barham et al.	2014	Quantitative
Effect of management practices on research collaboration	Beerkens	2013	Quantitative
How do business researchers' internationalization strategies influence their research performance?	Eisend, Schmidt	2013	Quantitative
Assessment of the relationship between interdisciplinary dissertation research and career-related indicators	Millar	2013	Quantitative
Investigation into using social capital to increase research impact	Li, Liao, & Yen	2013	Quantitative
Is participation in university research centers helping researchers' careers	Sabharwal, Hu	2013	Quantitative
Analysis of the influence of team composition on creativity of research results	Lee et al.	2015	Quantitative
Study of the impact of a laboratory's team composition on research productivity	Conti, Liu	2015	Quantitative
Comparison of scientific productivity of PhD students by their hiring background	Baruffaldi et al.	2016	Quantitative

3.3.2 Research management

Research management deals with aspects of individual-level research collaboration that can be helpful for research managers, e.g identifying structural attributes of organizations that can be a help or hindrance to research collaborations (Walsh & Maloney, 2007) or the development of a management framework to structure interdisciplinary research (König et al., 2013). A summary of publications is provided in table 16.

Table 16: Research on research management

Study focus	Study	Year	Type
Investigation of structural attributes of work organizations that help or hinder research collaborations	Walsh, Maloney	2007	Quantitative
Development of a "collaboration supportiveness" measure to quantify an individual researcher's collaboration ability in order to inform research managers	Liu et al.	2013	Theoretical
Development of a management framework for structuring of interdisciplinary research	König et al.	2013	Case study
Investigation of the influence of division of labour on serendipity in science	Murayama et al.	2015	Quantitative

3.3.3 Collaborative motives

Collaborative motives focuses on analyzing scientists' motives for collaboration and their impact on outcomes (Bozeman & Corley, 2004) or gender differences regarding collaboration motives and strategies (Bozeman & Gaughan, 2011). Table 17 provides a summary of the two publications in this category.

Table 17: Research on collaborative motives

Study focus	Study	Year	Type
Analysis of the impact of scientists' collaboration motives and strategies on public goods (scientific and technical human capital)	Bozeman, Corley	2004	Quantitative
Investigation into gender differences regarding collaborative motives and strategies of scientists	Bozeman, Gaughan	2011	Quantitative

3.3.4 Collaborative behavior

Collaborative behavior contains publications that deal with the analysis of collaborative interactions and behavior from a wide variety of angles like the resource-based view (Van Rijnsoever et al., 2008) or relational mechanisms that influence collaborative behavior of scientists (Jha & Welch, 2010). Table 18 summarizes the various publications related to *collaborative behavior*.

Table 18: Research on collaborative behavior

Study focus	Study	Year	Type
Analysis of collaborative interactions of researchers through the lens of the resource-based view	Van Rijnsoever et al.	2008	Quantitative
Previous collaboration experience reduces barriers to collaboration in distributed interdisciplinary research	Cummings, Kiesler	2008	Quantitative
Understanding the optimal conditions for interdisciplinary research on the level of individual researchers	Van Rijnsoever, Hessels	2011	Quantitative
Investigation into scientists' information-sharing behaviour	Haeussler	2011	Quantitative
Understanding the relational mechanisms that govern collaborative behaviour of researchers	Jha, Welch	2010	Quantitative
How do scientists coordinate collaboration across domains of expertise	Bruns	2013	Case study
How do interpersonal ties between researchers form and persist?	Dahlander, McFarland	2013	Quantitative
Investigation of the role of physical proximity on formation and results of scientific collaborations	Kabo et al.	2014	Quantitative
Examination of information sharing behavior in competing scientists	Haeussler et al.	2014	Quantitative
Analysis of Chinese overseas alumni scientists' collaborative behavior	Li et al.	2015	Quantitative
Study of the influence of collaborative behavior and individuals' collaboration networks on knowledge creation	Wang	2016	Quantitative

3.4 Technological Perspective

The technological perspective supplements the macro, meso, and micro perspectives of research collaboration suggested by Glänzel (2004) and Hou et al. (2007). Among the publications analyzed, the following clusters of publications within the technological perspective were identified: *'e-science'*, *'IT-supported research collaboration'*, and *'collaboratories'*.

3.4.1 e-Science

e-Science can be thought of as the overarching construct that informs the technological perspective of research collaboration. Owing to technological innovations in communication and collaboration technologies as well as in networking and computation with initiatives like grid or cloud computing, visions of new a new generation of tools to advance scientific work have been fostered (Dutton, 2011).

Consequently, several initiatives have emerged with the goal of using these new and emerging technologies for supporting scientific research. Among the labels assigned to digital research initiatives are collaboratories, e-Research, e-Science, e-Social Science, e-Humanities, computational science, cyberinfrastructure, digital scholarship, and many more that try to capture the next generation of research technologies (Borgman, 2006; Nentwich, 2003; Dutton, 2011). The broad area of e-Science constitutes the largest sub-cluster of the technological perspective. e-Science studies themselves are interdisciplinary in nature (Nentwich, 2003) and e-Science-related aspects are usually investigated in the even broader context of social shaping of technology (Park, 2010), due to e-science being a moving target (Nentwich, 2003). Depending on the viewpoint, the other three areas identified (IT-supported research collaboration, research support tools, and collaboratories) could also be thought of pertaining to e-science itself, but due to a distinct focus different from e-science as a phenomenon, they have been categorized to belong to different sub-clusters in their own right. A summary of the publications in the *e-Science* category is provided in table 19.

Table 19: Research on e-Science

Study focus	Study	Year	Type
Identification of paradoxical, non-technical challenges in a large e-Science project	Lawrence	2006	Case study
Investigation into scientific data collections as a distributed collective practice in e-Science projects	Cragin, Shankar	2006	Case study
Transferring findings from digital library studies and e-learning to e-Science	Borgman	2006	Case study
Understanding remote collaboration over video data to foster real-time e-Science in the social sciences	Fraser et al.	2006	Exploratory interviews
Development of a framework to use the Internet as a collaborative space for research	Pilson, Foster	2006	Systems Development
Understanding synchronous remote participation in experimental research	Birnholtz, Horn	2007	Exploratory interviews
Investigation into data re-use in e-Science projects and identification of data life cycles in different disciplines	Carlson, Anderson	2007	Case study
Systematic analysis of e-Science projects in South Korea using webometrics	Park	2010	Quantitative
How to democratize the next generation of research in computational networks?	Dutton	2011	Theoretical
Analysis of the governance of an emerging e-Science infrastructure	Barjak et al.	2013	Case study

3.4.2 IT-supported research collaboration

IT-supported research collaboration contains publications with a much narrower view than the previous category. Authors have contributed by proposing a layered model of collaboration to guide designers of collaboration systems (Briggs et al., 2009), by identifying needs of virtual researchers for specific types of support (Söldner et al., 2009), and by proposing a design of an integrated environment to help with sensemaking of research literature (Zhang et al., 2008). In addition, Jirotka et al. (2013) provide a broad overview of concepts, methods, and tools for supporting research collaboration. Table 20 provides a summary of the publications on *IT-supported research collaboration*.

Table 20: Research on IT-supported research collaboration

Study focus	Study	Year	Type
Development of a prototypical system to help in sensemaking of scientific literature	Zhang et al.	2008	Systems development
Proposition of a layered model to help software designers implement improved collaboration systems	Briggs et al.	2009	Systems development
Support needs of researchers in virtual teams	Soeldner et al.	2009	Case study
Development and evaluation of a maturity model for research portals	Becker et al.	2010	Case study
Exploration into IT's role in enabling collaboration	Smith, McKeen	2011	Case study
Comprehensive overview of the interrelationship of CSCW and e-Science research for supporting scientific collaboration	Jirotka et al.	2013	Case study
Proposition of an approach for partner selection in research collaboration environments	Schall	2014	Conceptual
Investigation of the influence of instant messaging technology use on team performance in collaborative research	Bertolotti et al.	2015	Quantitative

3.4.3 Collaboratories

The subcluster of *collaboratories* refers to publications that deal with a phenomenon that is defined in various different ways – typically as an extension of physical laboratories: according to Kling et al. (2000), collaboratories constitute laboratories where researchers can collaborate remotely from each other and from key equipment. In an early and seminal definition, a collaboratory has been defined as "a center without walls, in which researchers can perform their research without regard to a physical location – interacting with colleagues, accessing instrumentation, sharing data and computational resources, and accessing information in digital libraries" (Sonnenwald et al., 2003: p. 151). In a similar vein, Bos et al. (2007) define collaboratories in a broad fashion:

> *"A collaboratory is an organizational entity that spans distance, supports rich and recurring human interaction oriented to a common research are, and fosters contact between researchers who are both known and unknown to each other, and provides access to data sources, artifacts, and tools required to accomplish research tasks" (Bos et al, 2007: p 5).*

In addition, they propose a taxonomy of collaboratories that spans diverse entities from shared instruments and databases to virtual communities of practice (Bos et al., 2007). Other publications investigate the use of collaboratories from diverse disciplinary backgrounds, e.g. biology (Chin & Lansing, 2004) or from a theoretical perspective (Kling et al., 2000). Table 21 summarizes the identified publications regarding *collaboratories*.

Table 21: Research on collaboratories

Study focus	Study	Year	Type
Theoretical model of scientific collaboratories as socio-technical interaction networks	Kling et al.	2000	Theoretical
Evaluation of a scientific collaboratory in the nanosciences	Sonnenwald et al.	2003	Case study
Development of a tool for enabling sharing of data in a collaborator in the biological sciences	Chin, Lansing	2004	Systems development
Examination of coordination and social practices of collaboratories	Lee et al.	2006	Theoretical
Proposition of a comprehensive taxonomy of collaboratories	Bos et al.	2007	Case study

4 Social Software: Research Categories

This chapter presents the categorization of the identified publications in the area of *social software*. Initially, the approach used to categorize the 511 publications into seven comprehensive categories is described. Then, research done in each of the seven categories is summed up.

The final selection consisting of 511 journal and conference papers was first read and categorized based on a full-text analysis. Each publication was tagged with three to four keywords such as privacy, trust, motivation, academic use, marketing, design recommendation, etc. Then the publications were clustered into sub-groups of the seven broad categories based on the keyword tags assigned to them. The largest sub-group consists of 154 publications and the smallest of 13 publications. The categorization was organically developed and incrementally refined during the literature screening since no extant categorization was found in the literature. Formal content-coding was not applied for this categorization, so the categories should only be seen as an organizing tool that helps get a clear overview of published research in the field of social software, and not as a definitive categorization of extant research.

Table 22 lists the seven broad categories with a summary of the topics included and the number of publications for each category.

Table 22: Research categories in the field of social software

Areas	Topics included	No. of publications
Theoretical view	Theory use in social media, information diffusion in social media, Web 2.0 overview articles, social computing and social information systems, data quality in social media, social media analysis	77
Social and behavioral view	Social capital, self presentation and information disclosure, information overload, mood and habit, motivation and intention, adoption and continuance, trust, and privacy	154
Organizational view	Enterprise 2.0, social software for organizational knowledge and innovation management, organizational adoption of Web 2.0 technologies, volunteering 2.0, digital health, crisis management, governmental use	145

Areas	Topics included	No. of publications
Design view	Principles and practices of design for social software, design of collaborative social software, design of social tagging and bookmarking systems	25
Business view	Marketing, sales, and advertising; social business intelligence and social media analytics; information security; business strategy; business processes	73
Political view	Social software for political campaigning; social software to enable e-democracy and e-participation	13
Academic use view	Social software to support teaching and learning; social software to support research collaboration	24
Total number of publications		**511**

Figure 9 depicts the classification framework of the main categories that was organically developed during the screening and subsequent in-depth analysis of the literature.

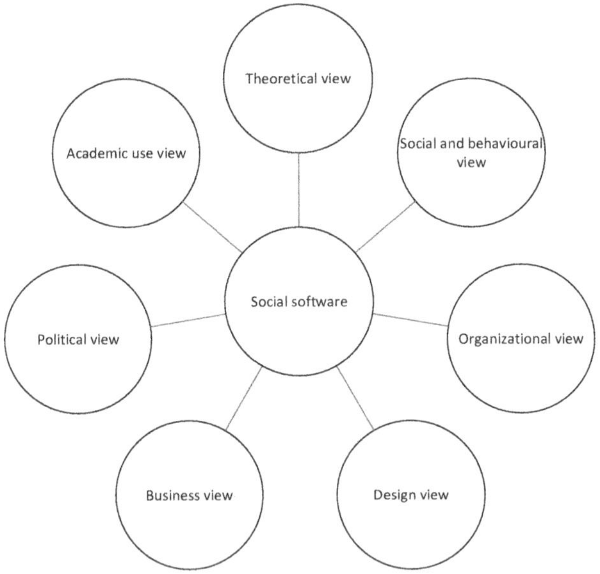

Figure 9: Overview of categories in the area of social software

Below research from each of the seven categories is summed up in a systematic manner. First, each category is briefly explained and the sub-groups contained are listed. Then research from each sub-group is presented and summarized.

4.1 Theoretical View

The theoretical view contains publications that deal with a wide range of theoretical subjects and overview articles relating to social software. These publications have been split into six sub-groups: '*social computing / social information systems*', '*Web 2.0*', '*social network analysis*', '*information diffusion in social media*', '*theory use in social media*', and '*data quality in social media*'.

4.1.1 Social computing and social information systems

Social computing and social information systems captures publications that deal with an emerging research discipline in which the number of publications has increased by 120% year-over-year between 2008 and 2011 according to Li & Joshi (2012). Social computing is assumed to embody a new phase on the web (Parameswaran & Whinston 2007) and to empower individual users and ultimately mitigate the information asymmetry by improving the information flow thanks to broadband connectivity and powerful personal computing devices (Li & Joshi, 2012). The eight papers pertaining to this category all take a bird's eye view of the field and present either reviews of the genre or focus on research issues. Table 23 summarizes the publications on *social computing and social information systems*.

Table 23: Research on social computing and social information systems

Study focus	Study	Year	Type
Broad overview of research issues in social computing	Parameswaran, Whinston	2007	Literature review
Highlighting the importance of a social informatics perspective in Web 2.0 research	Allen et al..	2007	Position paper
Overview of systems that provide virtual worlds as an aspect of social computing	Messinger et al.	2009	Literature review and case study
Analysis of social technology usage by individuals with the help of genre theory	Davison et al.	2010	Literature review
Proposal of a framework and a research agenda for the area of social information systems	Schlagwein et al.	2011	Literature review

Study focus	Study	Year	Type
Literature review of social computing using the latent semantic analysis technique	Li, Joshi	2012	Literature review
Overview of research agenda in social computing and social networking services	Chen, Liu	2014	Editorial
Description of a research agenda to tackle challenges in social web research issues	Appleford et al.	2014	Position paper

4.1.2 Web 2.0

Web 2.0 contains publications that mostly offer an overview of technologies that are commonly associated with the umbrella term 'Web 2.0'. This term gained popularity after the publisher O'Reilly first organized a conference under that name in 2004 (Steininger et al., 2011). Publications in this sub-category encompass papers like Boyd and Ellison's (2007) seminal paper on social network sites, overview articles that point out research streams in social networks (Oinas-Kukkonen et al., 2010) or specialized articles that investigate into the features of social media tools (Alfaro et al., 2012). A summary of publications is provided in table 24.

Table 24: Research on Web 2.0

Study focus	Study	Year	Type
Investigation into usage patterns of Facebook users in the early days of the platform's availability	Lampe et al.	2006	Quantitative
Comprehensive portrayal of the history of social network sites and a review of existing research	Boyd, Ellison	2007	Literature review
Propositition of a framework to better understand Web 2.0 offerings	Ganesh, Padmanabhunii	2007	Case study
Discussion of social network sites in response to previous paper by Boyd and Ellison (2007)	Beer	2007	Literature review
Study of change of usage patterns and perception of Facebook over a period of three years	Lampe et al.	2008	Quantitative
Review of research streams in social networks	Oinas-Kukkonen et al.	2010	Literature review
Proposition of a framework to systematize research on Web 2.0	Steininger et al.	2011	Theoretical
What is the impact of new features in social networking services on users's communication patterns and activities?	Demetz et al.	2011	Quantitative
Analysis of social media tools on a feature level	Alfaro et al.	2012	Case study
Proposition of algorithm for estimating the number of active users and prediction of future participation	Sivan et al.	2012	Quantitative

Study focus	Study	Year	Type
Development of a framework for the explanation of the survivability of user-created content	Park et al.	2013	Quantitative
Analysis of three social networks for affordances to identify software features	O'Riordan et al.	2012	Case study
Investigation of which social media type is preferred by information seekers	Osatuyi	2012	Quantitative
How do interaction on social networks influence relationships?	Schöndienst, Dang-Xuan	2012	Quantitative
Investigation into language usage in social networking services	Cunliffe et al.	2013	Mixed Mode
Social media features can undermine communicative purposes on websites and may sometimes not be desirable	Jensen et al.	2013	Quantitative
Discussion and comparison of the status of social media and social networking in different countries around the wolrd	Shim et al.	2013	Quantitative
Juxtaposition of a typology of traditional offline social networks and technologically-mediated online social networking services	Kane et al.	2014	Mixed mode
Comprehensive literature review on social networking services	Berger et al.	2014	Literature review
Overview of Wikipedia's little known sister project Wikidata as a free and collaborative knowledgebase	Vrandecic, Krötzsch	2014	Overview article
Investigation of the role of societal culture for usage of social media	Schlagwein, Prasarnphanich	2014	Quantitative
Systematic literature review on research on social networks in information systems	Cao et al.	2015	Literature review
Overview and position paper on developments around Web 2.0 technologies	Kulathuramaiyer, Maurer	2015	Position paper
Analysis of the influence of authors' reputation on the quality of wiki websites	Wöhner et al.	2015	Quantitative
Discussion paper on Web 2.0 and future directions towards a Web 3.0	Newman et al.	2016	Conceptual

4.1.3 Social network analysis

Social network analysis contains publications that focus on an examination of social networks and of their structures and properties often with a mathematical or theoretical lens. Areas of study are typically abstract concepts like metrics of connectedness in social networks (Landherr et al., 2010), visualizing the concepts of social networks (Zhu et al., 2010), the proposal of an algorithm and mathematical methods on how to explore the organizational structure in social networks (Qiu & Lin, 2011), or an algorithm for extracting a subpopulation in large social networks (Zhang et al., 2011), to name just a few representative examples for that sub-group. Publications in that area are summarized in table 25.

Table 25: Research on social network analysis

Study focus	Study	Year	Type
Discovery of principles in online social networks	Ganley, Lampe	2009	Quantitative
How do economists study the structure and composition of social networks?	Mayer	2009	Quantitative
Examination of social structure in a social networking service	McLure Wasko et al.	2009	Quantitative
Identiying key people in social networks via metrics of connectedness	Landherr et al.	2010	Mathematical
Proposition of a new approach to visualize social network concepts	Zhu et al.	2010	Conceptual
Proposition of an algorithm to identify key users in social networks via a PageRank-based approach	Heidemann et al.	2010	Conceptual
Development of a new algorithm to help explore the organizational structure in a social network	Qiu, Lin	2011	Conceptual
Proposition of a new method to extract a subpopulation in a social network	Zhang et al.	2011	Conceptual
Description of a new algorithm to build recommendations in social networks	Li, Wang	2012	Conceptual
Impact of network structure (weak/strong ties) on information value in social networking services	Koroleva, Stimac	2012	Quantitative
Analysis of approaches how to identify influential users in social network services	Probst	2013	Literature review
How do participants in social network services interact with organizing structures	Moser et al.	2013	Mixed mode
How do previously existing offline relationships influence subsequently formed online connections on Twitter	Kim et al.	2016	Quantitative

4.1.4 Information diffusion in social media

Information diffusion in social media refers to a research topic that has become a focal area in recent years with the more widespread use of social networks and social media such as blogs. Topics researched range from framework and algorithm generation (Cheng et al., 2011) to an examination of the role centrality plays for information diffusion in social networks (Mochalova & Nanopoulos, 2013). Table 26 summarizes the publications on *information diffusion in social media.*

Table 26: Research on information diffusion in social media

Study focus	Study	Year	Type
Examination on bloggers' influence on information diffusion in a large Chinese blogging community	Jiang, Wang	2009	Quantitative
Proposition of a recommendation framework to extract useful information from micro-blogging sites	Cheng et al.	2011	Conceptual
Development of an empirical approach for the measurement of information diffusion in social network services	Garg et al.	2011	Conceptual
Analysis of recommendation behaviour in social networking services	Ebermann et al.	2011	Quantitative
What is the influence of seed members in social networks on information diffusion?	Mochalova, Nanopoulos	2013	Mathematical
Proposition of a method to restrict "online firestorms" in social networking services	Mochalova, Nanopoulos	2014	Mathematical
Statistical investigation into content sharing behaviour on Twitter	Shi et al.	2014	Quantitative

4.1.5 Theory use in social media

Theory use in social media deals with publications that concentrate on developing and using theory in social media. Theory building represents a major issue in the IS field (Urquhart & Vaast, 2012), and there is a concern in the IS community, that theory development in social media is currently still insufficient (Albert & Salam, 2013). Papers identified deal with issues such as where is the theory in wikis (Majchrzak, 2009) or how to deal with the wide variety of theoretical approaches to better understand social media (Quinio & Marciniak, 2013). Publications on *theory use in social media* are summarized in table 27.

Table 27: Research on theory use in social media

Study focus	Study	Year	Type
How to create theories for wikis	Majchrzak	2009	Personal comment
Proposition of a model to understand antecedents of use of social networking services based on self-determination theory and socio-emotional selectivity theory	Jacks, Salam	2009	Conceptual
Analyzing the effects of long tail economics on a blog platform	Evans	2009	Case study
Modelling of the underlying economics of user-generated content	Shim, Lee	2009	Conceptual
Applying a sociomateriality perspective to social networking services	Thambusamy, Nemati	2011	Mixed mode
Building social media theories from case studies	Urquhart, Vaast	2012	Conceptual
Building a theory on the impact of social media on the entrainment of contention to innovation	Kim	2012	Conceptual
Philosophically-infused conception of blogging as "technologies of the self"	Siles	2012	Mixed mode
Proposition of a generic definition for virtual social networks that encompasses other phenomena	Quinio, Marciniak	2013	Literature review
Development and test of a research model to understand factors of social networking services usage drawing on social exchange theory	Chen	2013	Quantitative
Using social discourse analysis as a means for theory development in social media	Albert, Salam	2013	Conceptual
Understanding how people will use social media at different stages of life through the lens of stages of psychosocial development theory	Kane	2013	Conceptual
Analysis of social media use through the lens of sociomateriality theory	Freeman et al.	2013	Case study
Proposition of new methodologies to understand member engagement in social networking services	Germonprez, Hovorka	2013	Case study
Presentation of a research agenda for using ontologies to improve on social media analytics	Alt, Wittwer	2014	Conceptual
Proposition of an alternative definition of strong and weak ties based on previous knowledge about the structure of a social networking service	de Meo et al.	2014	Conceptual
Application of affordance and sociomateriality perspective on studying enterprise social networking services	Ulmer, Pallud	2014	Case study
Proposition of a conceptualization of online community health	Wagner et al.	2014	Conceptual
Investigation of communication types in social networking services through the lens of social presence theory	Köster et al.	2015	Quantitative
Examination of message exchanges in a social networking service with spatial preference theory	Recker, Lekse	2016	Quantitative
Investigation of the role of organizational identification on the motivation of stakeholders to react to organization-directed negative feedback	Nguyen, Sidorova	2016	Conceptual

4.1.6 Data quality in social media

Data quality in social media constitutes the smallest sub-group consisting of three publications. Social media is regarded as the next generation of knowledge management systems since it combines the collaboration and codification capabilities of earlier systems (Kane & Ransbotham, 2012). Since the way knowledge is managed in social software-based systems is different from traditional knowledge management systems, questions about data quality are amongst the research issues arising out of the more and more widespread use of these tools (Probst & Görz, 2013; Kane & Ransbotham, 2012). Table 28 summarizes the publications dealing with *data quality in social media*.

Table 28: Research on data quality in social media

Study focus	Study	Year	Type
Analysis of information quality in a large dataset of Wikipedia articles	Kane, Ransbotham	2012	Quantitative
Examination of currency of user data in the business network xing	Probst, Görz	2013	Quantitative
Investigation into what factors influence content quality on blogs	Zülch et al.	2014	Quantitative

4.2 Social and Behavioral View

The widespread and mainstream use of social networks raises the question as to why users are so willing to disclose very personal information, not only to their family and friends but also to outsiders so that the information can easily be (ab)used. Papers that deal with such and similar issues, as well as positive and negative psychological outcomes of social software use, have been categorized to pertain to the social and behavioral view. These publications have been split into eight sub-groups: '*social capital*', '*self-presentation and information disclosure*', '*information overload*', '*mood and habit*', '*motivation and intention*', '*adoption and continuance*', '*trust*', and '*privacy*'.

4.2.1 Social capital

Social capital contains publications that investigate the use and usage patterns of social media, predominantly social networking services, social capital formation, and related aspects. Representative studies find that sensible use of services like Facebook can lead to increased social capital (as regards the number and the quality of connections) as well as improved academic performance in students (Shah et al, 2012). Koroleva et al. (2011) discover that the differentiated network structure and the enhanced social connectedness help the users of social networking services reap the four benefits of social capital: emotional support, networking value, broadening of one's own mental horizon, and offline activities. Goswami et al. (2010) describe the features of social networking services that help increase social connectedness in elderly users. Table 29 provides a summary of research on *social capital*.

Table 29: Research on social capital

Study focus	Study	Year	Type
Does Facebook influence attitudes and behaviors in students that lead to an increase in social capital?	Valenzuela et al.	2009	Quantitative
What features of social networking services can help increase the social connectedness of elderly users	Goswami et al.	2010	Quantitative
Examination of the relationship between the use of blogs and the development of social capital	Vaezi et al.	2011	Quantitative
How do distinct users of social networking services generate social capital benefits	Koroleva et al.	2011	Quantitative
Research proposal on how social networking technologies can change social capacity	Adams	2011	Conceptual
Inquiry into the implications of using social networking services on four dimensions of social capital	Brandzaeg	2012	Quantitative
Analysis of knowledge sharing behaviour in social networking services	Chung, Koo	2012	Quantitative
What are the beneficial (e.g. increased social capital) and adverse (e.g. lowered academic performance) consequences of Facebook use	Shah et al.	2012	Quantitative
Proposal of research framework based on social capital theory to understand factors influencing knowledge sharing among bloggers	Chai et al.	2012	Quantitative
Analysis of the role of an individual's social capital in a social networking service on job search behaviour	Garg, Telang	2012	Quantitative
How does information in a social networking service influence perceptions of social capital in teams	Cummings, Dennis	2014	Quantitative
Higher self-disclosure in communication on social media platforms can foster the building of social capital	Risius	2014	Quantitative
Investigation of the influence of friendship patterns on social capital in social networking services	Liu et al.	2014	Quantitative
Participation in enterprise social networks is more helpful for boding social capital than for bridging social capital	Riemer et al.	2015	Quantitative
Study of the effects of social media use on job performance as mediated by social capital	Ali-Hassan et al.	2015	Quantitative

4.2.2 Self-presentation and information disclosure

Self-presentation and information disclosure encompasses publications that investigate how self-presentation and information disclosure in the context of online social networking services is different from its analogous counterparts in traditional face-to-face relationships, a phenomenon which has been amply studied in the past (Hollenbaugh & Everett, 2013). Self-disclosure represents an important enabler for increasing the breadth and depth of relationships, but thanks to the anonymity afforded by the Internet, self-disclosure has undergone a transformation towards decreased inhibitions and thus increased self-disclosure (Hollenbaugh & Everett, 2013). Studies in this category investigate the effect of self-disclosure and presentation on impression formation in hiring processes (Pike et al., 2012), explore the online disinhibition effect as a result of the anonymity in blogs (Hollenbaugh & Everett, 2013), or the self presentation-related challenges users encounter in online social networking services like Facebook (Karakayali & Kilic, 2013). A summary of the publications on *self-presentation and information disclosure* is presented in table 30.

Table 30: Research on self-presentation and information disclosure

Study focus	Study	Year	Type
Proposal for an alternative way of describing one's own person on social networking services	Dugan et al.	2008	Quantitative
Development of a theoretical framework to understand information disclosure behavior in social networking services	Xu et al.	2010	Conceptual
What are the motivations of users to disclose personal information in social networking services	Krasnova et al.	2010	Quantitative
Why do users of social networking services disclose personal information?	Tow et al.	2010	Quantitative
How do extraversion and surrounding factors influence an individual's popularity in social networking services	Utz	2010	Quantitative
How does self-presentation in social networking services affect impressions by potential employers	Pike et al.	2012	Quantitative
Investigation of the role of culture and gender on self-disclosure	Krasnova et al.	2012	Quantitative
What influence does personality (in terms of the 'Big Five' personality characteristics) have on self-disclosure behavior in social networking services	Loiacono et al.	2012	Quantitative
How do community and personal goals influence self-presentation in social networking services	Schwämmlein, Wodzicki	2012	Quantitative
Investigation into self-disclosure behavior exhibited in social networking services	Chen	2013	Quantitative

Study focus	Study	Year	Type
What are the determinants that explain why individuals exhibit informational nonconformity in social networking services	Neben, Lips	2013	Conceptual
Examination of the relationship between emotions (sentiment in social media) and information diffusion in social media	Stieglitz, Dang-Xuan	2013	Quantitative
Analysis of the influence of anonymity on self-disclosure in blogs	Hollenbaugh, Everett	2013	Quantitative
Examination of how Facebook users deal with self-presentation challenges	Karakayali, Kilic	2013	Case study
Investigation of self-disclosure behavior in social networking services through the lens of social exchange theory	Loiacono	2015	Quantitative
How does affect influence self-disclosure behavior on social networking services	Yu et al.	2015	Quantitative
Proposition of a research model to help understand the influence of characteristics of social media platforms on users' self-disclosure behavior	Pu et al.	2016	Conceptual
Duration and intensity of a negative emotional state influence users' disclosure behavior on social networking services	Cho	2016	Quantitative

4.2.3 Information overload

Information overload deals with publications that discuss the negative effects of social media use. The information overload hypothesis assumes that there exists a threshold point in any individual beyond which additionally received information can lead to a decline in processing ability, information overload, and finally even stress and anxiety (Koroleva et al., 2010). As a side observation, out of the ten publications that were categorized as having a focal topic of information overload, seven publications (70%) were authored by German researchers. The empirical field of most publications in this category was the social networking service Facebook. Table 31 summarizes the publications dealing with *information overload*.

Table 31: Research on information overload

Study focus	Study	Year	Type
Exploration of information overload on Facebook and derivation of recommendations for providers of networks	Koroleva et al.	2010	Case study
Analysis of the influence of heuristic cues in Facebook on users' attitude and potential information overload	Koroleva et al.	2011	Quantitative
Analysis of impact of network and information characteristics on Facebook users' attitude towards information overload	Weinert et al.	2012	Quantitative
Why do Facebook users experience fatigue when using a social networking service that is intended to provide fun and hedonic value?	Maier et al.	2012b	Quantitative
Exploration of information overload on Facebook users and the factors associated with it, generation of design recommendations for user interfaces to mitigate overload	Shrivastav et al.	2012	Quantitative
Examination of sources and impact of stress in users of social networking services	Maier et al.	2012a	Quantitative
How is the structure of a social networking service related to positive and negative outcomes (social overload)?	Wang	2013	Quantitative
Analysis of how communication characteristics contribute to social interaction overload	Maier et al.	2013a	Quantitative
How do connection demands in various media channels impact affect in users	Lee et al.	2013	Quantitative
What are the roles of addiction and strain in the behaviour of users of social networking services?	Maier et al.	2013b	Quantitative
Proposition of a model of continuance intention to use social networking services and confirmation of the role of habit on information overload	Kefi et al.	2015	Quantitative

4.2.4 Mood and habit

Mood and habit contains publications that investigate the effect of social media use on mood aspects, habit, and mood-related behavior. The empirical field of almost all the identified studies – all of which are either quantitative or are conceptual research proposals of quantitative studies – is the social networking service Facebook. Topics range from very negative aspects like depression contagion on social networking services (Xu et al., 2013), over more neutral topics like how status message use on Facebook contributes to social connectedness (Köbler et al., 2010), to positive effects like the psychological empowerment of women through blogging (Stavrositu & Sundar, 2012). An overview of the publications on *mood and habit* can be found in table 32.

Table 32: Research on mood and habit

Study focus	Study	Year	Type
Investigation into the role of network structure on mood and tension in social networking services	Binder et al.	2009	Quantitative
In-depth analysis of the role of a social networking service on teenagers' mood and activities	Greenhow, Robelia	2009	Case study
Use of status update message in social networking services helps generate feelings of connectedness between users	Köbler et al.	2010	Quantitative
Feelings of satiation motivate users to seek variety on Facebook	Church, Salam	2010	Quantitative
What is the role of technology dependency in habit formation among users of social networking services	Thadani, Cheung	2011	Quantitative
What is the effect of using social networking services on environmental behaviour	Oakley, Salam	2011	Quantitative
Examination of negative and positive outcomes of social networking services use on romantic relationships	Utz, Beukeboom	2011	Quantitative
Exploration of the relationship between blogging and psychological empowerment in women	Stavrositu, Sundar	2012	Quantitative
Analysis of sentiment exchange in social networking services	Hillmann, Trier	2012	Quantitative
What are the antecedents of habit in users of social networking services?	Wu, Tseng	2012	Quantitative
Proposition of a research model to explain compulsive use of Facebook	Cheung et al.	2013	Quantitative
Proposition of a research framework that links tense moods to habitual use of Facebook	Lee, Jahng	2013	Conceptual
Investigation into depression contagion on social networking services	Xu et al.	2013	Conceptual
What is the influence of sentiment on communication and behaviour in social networking services?	Hillmann, Trier	2013	Quantitative
Understanding users' reactions and responses to social predicament in social networking services	Choi, Jiang	2013b	Quantitative
Development of a framework to understand antecedents and consequences of sense of community in social networking services	Mamonov	2013	Quantitative
Investigation of relationship attachment and vitality as results of social networking services use	Islam, Mäntymäki	2014	Quantitative
Analysis of the impact of Facebook use on well-being and life satisfaction in teenagers	Wenninger et al.	2014	Quantitative
Development of a model to explain the influence of relationship characteristics and features of online social networking services on perceived loneliness	Matook et al.	2015	Quantitative
Analysis of the influence of social media use among students on academic performance and satisfaction with life	Hassell, Sukalich	2015	Quantitative
Examination of drivers and consequences of frustration in Facebook users	Wirth et al.	2015	Quantitative
Analysis of the causes of addiction among Facebook users	Kisyovska et al.	2015	Quantitative

Study focus	Study	Year	Type
Connection between mood and communication on social networking services depends on selection of communication partners	Kraut, Burke	2015	Review article
Proposition of a research model that links member satisfaction and member loyalty in social networking services users	Krishen et al.	2015	Quantitative
Examination of the influence of habitual Facebook use on susceptibility to fraud	Vishwanath	2015	Quantitative
Investigation into the development of psychological dependence on social media among microblogging users	Wang et al.	2015	Quantitative
Examination of Facebook users' impulse buying behavior	Chen et al.	2016	Quantitative
Expanded version of the study by Kraut and Burke (2015) on the connection between Facebook use and mood	Burke, Kraut	2016	Quantitative
Analysis of the influence of Facebook use and its characteristics on mood and psychological well-being	Seo et al.	2016	Quantitative
Development of a model to explain cyberbullying on social networking services	Zhang et al.	2016	Quantitative
Proposition of a framework to examine user passion and affect on social networking services	Wakefield, Wakefield	2016	Quantitative
Investigation of the influence of social networking services users' personality traits on psychological well-being	Sharma	2016	Conceptual

4.2.5 Motivation and intention

Motivation and intention refers to publications that investigate what constitutes motivations, goals, and intentions to use social networking services. Papers in this category deal with questions like 'what is the moderating role of utilitarian and hedonic user motivation on users' behavior in Web 2.0 applications?' (Wang et al., 2009) or the development of frameworks that help better understand the motivations of users of social networking services (Wu, 2009b). Table 33 provides a summary of the studies on *motivation and intention*.

Table 33: Research on motivation and intention

Study focus	Study	Year	Type
Analysis of usage motivations and gratifications derived from Facebook use	Joinson	2008	Quantitative
Systematic analysis of motivation and usage patterns of social networking services	Schaefer	2008	Quantitative
Analyis of log data in Facebook to understand newcomers' motivations for contributing content	Burke et al.	2009	Quantitative
Study of users' behavioural intentions in a web 2.0 environment	Wang et al.	2009	Quantitative
Proposition of a framework for understanding the motivation of users of social networking services	Wu	2009b	Conceptual
Exploration of the hedonic and utilitarian values of social networking services	Wu	2009a	Quantitative
Examination of gender differences in the development of we-intention to participate in collaboration in social networking services	Shen et al.	2010	Quantitative
Development of a theoretical model to understand network construction behaviour in social networking services	Krasnova et al.	2010	Conceptual
Exploration of gift-giving as theoretical framework to understand social behaviour and motivation in social networking services	Skageby	2010	Conceptual
Proposition of a model to understand why people use social networking services	Cheung, Lee	2010	Quantitative
Understanding factors that influence users' motivations to use Web 2.0 tools	Yeh et al.	2012	Quantitative
Examination of the hedonic motivation of social media users in the case of musicians' Facebook pages	Sopha, Raghu	2012	Quantitative
Analysis of the influence of self-identity and social influence on users' intentions to use social software	Vannoy, Medlin	2013	Conceptual
Proposition of a mathematical model to predict users' interest in microblogging	Bao et al.	2013	Conceptual
Influence of envy on users' intention to use social networking services	Wu, Srite	2014	Quantitative
Investigation into the reasons why users share location-related information on social networking services	Luarn et al.	2015	Quantitative

4.2.6 Adoption and continuance

Adoption and continuance, with 33 publications presumably the most widely explored aspect in the social and behavioral view of social software, deals with questions of adoption, non-adoption, and continuance of mostly social networking services, both of a hedonic nature (like Facebook) and a utilitarian nature (enterprise social networking services). There is a very wide array of studies that explore these issues in the context of hedonic social networking services, studies on professionally used services are few (e.g. Kügler et al., 2012). An overview of the publications on *adoption and continuance* is given in table 34.

Table 34: Research on adoption and continuance

Study focus	Study	Year	Type
Proposition of a research model to explain the acceptance of hedonic information systems and the intentions of users	Rosen, Sherman	2006	Mixed mode
What are the antecedents for adoption and use of hedonic social networking services?	Sledgianowski, Kulviwat	2008	Quantitative
Investigation of the influence of the 'big five' personality traits on the acceptance of social networking services, using a new framework that targets acceptance of hedonic information systems	Rosen, Kluemper	2008	Quantitative
Examination of the impact of social ties on the adoption of a social networking service in the field of bodybuilding	Ploderer et al.	2008	Case study
Analysis of factors that influence users to continue using social networking services after initial acceptance	Hu, Kettinger	2008	Conceptual
Examination of continuance usage intentions in twitter users	Barnes, Böhringer	2009	Quantitative
Study of bloggers' post-adoption behaviour	Zhang et al.	2009	Quantitative
Proposition of a new construct, change in intended use, to understand users' satisfaction with social networking services	Harden	2010	Quantitative
Investigation of the influence of gender and the degree of shyness on the continuance of usage intention of a hedonic social networking service	Kefi et al.	2010	Quantitative
Development and test of a theoretical model to help explain the adoption of Web 2.0 services	Soliman, Beaudry	2010	Quantitative
Proposition of a research model based on expectation-confirmation model of information systems continuance to understand users' continuance intention of social networking services	Yin et al.	2011	Quantitative
How to motivate nonadopters to accept social networking services	Hu et al.	2011	Quantitative
Exploration of factors that influence the adoption of Web 2.0 applications using the technology acceptance model	Dwivedi et al.	2011	Quantitative
Extension of information systems continance model to help better understand the user experience of professional social networking services	Islam, Mäntymäki	2012	Quantitative
Analysis of users' loyalty of social networking services through the lens of social exchange theory and satisfaction	Shin, Hall	2012	Quantitative
Proposition of a model to understand adoption of enterprise social networking services	Kügler et al.	2012	Quantitative
Development of a research model to understand post-adoptive use intention of social networking services	Jung et al.	2012	Quantitative
Refinement of the commitment-trust model of website stickiness in the context of social networking services	Xu et al.	2012	Quantitative

Study focus	Study	Year	Type
Proposition of a model based on expectation confirmation theory to understand continuance intention in users of social networking services	Johnson	2012	Quantitative
Exploration of the antecedents of the perceived enjoyment and perceived usefulness constructs of the technology acceptance model in the context of social networking services	Ernst et al.	2013	Quantitative
Building of a predictive model of technology acceptance of social networking services	Li et al.	2013	Quantitative
Understanding the antecedents and effects of computer self-efficacy in the context of Asian social networking service users	John	2013	Quantitative
Proposition of a research framework to understand social media non-adoption	Gupta et al.	2013	Case study
Analysis of continuance participation on Facebook based on an extension of the theory of planned behavior	Al-Debei et al.	2013	Quantitative
Investigation of usage continuance of social networking services	Mlaiki et al.	2013	Mixed mode
Extension of the unified theory of acceptance and use of technology (UTAUT) to understand individual use of social networking services	Zhao, Srite	2013	Conceptual
Understanding the adoption of social networking services among elderly people	Vyas, Choudrie	2013	Quantitative
Investigation of factors that influence the adoption of blogs by elderly users	Liu, Shi	2014	Quantitative
Examination of antecedents of social networking service switching intention	Chang et al.	2014	Quantitative
Investigation of discontinuance intentions in users of social networking services	Maier et al.	2015	Quantitative
Literature review of factors that influence the adoption of social commerce by consumers	Friedrich	2015	Literature review
Influence of curiosity on user acceptance of social networking services	Oehlhorn et al.	2016	Quantitative

4.2.7 Trust

Trust, a well-researched phenomenon in information systems usage and particularly computer-mediated communication (Shin & Hall, 2013), is getting increased attention among researchers of social networking services. This category contains nine publications that investigate the role of trust on a variety of users' behavioral aspects like continuance usage (Shin & Hall, 2013), but also explores antecedents of trust (Salehan, 2013) or the role of culture and cultural diversity on trust among users of social networking services (Krasnova et al., 2011; Musembwa & Paul, 2012). Some of the publications in this category are also closely related to the category of privacy, which is discussed in the following section. An overview of the studies dealing with *trust* is given in table 35.

Table 35: Research on trust

Study focus	Study	Year	Type
How do trust and privacy concerns influence human interactions on social networking services?	Dwyer et al.	2007	Quantitative
How to enable providers of social networking services to address problems of trust and privacy	Krasnova et al.	2010	Quantitative
Examination of the influence of self-construal on the building of trust on social networking services	Chen, Mitchell	2010	Quantitative
Analysis of the influence of culture on trust in social networking services	Krasnova et al.	2011	Quantitative
Proposition of a model to understand the effects of trust, diversity, and social capital on the willingness of users cto take an active role in social networking services	Musembwa, Paul	2012	Conceptual
Proposition of a peer-to-peer reputation system for increasing trust on social networking services	Ganesh, Sethi	2013	Conceptual
Exploration of the role of trust on social networking services, leveraging social exchange theory and expectation confirmation model	Shin, Hall	2013	Quantitative
Investigation of users' trust perceptions on social networking services via a brain imaging experiment and a behavioural study	Kopton et al.	2013	Mixed mode
What are antecedents and consequences of trust in social networking services?	Salehan et al.	2013	Quantitative
Investigation of how employee behaviour in social networking services influences customer trust	Ivens, Schaarschmidt	2015	Quantitative

4.2.8 Privacy

Privacy has been similarly well researched like trust in the general literature on information systems, but as of 2009, there has been little published research on privacy on the then-upcoming phenomenon of social networking services (Nov & Wattal, 2009). This situation has changed considerably since then – the category of *privacy* contains 20 publications that explore and analyze privacy-related issues in social software and primarily in social networking services. A summary of publications on *privacy* is provided in table 36.

Table 36: Research on privacy

Study focus	Study	Year	Type
Analysis of the impact of privacy concerns and its antecedents in social networking services	Nov, Wattal	2009	Quantitative
Identification of three user types with different perceptions of privacy using conjoint analysis	Krasnova et al.	2009	Quantitative
Study of privacy policies of social networking services	Rizk et al.	2010	Case study
Proposition of a concept to enable digital expiration to protect privacy	Karla	2010	Conceptual
Proposition and test of a research model to understand why users of hedonic social networking services exchange privacy for pleasure	Thambusamy et al.	2010	Quantitative
Examination of the influence of privacy concerns and trust on the willingness to share personal information with different user groups on Facebook	Lo, Riemenschneider	2010	Quantitative
Discussion of privacy challenges in Web 2.0	Buhl, Müller	2010	Overview article
Proposition and empirical validation of a privacy concept that matches the features of interaction in social networking services	Zhang et al.	2011	Quantitative
Investigation into factors that explain motivations of SNS users' to use individual privacy settings	Deuker	2012	Quantitative
Analysis of the privacy practices of Facebook users and longitudinal comparison with a previous study of 2007	Collins et al.	2012	Quantitative
Perceived privacy and trust in other users of a social networking service are positively correlated with trust in the social networking service	Harden et al.	2012	Quantitative
Proposition and operationalization of a framework to analyze privacy concerns in social software	Choi, Jiang	2013a	Conceptual
Understanding the influence of privacy perceptions on users' behaviour with Facebook's application and permission dialogs	Krasnova et al.	2013	Quantitative
Proposition of a model to help understand the influence of privacy settings on self-disclosure in the social networking service Facebook	Tschersich, Botha	2013	Quantitative
Exploration of privacy preserving activities of elderly people on Facebook	Chakraborty et al.	2013	Quantitative
Investigation into privacy issues of underage users of social networking services	Livingston et al.	2013	Quantitative
Definition of objectives for identity and privacy protection	Dhillon, Chowdhuri	2013	Quantitative
How can privacy concerns be counterbalanced by perceived social benefits attained in using a social networking service	Wilson et al.	2014	Quantitative
Experimental investigation into the relationship of social network providers' privacy policies and the reactions of users	Gerlach et al.	2015	Quantitative
Examination of interpersonal boundary regulation to understand the conflict of privacy protection on social networking services and interacting with other users	Wisniewski et al.	2016	Mixed mode

4.3 Organizational View

Over the last decade, a variety of Web 2.0 and social software applications have been widely adopted by individual users, a fact that has also been noticed and received considerable attention from organizations. Although an increasing share of organizations has started to use Web 2.0 technologies and social software application with the aim of fostering innovation and improving collaboration, some researchers noted that only a few theoretical perspectives are found in the literature that help understand the phenomenon of adoption of Web 2.0 technologies by organizations and enterprises (Huang et al., 2010). This section sheds some light on the perspectives of extant publications that broadly deal with the use and adoption of social software in an organizational context. The rather extensive literature base that has been identified to belong to the organizational view has been split into seven sub-groups that encompass a wide range of topics: '*Enterprise 2.0*', '*social software for organizational knowledge and innovation management*', '*organizational adoption of Web 2.0 technologies*', '*volunteering 2.0*', '*digital health*', '*crisis management*', and '*governmental use*'.

4.3.1 Enterprise 2.0

Enterprise 2.0 denotes the use of social software platforms by organizations to pursue their goals (McAfee, 2009). With 58 papers in this category, it constitutes a fairly large and rather generic subgroup of the identified publications on social software within the organizational view. More specialized publications on the use of social software for organizational knowledge and innovation management can be found in the next section. The papers of this category cover a broad range of topics ranging from overview and literature review articles (e.g. Bächle, 2007; Stenmark, 2008; Nath et al., 2009; Richter et al., 2011) to use case-specific analyses of Enterprise 2.0 applications (e.g. Gonzalez et al., 2013; Seebach et al., 2011). Table 37 provides a summary of the papers on *Enterprise 2.0*.

Table 37: Research on Enterprise 2.0

Study focus	Study	Year	Type
Analysis of an enterprise social bookmarking service	Millen et al.	2006	Quantitative
Research framework for using social software in organizational settings	Ip	2007	Conceptual
Review of products for enterprise social networking	Koch et al.	2007	Review article
Analysis of users' motivations for adopting social networking services in a work context	DiMicco et al.	2008	Case study
Proposition of a framework to analyze the business value of social networking services	Kettles, David	2008	Conceptual
Overview article of Enterprise 2.0, social commerce, and open innovation as business and organizational applications of Web 2.0 technologies	Bächle	2008	Review article
Does Web 2.0 constitute a useful concept for business use?	Stenmark	2008	Literature review
Development of a conceptual foundation to understand value propositions of Web 2.0 technologies	Nath et al.	2009	Literature review
How can social networking services support collaboration in enterprises?	Richter, Koch	2009	Case study
Development of a prototype of a enterprise social networking service as a management tool for technical systems	Bente, Karla	2009	Conceptual
Analysis of requirements for using Web 2.0 technologies in small and medium enterprises	Blinn et al.	2009	Case study
Mechanisms for improvement in corporate blogging	Yardi et al.	2009	Mixed mode
Practitioner review article of Enterprise 2.0 characteristics and value proposition	McAfee	2009	Review article
Attributes of social software and organizational benefits	Ali-Hassan, Nevo	2009	Quantitative
Usage potential of enterprise microblogging	Riemer et al.	2010a	Case study
Proposition of an Enterprise 2.0 management framework	Patten, Keane	2010	Conceptual
Expanded and re-published version of the framework proposed by Nath et al. (2009)	Nath et al.	2010	Literature review
Expanded and re-published version of the Web 2.0 requirements analysiy by Blinn et al. (2009)	Blinn et al.	2010	Case study
Can enterprise microblogging platforms be used productively in a corporate context?	Riemer et al.	2010b	Case study
How can organizations become Enterprise 2.0?	Seo, Rietsema	2010	Case study
Development of a framework that integrates opportunities and challenges of adoption of social networking services	Turban et al.	2011	Case study
Evaluation of a social collaboration platform regarding support for situation awareness	Seebach et al.	2011	Case study
Development of a model for analyzing the influence of an organizational social web site on work performance	Raeth et al.	2011	Conceptual
Comprehensive literature review on Enterprise 2.0	Richter et al.	2011	Literature review
Analysis of corporate use of enterprise microblogging for context building	Riemer et al.	2011	Case study
Understanding the influence of Web 2.0 usage at home on usage intention of Enterprise 2.0 tools	Majumdar, Krishna	2012	Quantitative

Study focus	Study	Year	Type
Assessing organizational readiness for Enterprise 2.0 tools via organizational semiotics methods	Jacobs, Nakata	2012	Case study
Analysis of the influence of usage of social networking service on organizational identification	Larosiliere, Leidner	2012	Quantitative
Understanding the contextual aspects of Enterprise 2.0 tools	Richter, Riemer	2013	Case study
Proposition of a framework for guidelines of Enterprise 2.0 tools	Krüger et al.	2013	Case study
Benefits of adoption of social software for corporate use	Majumdar et al.	2013	Case study
Analysis of the relationship of enterprise social software and boundary spanning	Van Osch, Steinfield	2013	Quantitative
Influence of social media usage on organizational commitment and socialization	Gonzalez et al.	2013	Quantitative
Examination of innovation-related content flows in enterprise social networking services	Malsbender et al.	2013	Conceptual
Using an enterprise social network service as part of an effort to change internal culture	Koch et al.	2013	Case study
Analysis of users' perceptions of the profiles of other users in enterprise social networking services	Cummings, Reinicke	2014	Quantitative
What do management consultants advise organizations wanting to engage in social media	Stenmark, Zaffar	2014	Case study
Analysis of influencing factors on enterprise social media usage	Aoun et al.	2014	Quantitative
Proposition of a framework that categorizes enterprise social software according to control and interaction	Razmerita et al.	2014	Mixed mode
Investigation of role and influence of users that add value in enterprise social networking services	Berger et al.	2014	Mixed mode
Proposition of social fabric as a theoretical framework to help understand interactions on enterprise social networking services	Dyrby et al.	2014	Case study
Investigation into factors that influence the use of enterprise social networking services	Chin et al.	2015	Case study
Proposition of affordances for social software that helps in corporate communications	Argyris, Monu	2015	Conceptual
Analysis of online social networking by applying a deep structure framework	Trier, Richter	2015	Case study
Investigation of the influence of organizational hierarchies on users' behaviour on enterprise social networking services	Behrendt et al.	2015	Mixed mode
Proposition of a framework to help guide the evaluation of enterprise social networking services	Herzog et al.	2015	Case study
Teaching case about a large organization that abolished email in internal communication	Silic et al.	2015	Case study
Analysis of activities within enterprise social networking services and their influence on team collaboration	Merz et al.	2015	Case study
Examination of the influence of organizational climate on contributive and consumptive usage of enterprise social networking services	Kügler et al.	2015	Quantitative

Study focus	Study	Year	Type
Proposition and test of a model that investigates the influence of usage of corporate blogs on job performance	Lu et al.	2015	Quantitative
Case study portraying a successful implementation of an enterprise social networking service	Chin et al.	2015	Case study
Exploration of users' behaviour on enterprise social networking services	Chen et al.	2015	Conceptual
Investigation of the impact of enterprise social networking services on employee performance	Kuegler et al.	2015	Quantitative
Exploration of the role of habit to help explain adoption of enterprise social networking services as an email replacement	Pillet, Carillo	2015	Quantitative
Development of a framework to classify and analyse corporate blogs	Dennis et al.	2016	Conceptual
Business users of enterprise social networking services behave in a less social way than private users of hedonic social networks	Mettler, Winter	2016	Quantitative
Editorial relating enterprise social networking services and organisational change	Kumar et al.	2016	Editorial
What team boundary-spanning activities are carried out in enterprise social networking services?	van Osch, Steinfield	2016	Mixed mode
Exploration of relationship between users' experience of enterprise social networking services and their assessment of collaboration quality	Wyatt et al.	2016	Quantitative

4.3.2 Social software for organizational knowledge and innovation management

Knowledge is widely accepted as the strategically most important resource for organizations to create sustainable competitive advantage (Bharati et al., 2012). The rise of social software technologies like wikis, blogs, and social networking systems and their potential benefit for organizations like improving bottlenecks commonly associated with knowledge management (Arazy & Gellatly, 2013) has inspired a host of research on the topic of *social software for organizational knowledge and innovation management*. The large number of publications that fall into this category mirrors this interest in the positive outcomes of social software use in an organizational context, with scholars suggesting that social software may change and improve processes in organizations in fundamental ways (Manour et al., 2013). Table 38 provides a summary of publications on *social software for organizational knowledge and innovation management*.

Table 38: Research on social software for organizational knowledge and innovation management

Study focus	Study	Year	Type
Investigation of how Web 2.0 technologies can support innovation and knowledge management processes	Benlian & Hess	2008	Quantitative
Using community blogs for organizational knowledge management	Silva et al.	2008	Case study
Proposition of a framework that investigates the suitability of Web 2.0 tools for organizational learning	Boateng et al.	2009	Conceptual
Examination of influences on user's intention to share knowledge on Enterprise 2.0 tools, leveraging expectation confirmation theory	Kim et al.	2009	Quantitative
Understanding the use of blogs for knowledge production	Wei	2009	Quantitative
Critical investigation into the usefulness of Web 2.0 communities for knowledge production	Javadi & Gebauer	2009	Case study
Using wikis to enhance the documentation and analysis of enterprise architecture	Buckl et al.	2009	Conceptual
Proposition of a social software-based tool to support knowledge management	Spiekermann et al.	2009	Conceptual
How enterprise wikis can be used as a collaborative information repository in knowledge management	Bibbo et al.	2010	Case study
Proposition of a research framework of success factors of wiki technology in an enterprise context	Chai et al.	2010	Conceptual
Proposition of a model to help understand organizational use of Web 2.0 tools to foster innovation	Huang et al.	2010	Conceptual
How can wikis be leveraged to improve team performance?	Zhang et al.	2011	Quantitative
Using social bookmarking systems to improve innovativeness	Gray et al.	2010	Quantitative
Proposition of a strategic research agenda on the potential of Web 2.0 tools to foster and change knowledge management	von Krogh	2012	Conceptual
How can Web 2.0 tools help organizations improve knowledge management and knowledge quality?	Bharati et al.	2012	Quantitative
Exploration of how social media can foster innovation in an organizational setting	Helms et al.	2012	Mixed mode
Proposition of a framework to explain how organizational use of Web 2.0 can foster knowledge management and organizational learning	Huang, Güney	2012	Conceptual
Exploration of the affordance of wiki systems to continuously improve contributions in an enterprise wiki	Majchrzak et al.	2013	Quantitative
Investigation into usage motivations of organizational wiki systems	Arazy, Gellatly	2013	Quantitative
Analysis of the influence of social media use on competitive advantage and performance of enterprises	Hu, Schlagwein	2013	Case study
Understanding wiki affordances for organizational knowledge management practice	Mansour et al.	2013	Case study
Exploration of the suitability of Web 2.0 tools to help organizations assimilate knowledge	Limaj, Bernroider	2013	Quantitative

Study focus	Study	Year	Type
Proposition of a research model to understand the potential of microblogging to facilitate knowledge creation	Cleveland, Ellis	2013	Conceptual
Understanding tensions in organizations with Web 2.0 tools like Facebook and Twitter challenging traditional approaches to knowledge management	Ford, Mason	2013b	Mixed mode
Investigation of the influence of social media on team performance in knowledge work	Nissen, Bergin	2013	Quantitative
How can social software technology foster informal knowledge sharing in the enterprise	Jarrahi, Sawyer	2013	Case study
Exploration of social media on knowledge management models	Hemsley, Mason	2013	Mixed mode
Overview of current trends in social software use for knowledge management and proposition of a framework to tackle open research questions	Pawlowski et al.	2014	Overview and conceptual
Literature review on how social software can be leveraged in new product development (NPD)	Rohmann et al.	2014	Literature review
Enterprise social networking services can increase accuracy of users' metaknowledge at work	Leonardi	2015	Quantitative
What are barriers and challenges that impede the success of social software tools to support new product development (NPD)	Rohmann et al.	2015	Case study
Investigation of how the use of enterprise social networking (ESN) services moderates the relationship between stressors and employee innovation	Ding et al.	2015	Quantitative
Proposition of a model to understand the impact of microblogging capacities on employee attitude on knowledge sharing	Ellis	2015	Conceptual
Proposition of a new archetype of project leadership to facilitate institutionalising wiki-based knowledge-management systems	Argyris, Ransbotham	2016	Case study
Extrinsic factors motivate employees to share knowledge in enterprise social networking services	Rode	2016	Quantitative
How can the affordances of enterprise social networking services be leveraged to help users cope with institutional complexity	Oostervink et al.	2016	Case study

4.3.3 Organizational adoption of Web 2.0 technologies

Organizational adoption of Web 2.0 technologies deals with publications that investigate the challenges associated with the efficient and effective deployment of social software technologies in organizations and their adoption thereafter. Studies in these categories comprise the proposition of new models and metrics to help understand the success of social software tools in organizational environments (e.g. Raeth et al., 2009; Muller et al., 2009; Pishdad & Haider, 2012), empirical tests of such models (e.g. Saldanha &

Krishnan, 2012) and case studies of organizational adoption in various verticals (e.g. Ramotar & Baptista, 2013). Table 39 summarizes the papers of this category.

Table 39: Research on organizational adoption of Web 2.0 technologies

Study focus	Study	Year	Type
Proposition of models to assess the success of wikis and blogs in an organizational environment	Raeth et al.	2009	Conceptual
Proposition of the metric 'Return on Contribution' for managing enterprise social software	Muller et al.	2009	Conceptual
Empirical test of a model of Web 2.0 adoption in business	Saldanha, Krishnan	2010	Quantitative
Analysis of the influence of network externalities on adoption of blogs in organizations	Wattal et al.	2010	Quantitative
Adoption of Web 2.0 technologies in Australian organizations	Singh et al.	2010	Case study
Acceptance of microblogging technologies in enterprises	Mayer, Dibbern	2010	Case study
Factors influencing adoption of Web 2.0 in business	Kosalge, Tole	2010	Quantitative
Adoption of Web 2.0 in large businesses through a process perspective	Raeth et al.	2010	Case study
Proposition of research framework for analyzing organizational adoption and diffusion of Web 2.0 technologies	Pishdad, Haider	2012	Conceptual
Case study on adoption of enterprise social networking service in a large consultancy	Riemer et al.	2012	Case study
Proposition and test of model of factors to explain organizational adoption of Web 2.0 technologies; expanded version of Saldanha & Krishan (2010)	Saldanha, Krishnan	2012	Quantitative
What are consequences of adoption of social media by organizations?	de Oliveira, Watson-Manheim	2013	Case study
Exploration of internal processes of organizations to support adoption of social media	Alfaro et al.	2013	Quantitative
Investigation of use of metrics and methods used by organizations for measuring success of enterprise social software	Herzog et al.	2013	Case study
Case study on social media adoption in a financial services organization	Ramotar, Baptista	2013	Case study
How can organizational support influence the adoption of Enterprise 2.0 software?	Alqahtani et al.	2014	Case study
Investigation of recruiters' intention to adopt social software	Alalwan	2014	Quantitative
Identification of employees' post-adoptive behaviors in the use of enterprise social networking services	Kügler, Smolnik	2014	Quantitative
Investigation of strategies employed to control enterprise social networking services and the symbolic capital generated by the adoption of such systems	Karoui et al.	2015	Case study
Analysis of the influence of system design features on the acceptance of enterprise social media	Paluch et al.	2015	Mixed mode
Exploration of enterprise social software adoption through the lens of resistance and workarounds	Choudrie, Zamani	2016	Case study
Investigation of factors that influence the adoption of Facebook in Cameroonian workplaces	Nzabandora et al.	2016	Quantitative

4.3.4 Volunteering 2.0

With five publications, the area of *Volunteering 2.0* investigates how volunteer organizations can leverage social networking services and social media to improve volunteer retention (Connolly & Jones, 2012a; Connolly & Jones, 2012b), how non-profit organizations can engage volunteers and stakeholders with the microblogging service Twitter (Lovejoy & Saxton, 2012) and how Facebook can be leveraged to help in the self-organization of volunteers (Kaufhold & Reuter, 2015). Table 40 provides a summary of the studies dealing with *Volunteering 2.0*.

Table 40: Research on Volunteering 2.0

Study focus	Study	Year	Type
Using social networking services for volunteer retention	Connolly, Jones	2012a	Conceptual
How can volunteer organizations leverage social networking services	Connolly, Jones	2012b	Mixed mode
Social media use in non-profit organizations	Lovejoy, Saxton	2012	Quantitative
Case study on the usage of a Chinese microblogging platform to support a volunteering organization	Zheng, Yu	2014	Case study
Development and evaluation of a Facebook-based application to help in volunteers' self-organization	Kaufhold, Reuter	2015	Conceptual

4.3.5 Digital health

Digital health contains publications that deal with the potential of social networking services for health care and management and building digital health communities. Kühne et al. (2011) look at the diffusion of Web 2.0 tools in German health insurance companies, Lux et al. (2013) investigate the benefits of using social networking services in hospital recruitment, Kordzadeh and Young (2015) explore Facebook posts to further the understanding of how hospitals use social media, and Ba and Wang (2013) analyze the effect of digital health communities on their users' motivations. Table 41 summarizes the publications on digital health.

Table 41: Research on digital health

Study focus	Study	Year	Type
How are Web 2.0 tools used by German health insurance companies?	Kühne et al.	2011	Quantitative
Using social networking services for recruiting in hospitals	Lux et al.	2013	Quantitative
How can health-related social networking services motivate users to change their lifestyles	Ba, Wang	2013	Quantitative
Examination of the usage potential of social media to support the interaction of patient and physician	Dantu et al.	2014	Conceptual
Proposition of a typoplogy of social media-based interactions between health care providers and consumers	Smailhodzic et al.	2015	Quantitative
How can participation in digital health communities on social networking services improve health-promoting behaviors in patients?	Tan	2015	Mixed mode
Analysis of Facebook posts to understand the use of social media by hospitals	Kordzadeh, Young	2015	Mixed mode

4.3.6 Crisis management

Using social software in the context of *crisis management* is a research topic that started to emerge between 2010 and 2012 with three publications that were still in the research-in-progress state at the time of publication within the International Conference of Information Systems proceedings in 2010, 2011, and 2012 respectively. All three publications investigate the usage potential of social software and social networking services for emergency and crisis management. In subsequent years, the topic has gained broader traction and publications include a comprehensive literature review (Simon et al., 2015), apart from several case studies and quantitative analyses (e.g. Stieglitz et al., 2015) that examine the usage (potential) and adoption of social media for emergency and crisis management. Table 42 summarizes the publications dealing with *crisis management*.

Table 42: Research on crisis management

Study focus	Study	Year	Type
Usage potential of social networking services for emergency management	Ada et al.	2010	Conceptual
Exploration of the usage potential of social media for disaster management	Ahmed	2011	Conceptual
Use of microblogging for emotion management during a crisis	Vaast et al.	2012	Conceptual
Analysis of adoption and usage potential of social networking services by emergency management agencies	Gill et al.	2014	Case study
Application of social network analysis (SNA) on emergency responses	Stojmenovic, Lindgaard	2014	Case study
Examination of the use of social networking services in crisis management of natural disasters	Leong et al.	2015	Case study
Investigation into social media strategies during product-harm crises at the example of a plane crash in 2015	He et al.	2015	Quantitative
Literature review of usage of social media in crisis and emergency situations	Simon et al.	2015	Literature review
Proposition of an approach to dynamically assess user-generated content on social media in the context of emergency situations	Ludwig et al.	2015	Case study
Investigation of the usage of social media by emergency management agencies	Van Gorp et al.	2015	Case study
Analysis of crisis-related communication on Twitter	Stieglitz et al.	2015	Quantitative
Examination of the importance of key words in emergency management-related social media	Yates, Paquette	2016	Quantitative

4.3.7 Governmental use

Governmental use refers to publications that investigate the usage potential for social software and social networking services in government. Researchers assume that social media offers the potential to support, enhance, and transform governmental activities and functions (Ferro et al., 2013) since it facilitates communication of a government with its citizens and is assumed to increase participation and foster e-democracy (Magnusson et al., 2012), thus calling for more research on the use of social software in that area (Ferro et al., 2013). Table 43 provides a summary of the publications.

Table 43: Research on governmental use

Study focus	Study	Year	Type
Exploratory case study of Facebook use in governmental settings	Magnusson et al.	2012	Case study
Proposition of a framework to evaluate social software potential for governmental usage	Ferro et al.	2013	Conceptual
Investigation into governments' rationales and strategies of social media use	Hofmann	2014	Case study

4.4 Design View

The design view contains publications that deal with a wide range of design-related subjects and overview articles. These publications have been split into three sub-groups: *'principles and practices of design for social software'*, *'design of collaborative social software'*, and *'design of social tagging and bookmarking systems'*.

4.4.1 Principles and practices of design for social software

Principles and practices of design for social software captures publications that deal with general questions of how to design social software and takes up approaches as diverse as positive design, social facilitation, or soft systems methodology. In addition, concrete examples of design social software systems for special use cases are explored. Authors agree that social computing can be viewed as the new and prevalent paradigm of human-computer interaction made possible by a range of Web 2.0 technologies such as microblogging, tagging and social bookmarking, blogging, wikis, social networking services, and collaborative filtering and recommendation systems (Carroll, 2010). As such, this now prevalent paradigm has impacted and transformed the design practice of the world wide web towards a more collaborative fashion (Carroll, 2010) and allows for technologically-mediated social relations to be almost as meaningful and rich as real-world social interactions (Bouman et al., 2007). Table 44 summarizes the publications dealing with *principles and practices of design for social software.*

Table 44: Research on principles and practices of design for social software

Study focus	Study	Year	Type
Deriving implications for the design of information sharing systems from an analysis of del-icio.us	Lee	2006	Quantitative
Understanding the concept of sociality for improving the design of social software	Bouman et al.	2007	Case study
Proposal of a design for a social networking service in the domain of emergeny management	Plotnick et al.	2009	Conceptual
How to design an interactive name translation system	Zhou	2009	Conceptual
Supporting activity awareness in social software with positive design	Carroll	2010	Conceptual
Design proposition of friend suggestion and friend browsing modules for social networking services	Chau	2010	Conceptual
Using source cues to influence reading choice	Winter, Krämer	2012	Quantitative
How can organizations design and use social software for improving task performance	Niehaves, Tavakoli	2012	Quantitative

4.4.2 Design of collaborative social software

Design of collaborative social software refers to publications that focus in detail on the collaboration-related aspects when designing social software systems. Topics cover a wide variety of aspects, e.g. Kasemvilas and Olfman (2009) focus on a wiki system to support collaborative writing through the lens of design science, Liao and Li (2008) investigate patterns for designing user interfaces for effectively managing connections at work, and Dwyer (2007) explores the dynamics of social networking sites using the task technology fit theory and the social-technical gap theory in order to better support the social requirements that arise out of the use of these platforms. Table 45 provides a summary of publications dealing with the *design of collaborative social software*.

Table 45: Research on design of collaborative social software

Study focus	Study	Year	Type
Combination of task technology fit and social-technical gap theory to help design collaborative social networking services	Dwyer	2007	Conceptual
Designing user interfaces for managing work connections efficiently and effectively	Liao, Li	2008	Conceptual
Design of an enterprise wiki to support a globally distributed research organization	Danis, Singer	2008	Mixed mode
Development of a framework to improve socio-emotional processes for improved performance in using a social networking service	Tan et al.	2009	Conceptual

Study focus	Study	Year	Type
Exploring design alternatives for a wiki system to support collaborative writing	Kasemvilas, Olfman	2009	Conceptual
Evaluation of recommendation algorithms in an enterprise social networking service	Chen et al.	2009	Mixed mode
How can online interactive spaces like Facebook event pages facilitate the temporal coordination of events	Khan, Jarvenpaa	2010	Mixed mode
Analysis of collaboration between bodybuilders on social network sites and derivation of design factors for fostering collaboration	Ploderer et al.	2010	Case study
Proposition of an approach to evaluate soft skills of social networking services' users to improve skill display in online profiles	Winkelmann, Bertling	2011	Mixed mode
Design implications for conception and implementation of enterprise wikis for the support of knowledge management	Stocker et al.	2012	Case study
Design for engagement in social media as an emergent process of learning	Spagnoletti et al.	2015	Mixed mode

4.4.3 Design of social tagging and bookmarking systems

Design of social tagging and bookmarking systems constitutes another sub-group of the design view. The five publications that have been identified as pertaining to that view all deal with social tagging techniques that can help users find and reuse information and support organizations in managing internal document repositories stored in intranets (Wu & Gordon, 2009). Tagging, probably first introduced as part of the del.icio.us social bookmarking website in 2003 (Millen et al., 2008), has found its way into many enterprise information systems today. According to Millen and his co-authors, traditional enterprise search has been shown to be rather ineffective, and thus social software that supports efficient and effective searching is an important topic to be explored in an enterprise context (Millen et al., 2008). A summary of publications is provided in table 46.

Table 46: Research on design of social tagging and bookmarking systems

Study focus	Study	Year	Type
Exploration of search tasks supported by social tagging to better understand usage patterns	Millen et al.	2008	Mixed mode
How do users choose the tags in collaborative tagging systems	Rader, Wash	2008	Quantitative
Proposition of a model to explain the role of social tags in knowledge acquisition and adaptation	Fu	2008	Quantitative
What social roles can be identified that describe audience-oriented tagging and what are the implications for the design of social software?	Thom-Santelli et al.	2008	Case study
Development of a model for sharing structural knowledge in Web 2.0	Wu, Gordon	2009	Conceptual
Proposition of a research model to understand whether the contributions of users to social bookmarking sites are of a motivational or circumstantial nature	Arakji et al.	2009	Quantitative

4.5 Business view

The disclosure behavior of individuals in social networking services constitutes an opportunity for businesses to learn about the emotions and opinions of people regarding their products and services, an area that has been widely researched in recent years. This section thus deals with papers that investigate the business potential of social software and social networking services. Publications have been divided into five sub-groups: '*marketing, sales, and advertising*', '*social business intelligence*', '*information security*', '*business strategy*', and '*business processes*'.

4.5.1 Marketing, sales, and advertising

Marketing, sales, and advertising contains publications that deal with the usage potential of social networking services and Web 2.0 tools for marketing, sales, and brand awareness purposes. Publications in this category focus on electronic word of mount (e.g. Aghakhani et al., 2016; Luo & Zhang, 2013; Cheung et al., 2012), how to use blogs in a corporate context for marketing and brand awareness purposes (e.g. Brecht et al., 2010), using social media for managing the reputation of a company (e.g. Benthaus, 2014; Seebach et al., 2012). The abundant research in this category emphasizes that using these tools can help firms be more effective and efficient in communicating and selling to the customer. Table 47 provides an overview of the studies on *marketing, sales, and advertising*.

Table 47: Research on marketing, sales, and advertising

Study focus	Study	Year	Type
Using wikis to foster customer centricity	Wagner, Majchrzak	2006	Case study
How can social networking services be monetized via advertising?	Clemons	2009	Mixed mode
Enterprises need a social media team to manage community relations	Kane et al.	2009	Review article
How to analyse public sentiments with Web 2.0 technology	Zimbra et al.	2009	Case study
Investigation of the relationship of evaluations on social networking services on consumer loyalty	Xu et al.	2009	Quantitative
Proposition of a platform to help understanding customers' opinions on social networking services	Garcia-Crespo et al.	2010	Conceptual
Framework for understanding use of social networking services for corporate marketing strategy	Peters, Salazar	2010	Quantitative
Examination of the integration of social networking services and product networks	Goldenberg et al.	2010	Mixed mode
Analysis of corporate blogging practices for marketing and public relations	Brecht et al.	2010	Quantitative
Investigation of how to reach out to and connect with Web 2.0 customers	Wigand et al.	2010	Case study
Using blogs for monitoring and forecasting of a company's public image	O'Leary	2011	Quantitative
Proposition of a framework to align social media with organizational goals	Larson, Watson	2011	Conceptual
Development of a method to discover target groups for online marketing in social networking services	Xu et al.	2011	Conceptual
Proposition of a diffusion mechanism for delivering advertisement-related information in microblogs	Li, Shiu	2012	Conceptual
Analysis of content monitoring tools to support environmental scanning with social networking services	Lucas Junior, da Silva Ornellas	2012	Case study
How can employers use social networking services to attract IT professionals?	Brecht, Eckhardt	2012	Quantitative
Do social media fans of a company really purchase more?	Ping et al.	2012	Quantitative
Proposition of a research model to understand the influence of consumer engagement on brand loyalty in social networking services	Cheung et al.	2012	Quantitative
Analysis of the benefits of operating Facebook pages for brands	Chen et al.	2012	Quantitative
Analysis of the user-generated content in Web 2.0 hotel reviews	Chaves et al.	2012	Quantitative
What are critical factors for carrying out viral marketing in social networking services	Kahl	2012	Case study
How can social media influence public opinion of a company and how can organizations best leverage these technologies	Seebach et al.	2012	Quantitative
Development of a text mining model to extract information from social media postings	Abrahams et al.	2013	Conceptual
How can firms manage their corporate image via social media	Schniederjans et al.	2013	Mixed mode
Proposition of a model for consumer search on social media	Ghose et al.	2012	Quantitative

Study focus	**Study**	**Year**	**Type**
Understanding consumer attitudes in Web 2.0 media	Walther et al.	2012	Quantitative
Measuring the success of a company's fan page on Facebook	Huber	2012	Quantitative
Using social media to engage stakeholders and manage a brand	Heath, Singh	2012	Case study
Proposition of a framework to gain market intelligence by summarizing opinions on microblogs	Li, Li	2013	Conceptual
What are the effects of electronic word of mouth on movie sales?	Rui et al.	2013	Quantitative
Understanding accceptantce of electronic word of mouth for influencing customers' attitude	Aghakhani, Karimi	2013	Conceptual
How can electronic word of mouth predict the value of a firm?	Luo, Zhang	2013	Quantitative
What are the factors to allow firms to gain online attention in social networking services	Church et al.	2013	Quantitative
Proposition of a social media marketing typology	Coursaris et al.	2013	Mixed mode
Development of a best practices' framework to utilize Facebook for marketing purposes	Ng, Wang	2013	Case study
Cross-country and cross-industry analysis of usage of social software for e-business	Levina, Yavetz	2013	Case study
Influence of a social shopping network on product search and consumer outcomes	Grange, Benbasat	2013	Quantitative
Proposition of social recommender system for product recommendations	Li et al.	2013	Quantitative
Case study describing the challenges of a large electronics company faces with integrating social media into its existing marketing operations	Recine et al.	2013	Case study
Examination of how financial institutions employ organizational impression management to steer corporate reputation on social media	Benthaus	2014	Quantitative
Analysis of the effect of social media on brand purchase	Xie, Lee	2014	Quantitative
Investigation of the effects of firms' social media activities on firm performance and consumer behavior	Chung et al.	2014	Quantitative
Airlines' customer service operations take social media users with a large follower base more seriously	Gunarathne et al.	2014	Quantitative
Analysis of features of social customer relationship management products	Küpper et al.	2014	Case study
How can Facebook data be used to profile and cluster users connected to the company's Facebook website	Van Dam, Van de Velden	2015	Quantitative
Analysis of the effect of companies' Facebook activities on sales	Zhou et al.	2015	Quantitative
Investigation of the effect of Facebook "likes" on sales performance in social commerce	Lee et al.	2015	Quantitative
Facebook "likes" positively influence the acceptance of electronic word of mouth	Aghakhani et al.	2016	Quantitative
How can gamification elements be used by organizations to promote their brands on social media	Summers, Young	2016	Case study
Literature review and proposition of framework to understand consumer behaviour in social commerce	Zhang, Benyoucef	2016	Literature review

4.5.2 Social business intelligence and social media analytics

Social business intelligence and social media analytics contains publications that bridge two significant research fields and constitutes a nascent research field, with publications appearing mostly in domain-specific journals, and only a few in journals of the AIS Senior Scholars' basket (Dinter & Lorenz, 2012). Since that appraisal of the field by Dinter and Lorenz (2012), a couple of papers have been published focusing on applications of social business intelligence and social media analytics to better understand customers in the context of social commerce (e.g. Tanbeer et al., 2014), or to analyze sentiments of consumers (e.g. Risius & Akolk, 2015). In addition, several articles provide an overview of applications and trends in the area (e.g. Zafeiropoulou et al., 2015; Fan & Gordon, 2014). Table 48 summarizes the contributions on *social business intelligence and social media analytics.*

Table 48: Research on social business intelligence and social media analytics

Study focus	Study	Year	Type
Proposition of a framework to analyse business intelligence in blogs	Chau, Xu	2012	Case study
Literature review on social business intelligence	Dinter, Lorenz	2012	Literature review
Case study on how the Accor hotel group was leveraging social business intelligence tools to improve customer service	Fan, Gordon	2014	Case study
Application of a social business intelligence approach to foster understanding of the effectiveness of promotional events	Adamopoulos, Todri	2014	Quantitative
Using social data mining for e-commerce applications	Tanbeer et al.	2014	Quantitative
Literature review of business social media analytics	Holsapple et al.	2014	Literature review
Review article on topic discovery methods and challenges of their application in social media	Chinnov et al.	2015	Literature review
Development of a classification of corporate social media accounts and application of sentiment analysis to Twitter data	Risius, Akolk	2015	Mixed mode
Literature review of social media analystics studies	Zafeiropoulou et al.	2015	Literature review

4.5.3 Information security

Information security deals with publications that focus on the challenges associated with protecting confidential information that companies do not want to see shared on social media. Väyrynen et al. (2013) present a framework that integrates knowledge protection challenges with features and characteristics of social media. In a similar vein, Hekkala et al. (2012) and Braun & Esswein (2012) investigate risks of social media use for corporations. Syed and Dhillon (2015) use social media as a data source to further the understanding of the impact of data breaches on the information security reputation of organizations. Table 49 sums up the research in this area.

Table 49: Research on information security

Study focus	Study	Year	Type
Study of the challenges for information security that social media represents for corporations and organizations	Hekkala et al.	2012	Case study
Literature review and proposition of a risk management framework for corporate use of social networking services	Braun, Esswein	2012	Conceptual
Proposition of a framework that relates social media features with information security challenges	Väyrynen et al.	2013	Case study
Analysis of Twitter postings to help identify threats to the information security reputation of organizations	Syed, Dhillon	2015	Case study

4.5.4 Business strategy

Business strategy encompasses publications that explore the potential of social software technologies for strategic aspects of enterprises, such as firm performance (Kim & Miranda, 2013) or competitive advantage (Effing & Spil, 2016; Steininger et al., 2013). Table 50 provides a summary of the contributions.

Table 50: Research on business strategy

Study focus	Study	Year	Type
Using social media to increase firm performance through entrainment of innvation to contention	Kim, Miranda	2013	Conceptual
Social media as an enhancement of communities of practice (CoP) for business strategy	Annabi, McGann	2013	Conceptual
Exploration of success factors of electronic business models by comparing two major social networking services intended for professional use	Steininger et al.	2013	Case study
How can firms derive value for their business by leveraging social media technologies in the area of open innovation	Dong, Wu	2015	Quantitative
Evaluation of how social media management tools can be leveraged to help influence companies' public perception among Twitter users	Benthaus et al.	2016	Quantitative
Proposition of a framework to evaluate companies' social media strategies	Effing, Spil	2016	Case study

4.5.5 Business processes

Business processes contains publications that explore the potential of social software to extend traditional business process management (BPM), a topic of research in the intersection of business management and computer science, thus constituting a core area of business information systems research (Abramowicz et al., 2010). Web 2.0 technologies and social software, intended to enable open social networks, allow for the easy exchange of information and thus cooperation in distributed scenarios, which makes them suitable mechanisms to foster communication also within the context of business process management (Vanderhaeghen et al., 2010; Abramowicz et al., 2010). Table 50 summarizes the publications in this field.

Table 51: Research on business processes

Study focus	Study	Year	Type
Prototypical development of a business process management platform to show the technological potential of Web 2.0 for business process management (BPM)	Vanderhaeghen et al.	2010	Conceptual
Using social software technologies to make business process management more collaborative	Koschmider et al.	2010	Conceptual
Analysis of BPM-related LinkedIn profiles to investigate if women are underrepresented in the BPM field	Gorbacheva et al.	2015	Quantitative

4.6 Political view

The category 'political view' deals with online social networking services that can help provide a platform for supporting political discussion which can help to initiate political change or even democratization (Gonzales-Bailon et al., 2010; Ameripour et al., 2010). The nine publications pertaining to this category have been split into two sub-groups: '*social software for political campaigning*' and '*social software to enable e-democracy and e-participation*'.

4.6.1 Social software for political campaigning

The Internet has been perceived as a valuable tool for helping reverse the decline in political participation in Western societies since the time it gained widespread popularity in the late 1990s (Vergeer & Hermans, 2013). While supporting political campaigns with the first generation of Web technologies has been widely studied

(Vergeer & Hermans, 2013), the section *social software for political campaigning* deals with the application of Web 2.0 tools like Twitter or Facebook to support political parties in increasing participation. The four publications in this category explore the benefits of using social software in political campaigning (Jensen & Dyrby, 2013; Utz, 2010; Vergeer & Hermans, 2013) and study how social networking services can help bring about societal change in Iran (Ameripour et al., 2010). Table 52 summarizes the publications of this category.

Table 52: Research on social software for political campaigning

Study focus	Study	Year	Type
Why are some political candidates more likely to adopt Twitter for political campaigning and have more followers?	Vergeer, Hermans	2010	Quantitative
Exploration of benefits of social networking services for political campaigning	Utz	2009	Mixed mode
Examination of the influence of political campaigns on social networking services in Iran on societal change	Ameripour et al.	2010	Case study
What benefits can Facebook offer to political parties to facilitate political campaigning?	Jensen, Dyrby	2013	Case study

4.6.2 Social software to enable e-democracy and e-participation

In recent years, social software has drawn pronounced interest from information systems and media researchers as a valuable source for political information and news (Kim, 2012), as a means to increase e-participation (Johannessen & Bjorn, 2012), and to help drive e-politics and e-democracy forward (e.g. Wattal et al., 2010). The eight publications categorized to belong to this section investigate the potential of *social software to enable e-democracy and e-participation* and are summarized in table 53.

Table 53: Research on social software to enable e-democracy and e-participation

Study focus	Study	Year	Type
Political blogs as alternatives to traditional media	Meraz	2009	Case study
Conceptualization of blogs as alternative media in political journalism	Kenix	2009	Mixed mode
Discussion of how Web 2.0 technologies can change political processes and proposition of a research agenda how information systems can help with e-politics	Wattal et al.	2010	Quantitative
Proposition of a model to help analyze, compare, and classify political discussions in social networking services	Gonzalez-Bailon et al.	2010	Quantitative
Understanding the influence of social media on political change	Maghrabi, Salam	2011	Case study

Study focus	Study	Year	Type
Analysis of the perception of blogs as credible sources of political information	Kim	2012	Quantitative
Proposition of a framework to analyse the potential of social media to support e-participation	Johannessen, Bjorn	2012	Case study
Do politically interested users perceive social networking services as credible sources of information?	Johnson, Kaye	2014	Quantitative
Analysis of a social networking service run by a Norwegian party to investigate online political communication	Johannessen, Folstad	2014	Case study

4.7 Academic use view

The academic use view contains publications that explore and analyze the usage of social software, particularly blogs, wikis, and social networking services in an academic context. Publications that have been categorized to belong to the academic use view have been split into two sub-groups: '*social software to support teaching and learning*', and '*social software to support research collaboration*'.

4.7.1 Social software to support teaching and learning

Social software to support teaching and learning captures publications that investigate using tools like blogs, social networking services, and wikis in a classroom setting – a highly relevant research area since results from recent studies suggest that social media can help enhance students' learning experience (Zhang & Olfman, 2010). An overview of the different social software tools and potential contributions for improving teaching in an academic context is provided by Schröder et al. (2010). Further studies focus on more specialized aspects like the analysis of specific Web 2.0 tools for their suitability to provide a collaborative learning environment (Kam & Katerattanakul, 2010), using wikis to support collaborative writing among students of information systems (Menchen-Trevino et al., 2009), or using wikis and screen capture technologies in conjunction to create information systems courses (Makkonen, 2010). The publications are summed up in table 54.

Table 54: Research on social software to support teaching and learning

Study focus	Study	Year	Type
Proposition of a research agenda to explore the use of wikis to support collaborative writing in the classroom	Menchen-Trevino et al.	2009	Case study
Call on the information systems research community to explore the adoption of wikis for the support of teaching, doing research, and scholarly publishing in the IS discipline	Kane, Fichman	2009	Conceptual
Development of a Web 2.0-based platform to support academic teaching	Langbein	2009	Conceptual
Commentary on Kane and Fichman's call (2009) to leverage Web 2.0 and wiki technology to innovate core processes of the information systems discipline	Te'eni	2009	Conceptual
Exploration of teachers' and students' motivations for leveraging wikis to improve teaching and learning outcomes	Guo et al.	2009	Conceptual
Investigation of the usefulness of social networking services for students' learning outcomes	Yu et al.	2010	Quantitative
Analysis of blog usage for supporting social and constructivist learning in university students	Zhang, Olfman	2010	Case study
Review of the educational usage potential of different social software tools	Schröder et al.	2010	Case study
Analysis of a specific Web 2.0 tool to understand support potential for collaborative learning in university students	Kam, Katerattanakul	2010	Case study
Using wikis and screen capture videos to enhance a university course of information systems	Makkonen	2010	Case study
Designing an introductory MIS (management information systems) course with social networking technology	Ractham et al.	2010	Mixed mode
Investigation of how Facebook can be leveraged to improve the educational experience of university courses	Magro et al.	2012	Conceptual
Exploration of how Facebook can be used for educational purposes	Amirtharajan et al.	2014	Quantitative
How can Facebook be used to improve students' engagement with flipped classes?	Talaei-Khoei, Daniel	2016	Quantitative

4.7.2 Social software to support research collaboration

Social software to support research collaboration deals with publications that examine how social software and social networking services can be leveraged to support research collaboration between non-collocated scientists. This subgroup features only a few publications, considering the crucial importance of research collaboration, its associated challenges and the potential of social software to help mitigate these challenges, this constitutes an underresearched area compared to other topics in which more research is warranted. Table 55 provides a summary of the publications.

Table 55: Research on social software to support research collaboration

Study focus	Study	Year	Type
Development of a model of the collaborative research process and investigation of how social software can support individual stages of the process	Söldner et al.	2009	Case study
Proposition of a research model to study social networking services that support open science	Kalb et al.	2011	Quantitative
Investigation of a wiki system implemented specifically for an agency promoting scientific research	Hasani-Mavriqi et al.	2011	Case study
Proposition of a research model based on UTAUT to study acceptance of collaborative social research networking services	Bullinger et al.	2011	Quantitative
Development of a social network-based recommendation algorithm to help find suitable partners for research collaboration	Xu et al.	2012	Conceptual
Using social networking services to facilitate data collection in survey research	Mirabeau et al.	2013	Conceptual
Development of a "collaboration supportiveness" measure to assess the collaboration ability of a researcher in a social networking service	Liu et al.	2013	Conceptual
Proposition of a social networking-based research analytics framework	Silva et al.	2013	Conceptual
Do scientists use enterprise social networking services as part of their working practice?	Ortbach, Recker	2014	Quantitative
Development of a virtual crowdsourcing community to support collaboration in science	Michel et al.	2015	Conceptual

5 Discussion and Reflection

This systematic literature review has provided a description of the state-of-the-art in the fields of *research collaboration* and *social software*. Building on the identified literature, it has also presented a preliminary classification of the publications in these two fields. Overall, this research categorization assesses the contribution of 92 publications in the area of *research collaboration* and 511 publications in the field of *social software* by highlighting and analyzing their topics, theoretical and empirical findings as well as the methods used. It clearly shows key areas of research interests within the four categories in the field of *research collaboration* and seven categories in the field of *social software*, but also allows for the identification of research gaps within the different categories.

5.1 Research Gaps in the Field of Research Collaboration

This section identifies the central research gaps in the area of research collaboration for each of the four perspectives used in this literature review. Readers, who are interested in further researching one of the research gaps identified in each category, are advised to read the individual publications listed in the respective categories.

5.1.1 Macro-level perspective

Research on the macro-level perspective deals with 'international and interdisciplinary research collaboration', aspects of research collaboration that influence overall research policy, and also investigates the wider topic of changes in the way knowledge is produced. Extant research emphasizes that international research collaboration constitutes a networked system and thus requires networked communication. These collaborative networks emerge either based on policy decisions or due to individual researchers looking at collaboration as a means for procuring resources and gaining reputation (Wagner & Leydesdorff, 2005). There is a considerable dispute in the literature regarding the validity of theories that can help explain the immense growth of international collaboration and the antecedents and factors that lead to knowledge generation in collaborative networks. Researchers call for further testing of these theories in order to better understand the mechanisms of these collaborative networks. In addition, challenges associated with ensuring fairness and accountability within the networked system that our scientific system constitutes do not go unnoticed by current research. These challenges tend to be even greater within the context of interdisciplinary and international collaboration. As a long-term goal, new ways of thinking about knowledge distribution and credit assignment within the overall research systems are called for.

Research that investigates the hypothesized phenomenon of the 'new production of knowledge' (NPK) is at the same time seminal and visionary but also disputed regarding its validity and applicability. NPK is perceived to be successful as a manifesto and it has managed to attract a major amount of attention in science policy circles (Hessels & Van Lente, 2008). However, investigating undergoing changes in our contemporary science system is difficult due to the heterogeneity and diversity of scientific disciplines and national contexts. Clearly, much more research is needed to understand and conceptualize these changes in our science system.

5.1.2 Meso-level perspective

Research on the meso-level perspective has been found to focus on three main areas: university-industry collaboration, university research centers, and multi-university collaborations. The comprehensive literature review by Perkman et al. (2013) on university-industry collaboration identifies five areas that require further research in this field: (1) the organizational context in which university-industry relations take place, (2) the outcomes and impact of university-industry collaboration, (3) the interconnectedness between academic engagement with industry and ensuing commercialization, (4) deeper and more detailed study of institutional aspects, and (5) building and testing theory on university-industry collaboration.

University research centers are considered a vital arrangement for solving scientific problems and fostering collaboration amongst researchers (Boardman & Corley, 2008). Extant research features case studies of single centers, but comparisons based on multiple cases using combined qualitative and bibliometric approaches are lacking. In addition, only a few research questions have been addressed so far (Ponomariov & Boardman, 2010).

Multi-university collaborations is a widely explored topic considering the relatively many publications on that topic that showed up in the literature review. Scientists are encouraged to engage in multi-university collaborations following policy changes, e.g. by the EU framework program and the US National Science Foundation (Cummings & Kiesler, 2007; Katz & Martin, 1997). There is currently limited research on the long-term consequences of collaborations between multiple universities. Hence, further research should contribute to elucidating the impact of multi-university collaborations.

5.1.3 Micro-level perspective

Publications that have been found to belong to the micro-level perspective focus on four broad areas: research productivity, research management, collaborative motives, and collaborative behavior.

Research productivity is an area that has understandably received considerable attention by extant research and has been analyzed from a wide variety of different angles. Considering the numerous publications that deal with research productivity in its various aspects and in different contexts, first and foremost an in-depth and comprehensive literature review is lacking. In addition, while there is some research on the link between email communication and research productivity (e.g. Vasileidadou & Vliegenthart, 2009), research on the impact of using social software-based tools to support research collaboration on research productivity is completely absent so far. Therefore, further research should continue to explore research productivity and the potential of technological support in much more detail.

While *research management* is considered a vital task to make project-based interdisciplinary research collaborations successful (König et al, 2013), there are only a few publications that pertain to this field. It would be beneficial if future research would focus on investigating further how interdisciplinary research management can be organized and supported in order to solve pressing challenges associated with coordination. Information systems research can play a crucial role in reducing these difficulties with the design of technologies for collaboration support to address problematic characteristics of the work organization (Walsh & Maloney, 2007).

Scientists' *collaborative motives* and *collaborative behavior* constitute fields that have been addressed by a sizeable number of publications. Authors highlight that more research is needed in understanding the collaboration behavior of researchers from different scientific fields like social science or the humanities and not only natural sciences and engineering (Bozeman & Gaughan, 2011). In addition, more research is needed on various areas like the influence of grants on collaborative behavior, the impact of physical proximity on outcomes and dynamics of research collaborations (Kabo et al., 2014), on the impact of gender on collaboration and social capital, or on individuals' collaborative behavior and collaborative networks on knowledge creation (Wang, 2016).

5.1.4 Technological perspective

Current research on the technological perspective of research collaboration has been found to deal with three broad areas: e-Science, IT-supported research collaboration, and collaboratories.

e-Science is a topic that shows up in the publication channels under investigation since 2006 and can be considered an umbrella term that stands for a wide variety of different topics related to electronic support of science. The research that falls under this broad category spans very different topics from remote collaboration over video up to how data can be re-used in e-Science projects and many more topics in that vast field, which is considered to be interdisciplinary in nature (Nentwich, 2003). Consequently, research gaps are also tied to the specific topic under consideration and cannot be easily summarized. Many of the concrete issues found in e-Science projects are of a very generic nature, that show up in other, non-e-Science-related, projects as well, like the effective and efficient management of information, engaging participants in large projects, satisfying the needs of large, multidisciplinary projects (Lawrence, 2006), or institutional and social hurdles to sharing of research tools, data, and results generated in e-Science projects (Park, 2010).

IT-supported research collaboration has a much narrower view than the very fuzzy, broad, and interdisciplinary area of e-Science. Despite its importance for supporting collaborative research and mitigating its challenges, only a few publications have been found to deal with this specific area. However, since there is a much broader body of research related to generic collaboration, more can be found regarding the support of generic collaboration in CSCW and neighboring fields. The research gaps identified in the publications pertaining to the intersection of research collaboration and collaborative technologies dealt with rather specific questions like the development of maturity models for collaborative research portals (Becker et al., 2010). The comprehensive paper by Jirotka et al. (2013) serves as an important bridge between CSCW research and the research collaboration field and names several important research gaps in that area: further research on specific collaborative practices of different scientific disciplines, on technologies and socio-technical constellations related to supporting the gathering, distribution, and examination of research data, and on large-scale e-Science endeavors as virtual organizations is needed, among other things.

Collaboratories, defined as research centers without walls, that allow the remote interaction with colleagues, the access of scientific instruments, and the sharing of computing resources and data independent of physical location, promise manifold benefits. Research gaps exist primarily in their evaluation – if they live up to their promise – with fundamental and crucial research questions currently unanswered regarding the quality of the results attainable by distributed research if the benefits that are provided by collaboratories outweigh their disadvantages as seen from the perspective of the individual researcher, their adoption by scientists, and the influence of culture on the (non-)adoption of collaboratories (Sonnenwald et al., 2003). Due to the broad range of possible types of collaboratories, the question as to what technologies should be used to implement collaboratories is closely tied to the specific type of collaboratory under examination, as is the question of identifying best practices for the set-up and operation of collaboratories (Bos et al., 2007).

5.2 Research Gaps in the Field of Social Software

This section identifies the central research gaps in the area of social software for each of the seven categories used in this literature review. Readers who are interested in further researching one of the research gaps identified in each category are advised to read the individual publications listed in the respective categories.

5.2.1 Theoretical view

Publications that were categorized to pertain to the theoretical view focus on six areas: social computing and social information systems, Web 2.0, social network analysis, information diffusion in social media, theory use in social media, and data quality in social media.

Social computing and social information systems constitute an emerging paradigm that is dealing with the intersection of computing technology and human social behavior, fostering the creation and maintenance of social connections, contexts, and conventions through technology (Chen & Liu, 2014). Building on a long tradition of research on social networks over the last 40 years, social computing and social networking services have become a major research area thanks to the technological push provided by web-based collaborative software, in which many of the theories of social networks to-date can be re-examined (Oinas-Kukkonen et al., 2010; Appleford et al., 2014). Open research issues and opportunities for further research are manifold due to the broadness and the inherent interdisciplinarity of the topic, comprising questions like how to help organizations and businesses to understand and make use of opportunities and mitigate threats inherent in the social web with its large and ill-defined datasets; how can these datasets managed, presented, and visualized in a technically suitable way; and how to deal with the social issues involved like understanding and communicating with diverse communities and stakeholders stemming from very different social and cultural backgrounds (Appleford et al., 2014). These issues will be treated in more detail in the respective and more targeted sections below since the sub-category of *social computing and social information systems* can be considered at the same time to be the overarching, most generic area for the research below.

Web 2.0, as defined in 2005 by Tim O'Reilly, denotes web sites and services whose content is to a great part generated by their users, instead of dedicated editors and content creators (O'Reilly, 2005). Web 2.0 and related technologies and services have long since become mainstream and are part of the daily routines of many people. The many effects of its adoption and use by individuals, organizations, and businesses are treated in separate respective subsections of this systematic literature review. From a technological point of view, researchers are focusing on what features are required to create the next generation of the web, Web 3.0, and what is required to make it successful. According to Newman et al. (2016), this next generation of the web has already arrived and consists of a combination of the latest technologies (as of the time of writing), like Internet of Things (IoT), Cloud Computing, Big Data, and existing services commonly associated with the Web 2.0 like social networking services.

Extant research in the area of *social network analysis* has a long-standing tradition and due to the rise of online social networking services, a large field has emerged that offers the opportunity for the re-validation of existing research and new research topics, like the proposition and evaluation of new algorithms to identify key users (e.g. Heidemann et al., 2010) or investigating the influence of previously existing offline connections on online relationships in social networking services (Kim et al., 2016).

Research on *information diffusion in social media* is considered an area whose importance has recently increased with the development of social networking services that allow for global connection and exchange of information (Mochalova & Nanopoulos, 2014). Research gaps are mainly associated with measuring information diffusion and determining sources of influence (Garg et al., 2011). Thus, future research in this area will probably deal with the proposition and the evaluation of mathematical and algorithmic approaches to further improve on these measurement challenges.

Theory use in social media is comprised of the application of various and diverse theories to social networking services and social media. There is no distinct global direction for future research in this area since the individual publications stem from very different perspectives and have diverse goals.

Research on *data quality in social media* is considered of high importance, also summarized by the common phrase "content is king" and bears important implications for providers of blogs and social media services (Zülch et al., 2014). However, detailed questions regarding the source and drivers of content quality still remain open and constitute an area for future research.

5.2.2 Social and behavioral view

The social and behavioral view encompasses publications that deal with intricately interlinked phenomena: social capital, self-presentation and information disclosure, information overload, mood and habit, motivation and intention, adoption and continuance, trust, and privacy.

The impact of individuals' participation in social media and certain properties of their social networks on the formation of *social capital* constitutes in general a well-explored topic. Although existing research suggests that the use of social networking and microblogging contribute to the buildup of social capital, future studies can contribute to the understanding of the actual mechanisms involved in the formation of bonding and bridging social capital and which usage patterns of social media contribute to these.

Self-presentation and information disclosure in social networking services are phenomena that have attracted the attention of Information Systems (IS) scholars. Extant research has already made a connection of users' individual beliefs related to privacy, benefits, and cost to use with self-disclosure behavior (Pu et al., 2016). More research is needed to address research gaps like how properties of social media influence self-presentation and information disclosure.

Information overload constitutes the 'dark side' of information systems usage with a huge estimated negative impact on the economy (Kefi et al., 2015). Information overload appears to be overall well researched, however, future research could address a more diverse set of social networking services, as most research is using Facebook as its empirical field, and more aspects and variables should be taken into account (Weinert et al., 2012)

As social media has become an integral part of the daily lives of millions of users, their relationship with *mood and habit* has sparked considerable interest among scholars. Extant research is still lacking in providing clear and unambiguous answers on a number of issues, e.g. the link between Facebook use and markers of subjective well-being and mood (Wenninger et al., 2014) or how the use of social networking services can influence mood states like loneliness or frustration.

Motivation and intention related to users' engagement in social media constitutes an important field for future research, as little is known on the factors that influence users to engage in social media use (Vannoy & Medlin, 2013). Future research should contribute to further the understanding of technology use which is embedded in users' social behavior.

Adoption and continuance constitute important research aspects in information systems research. Although social technologies such as Facebook and Twitter have seen widespread adoption, further research should continue to investigate factors that influence adoption and (dis-)continuance of Web 2.0 applications.

Trust in social networking services constitutes an important predictor of users' propensity to share information on the service (Salehan et al., 2013). Future research should strive to expand the understanding of the properties of social networking services on trust to elucidate how these properties affect trust. In addition, research samples used often focus on students and lack cultural diversity, thus future research could profit from broadening and diversifying its research sample.

Privacy serves as an important regulator for our interactions with others (Wisniewski et al., 2016) and constitutes an important area in social media research as well as a major source of concern to users of social networking services due to the privacy policies of the providers of these services. Further research on how to mitigate privacy concerns by these providers is needed to help increase the adoption of their services (Wilson et al., 2016).

5.2.3 Organizational view

Publications that belong to the organizational view deal with the use and adoption of social software, and most prominently, social networking services in the context of organizations. Publications have been split into seven sub-groups: Enterprise 2.0, social software for organizational knowledge and innovation management, organizational adoption of Web 2.0 technologies, volunteering 2.0, digital health, crisis management, and governmental use.

Enterprise 2.0 refers to organizations using social software platforms in the pursuit of their goals (McAfee, 2009). Although there is extensive research on the individual social tools and the potential benefits they bring about, several areas are perceived to be under-researched. Future research should increasingly focus on the impact of these systems on the employees (Cummings & Reinicke, 2014; Kuegler et al., 2015), and the motivations and interaction patterns of organizational users (Mettler & Winter, 2016).

Social media platforms and enterprise social networking services are increasingly adopted by organizations to facilitate knowledge sharing and innovation management (Oostervink et al., 2016). In the topic area of *social software for organizational knowledge and innovation management*, scientific contributions focusing on the affordances of social software platforms indicate that these tools can definitely help facilitate knowledge sharing, but can also create frustrations. Future research should thus focus on other factors than affordances alone to help understand the larger context of enterprise social software use.

Social software tools have received increased attention from organizations in recent years. Research on the *organizational adoption of Web 2.0 technologies* is critical since adoption determines the success of Enterprise 2.0 implementations. Successful IT implementations are perceived as essential towards achieving productivity in organizations and thus generating competitive advantage (Choudrie & Zamani, 2016). While the adoption of social media in a private, hedonic context has been studied in-depth, more studies that investigate the impact of factors that influence organizational adoption are needed (Paluch et al., 2015).

Volunteering 2.0 deals with the application of social networking services to support volunteer organizations which constitutes a nascent research topic. While some research has been done in the related area of *crisis management*, e.g. analyzing data from social media in the context of crises and emergencies, the internal coordination of volunteering organizations with the help of social software remains understudied (Kaufhold & Reuter, 2015). Thus, future research should focus on how social media and social networking services can be leveraged to improve the recruitment, coordination, and organization of volunteers.

Digital health refers to the usage of social media in health care. Several publications have already explored the usage of social media by clinics and hospitals (Kordzadeh & Young, 2015) and between physicians and patients (Dantu et al., 2014). Future research should focus on proposing, validating, and refining models of physicians' and hospitals' usage of social media to foster the interaction between patients and physicians, improving the quality of health care while lowering the associated costs.

Social media tools like Twitter or Facebook are becoming more and more important for *crisis management*, and has been adopted by emergency management agencies, governments, and non-governmental agencies after initially being used by the general public (Simon et al., 2015). While the usage of Twitter for communicating during emergencies has already been widely researched, further studies should focus on the disaster management-related usage potential of these tools by governmental bodies and first responders.

Governmental use deals with publications that focus on the usage potential for social software and social networking services by governments to support governmental activities and functions and facilitate communication between the government and its citizens. While some initial research has been performed to understand the usage potential of social software for governmental use, more research is needed to further the understanding of the citizens' perspective, their experiences with governmental social media offerings, and their expectations.

5.2.4 Design view

Publications that belong to the design view are concerned with issues related to the design of social software. The publications that pertain to this view have been divided into three groups: principles and practices of design for social software, design of collaborative social software, and design of social tagging and bookmarking systems.

Principles and practices of design for social software captures publications that deal with broad area of design of social software without focusing on specific systems, instead remaining rather on a philosophical and theoretical level. Research gaps in this field are manifold due to the broadness and newness of the topic and encompass questions related to designing for sociality instead of functionality (Bouman et al., 2007). Future research should focus on the formulation and refinement of design principles that help guide in the development of social software.

Design of collaborative social software stands in the tradition of previous work in CSCW that has examined the role of technology to facilitate collaboration. With the advent of social networking services like Facebook, a new class of collaborative tools has been created that allows its users to perform a wide range of social interactions within online shared interactive spaces (Khan & Jarvenpaa, 2010), which holds the promise to make virtual social relations almost as rich as they are in real life (Bouman et al., 2007). While there have been studies on design-related aspects of social software to support collaboration in many diverse fields such as bodybuilding (Ploderer et al., 2010) or elderly care (Spagnoletti et al., 2015), future research should focus on studying aspects of design in a more systematic and methodological way, bringing together insights from the various fields in a more comprehensive way to help understand better how these technologies can best be designed to facilitate collaboration.

Design of social tagging and bookmarking systems constitutes a relevant topic for finding and reusing of information, since social tagging and bookmarking systems are instrumental in sharing structural knowledge – the relationship of concepts and documents (Wu & Gordon, 2009). While first exploratory studies have been performed, overall, more in-depth and comprehensive research in this field is still lacking, with the latest publication identified in this literature review that pertains to this field stemming from 2009.

5.2.5 Business view

Publications of the business view deal with various aspects related to use cases of social media for businesses: marketing, sales, and advertising, social business intelligence, information security, business strategy, and business processes.

Even though there is extensive research on the aspects of *marketing, sales, and advertising* and increasing attention is paid by research to the business value of social media, several research questions have not been adequately studied. A major research gap identified in the literature is how companies' use of social media does affect their (sales) performance (Chung et al, 2014; Zhou et al, 2015). Further research gaps exist in understanding and identifying a firms' customer base in social media (van Dam & van de Welden, 2015), or the effect of implicit and explicit electronic word of mouth in social commerce (e.g. Lee et al., 2015; Aghakhani, 2016).

Social business intelligence and social media analytics has emerged as a focal area within the field of analytics due to the rising popularity of social media in recent years (Holsapple, 2014). The amount of published research in that sub-field is still rather limited due to the fact that social media analytics and social business intelligence constitute fairly new phenomena. Dinter and Lorenz (2012) and Zafeiropoulou et al. (2015) provide an overview of previous research and also point out promising research topics in these areas, of which there are many and they are diverse. Thus, readers interested in these research gaps are advised to read these two publications.

Corporate risks within social networks and media is investigated in the sub-category *information security*. Since extant research in this area is still very scarce, there is a need for the establishment of a corporate risk management framework dealing with social media (Braun & Esswein, 2012) and its further validation.

Business strategy deals with how organizations can strategically use social media to reap their benefits – a task that many companies find challenging (Effing & Spil, 2016). Future research should propose and validate frameworks that help organizations implement social media successfully.

Tools that support the modeling of *business processes* are typically made for individual users – adding 'social' features to foster the sharing and reuse of process models and to leverage a social recommendation system are areas that warrant further investigation (Koschmider et al., 2010).

5.2.6 Political view

Publications of the political view are concerned with how social media can foster participation in political discussions, support parties' political campaigning, and enable e-democracy.

Social software for political campaigning constitutes a niche topic that has been dealt with by four publications identified in this literature review. Extant studies have been concerned with the political situation in specific countries like Iran (Ameripour et al., 2010), the Netherlands (Utz, 2009; Vergeer & Hermans, 2013), or Denmark (Jensen & Dyrby, 2013). The results can thus probably not be generalized to other countries (Utz, 2009). Due to the limited amount of contributions and their lack of generalizability, there is a huge potential for future research in this area, e.g. by investigating the role of social media in other political systems and countries, or by investigating social media use by political candidates after the campaigns and subsequent elections.

Social software to enable e-democracy and e-participation has been researched on by scholars from the information systems and media fields since it is considered a helpful tool to increase citizens' e-participation and promote e-politics and e-democracy (Johannessen & Folstad, 2014; Maghrabi & Salam, 2011; Wattal et al., 2010). While several high-quality studies have already been performed on the role of social networking services like Facebook to promote political discussions (e.g. Johnson & Kaye, 2014), scholars suggest that future research should focus on other social media services like YouTube or LinkedIn or replicate and expand on existing studies since using social networking services for political reasons was still an emerging topic when these studies were conducted.

5.2.7 Academic use view

Publications pertaining to the academic use view are concerned with the application of social software in academia and have been split into two sub-groups: '*social software to support teaching and learning*', and '*social software to support research collaboration*'.

Publications in the area of *social software to support teaching and learning* investigate the usage potential of these tools in a classroom or teaching context (e.g. Amirtharajan et al., 2014; Talaei-Kohei & Daniel, 2016; Schroeder et al, 2010). While some anecdotal research on how social networking services can be used to foster teaching and learning beyond traditional methods and contexts has been performed, future research should focus on studying how educators can effectively leverage these tools to enhance and improve the learning process.

While *social software to support research collaboration* holds great promise to foster collaborative research projects (e.g. Soeldner et al., 2009), studies in this area are few and have been published at conferences only, but not in journals. In addition, social networking services and social software that targets a scholarly audience like Mendeley, ResearchGate or Academia.edu have neither been studied systematically, if at all, nor have they been studied in the way that hedonic social networking services like Facebook have been. Future research should therefore look closely at these novel kinds of services created for an academic audience and among other things explore the motivations of their providers in order to lay the groundwork for further in-depth studies of research-oriented social networking services.

6 Conclusion of the Review

The overarching research question driving this literature review was the first research question as outlined in the introduction of this thesis:

What is the current state-of-the-literature regarding collaborative research and social software? Are these fields interlinked? What are research gaps and directions for future research?

This systematic review of the literature brings together widely scattered research in two broad areas – *research collaboration* and *social software* – over a period of 17 years in one document. However, in both areas, the body of research continues to be fragmented in separate streams, understandable considering the broadness of both fields, the interdisciplinarity of the research field when regarding the area of *research collaboration,* and the relative newness of research on *social software*. The systematic literature review has also pointed out research gaps and directions for future research in all categories. As shown in the literature review, there are unfortunately very few interlinkages between the two areas of *research collaboration* and *social software*. The call for more research on the structure of scientific collaborations and the role of communication technologies and strategies in reducing the challenges associated with making collaborative research more successful (Walsh & Maloney, 2007), remained more or less unanswered by academia, as the literature review has revealed. However, several projects to facilitate collaborative research have emerged since Walsh and Maloney's (2007) call for more research. These projects are driven by enthusiastic researchers and individuals, mostly within the academic community, however unnoticed and underrepresented in the traditional publication channels like conferences and journals. This leads to the second research question of this thesis which part III engages in answering:

What is the current state of technology regarding social software tools specifically relevant to an academic audience? What is their intended use by their providers and can they further be classified according to their functionalities and intended use?

Part III

Empirical Study 1:

Social Research Networking Sites - Market Overview, Features, and Intended Use

J.-H. Soeldner, *Understanding Social Research Networking Sites*,
Markt- und Unternehmensentwicklung Markets and Organisations,
https://doi.org/10.1007/978-3-658-31575-7_3

1 Needs and Goals[15]

Research collaboration has always been acknowledged as a necessary and essential activity for generating significant scientific discoveries (Wagner et al., 2015; Heinze & Kuhlmann, 2008; Haussler & Sauermann, 2013). Due to the growing complexity of research projects, their often interdisciplinary nature, and the increasing specialization of scholars (Katz & Martin, 1997; Laudel, 2002), researchers are compelled to collaborate more than ever to keep up with the fast pace of innovation and to be able to advance scientific knowledge (Haussler & Sauermann, 2013; He & Jeng, 2016). Driven by the rapid development of Internet-based communication technologies and the rise of social software and social networking services in recent years, a new class of tools has emerged that enables collaboration between scholars on the technological basis of social networking services (He & Jeng, 2016; Bullinger et al., 2010; Söldner et al., 2009). These tools are referred to in the literature as "social research networking sites[16]" (SRNS) or as "academic social networking sites", forming a sub-category of Web 2.0 tools or online platforms (such as Academia.edu, Mendeley, or ResearchGate) that help enable and facilitate research collaboration, exchange of information and publications between scholars, and building and maintaining networks between scholars (Bullinger et. al, 2010; He & Jeng, 2016; Meishar-Tal & Pieterse, 2017).

Although these tools have first come into existence around the year 2008, the systematic literature review on research collaboration and social software presented in *part II* of this thesis which was covering an ample timeframe from 2000-2016 has not yielded any substantial academic contributions that focused on these tools, their features, and affordances. Hence, the broad literature base on both research collaboration and social software has not yet come to grips with how to best support

---

[15] Note that minor parts of this study are based on previous research by the author that has been published as a paper (Bullinger et al., 2010) and presented at the *Americas Conference on Information Systems* (2010) by the author. The author of this thesis contributed substantially to the development of the research design, literature selection, data collection and analysis, and the editing of the paper.

[16] Also: social (research) networking services, as sites and services are often used interchangeably when referring to SNS or SRNS

research-related tasks such as academic exchange or collaboration through (social) software. There is obviously a gap between theory due to the lack of published scientific contributions in journals and conferences on this topic and practice since various dedicated tools have come into existence since around the year 2008 that specifically target researchers as their audience and promise to help in a variety of research-related tasks and to support collaborative research.

This leads to the research questions of this empirical study, which is to gain a better understanding of this new class of tools termed "social research networking sites" (SRNS) and to bridge this gap between emerging practices in the field and their lack of coverage by research in the information systems discipline.

Hence, the main research questions of this study are as follows:

What is the current state of technology regarding social software tools specifically relevant to an academic audience? What is their intended use by their providers and can they further be classified according to their functionalities and intended use?

To answer these questions, this study investigates in total eight SRNS tools in-depth. Seven of these tools constituted all relevant SRNS offerings on the market since the beginning of their existence in around 2008, while one SRNS has only emerged recently in 2014. Of those SRNS, three have now become defunct and were discontinued due to lack of success on the market, two (CiteULike and the more recently developed Trellis are currently playing a niche role) and the remaining three (Academia.edu, Mendeley, ResearchGate) are unanimously considered to be the current[17] market leaders in this space.

To reach the goals of this study, first, a basis for analysis needs to be established. This basis builds on previous contributions of the author. These are a generic framework of social networking services for professional use (Richter et al., 2009) and a framework derived from an empirical study that identified support requirements for collaborative research (Söldner et al., 2009).

---

[17] As of September 2017

Once this basis for analysis has been laid out, the eight SRNS platforms are investigated along the lines of this framework, with the three surviving platforms investigated in-depth, while also uncovering causes for the lack of success of these SRNS platforms that are now defunct. The analysis itself has been carried out as a case study and draws on a multitude of sources, among them interviews with their founders, exploration of the platforms and their functions by two independent researchers, and extensive study of blogs, webcasts, and other materials made available by the platforms' providers and other parties.

The remainder of this empirical study is organized as follows: Chapter 2 describes the development of a framework for the analysis of these SRNS platforms. Chapter 3 explains the methodology underlying this study as well as how data was collected and analyzed. The eight cases are then presented within chapter 4. Chapter 5 provides the results of the analysis and describes the findings. Chapter 6 summarizes this study and identifies an area that requires further research in order to provide a more holistic picture of SRNS platforms.

2 Development of an analysis framework

In order to carry out a sound investigation into the current state of technology of *social research network sites* (SRNS), a framework for analysis needs to be established. This is particularly necessary since the SRNS evaluated in this *part* offer widely varying features, which makes a comparison and an evaluation of their suitability to support different research-related activities harder. A thorough evaluation of such applications is of crucial importance since they have a substantial influence on the activities and processes of their users and thus their organizations (Scholtz & Steves, 2004). Applications from the field of computer-supported cooperative work (CSCW) to which social research network sites also belong to are particularly hard to compare and evaluate (Grudin, 1988). While this general problem of the evaluation of CSCW applications which was pointed out by Grudin (1988) has not been solved yet, applying a structured framework helps in producing a meaningful and sound analysis (Scholtz & Steves, 2004). Utilizing such a framework is necessary as a tool for orientation during requirements analysis and evaluation regardless of if the software system is developed in-house or an existing tool is procured on the market (Richter et al., 2009).

Since social research network sites constitute a fairly recent class of tools starting with the first offerings around the year 2008 and existing literature has not come up with a suitable framework for the analysis of these applications so far, this *chapter* lays out the development of a structured framework for comparing and evaluating social research network sites.

This framework takes into account generic properties of these sites, i.e. properties that also apply to other social networking services targeted towards professional use, as well as features and affordances specific to research work and research collaboration. The generic properties of social network research sites are analyzed based on a modified and expanded version of the frameworks for the evaluation of enterprise social networking services proposed by Richter et al. (2009)[18] and Kietzmann et al. (2011). The research- and research collaboration-specific aspects of social research network sites are evaluated through the lens of research support functions, based on a modified and expanded version of the framework of research support functions proposed by Söldner et al. (2009). The details of the resulting framework for the evaluation of social research network sites are explained in the next sections of this *chapter*.

2.1 Framework Development to Evaluate the Generic Properties of Social Research Networking Sites

Since social research networking sites (SRNS) constitute a specialized variant of enterprise social networking services (ESN), their *generic* properties can be analyzed through the lens of frameworks that help understand the features and properties of enterprise social networking services. The following sections describe the fundamentals of social networking services and the development of the framework used here for the evaluation of generic properties of social research networking sites.

2.1.1 What are social networking services?

Social networking services have become a ubiquitous class of social software applications and are now a part of the daily lives of many people, both for utilitarian and hedonic purposes. To analyze the suitability of enterprise social networking services for usage in a professional environment, Richter et al. (2009) and Kietzmann et al. (2011) have proposed well-respected frameworks that are well suited to provide guidance in the evaluation of the generic properties, i.e. those aspects not specific to the research-related features of the SRNS - with some minor modifications.

The evaluation framework proposed by Richter et al. (2009) is constructed based on two widely accepted definitions of social networking services:

---

[18] The author of this thesis is a co-author of the framework proposed by Richter et. al. (2009)

> *"We define social network sites as web-based services that allow individuals to (1) construct a public or semi-public profile within a bounded system, (2) articulate a list of other users with whom they share a connection, and (3) view and traverse their list of connections and those made by others within the system." (Boyd and Ellison, 2007, p. 2)*

According to the alternative definition proposed by Koch et al. (2007), social networking services are defined as

> *"application systems offering their users functionalities for identity management (for representing one's own person, typically by means of a profile) and for networking with other users of the system (and thus also offering features for managing one's contacts and maintaining one's personal network)" (Koch et al. 2007, p. 3).*[19]

According to Koch et al. (2007), the fundamental functionalities of social networking services are:

- identity management: creating and modifying a profile allowing to represent different aspects of one's own personality
- relationship or contact management: managing one's contacts and maintaining one's network
- visualization of profiles and networks (implemented in various ways, e.g. as a graph or a set of paths between contacts)

In addition to these basic functionalities, they have identified further functionalities that some (but not all) professional social networking services offer:

- (semi-automatic) discovery of relationships and networks
- usage of these networks for searching for and discovering experts and for a (potentially automatic) recommendation of additional interesting contacts and experts
- communication functionalities, e.g. online communities and other features for communicating and exchanging information in a shared context (like forums, etc.)

---

[19] Translated by the author

- awareness features like notifications of changes in the professional status of a contact or the display if a contact is currently online in the system

The business value of these social networking services is derived from their capability to provide an overview of one's own network and every user with the most current information about their connections. In addition, the creation of new connections to other users is facilitated and presenting one's own qualifications and achievements to a larger audience is very easy, while at the same time being able to exchange more information with other users in less time and to find a shared context for more in-depth conversations (Koch et al., 2007; Teten & Allen, 2005).

The attributes of social networking services listed above (Koch et al., 2007) have been further condensed into five activities supporting six core functionalities (identity management, search for experts, context awareness, contact management, exchange of information and communication, and network awareness) and have been arranged into the process model of IT-supported social networking (Richter and Koch, 2008), depicted in figure 10.

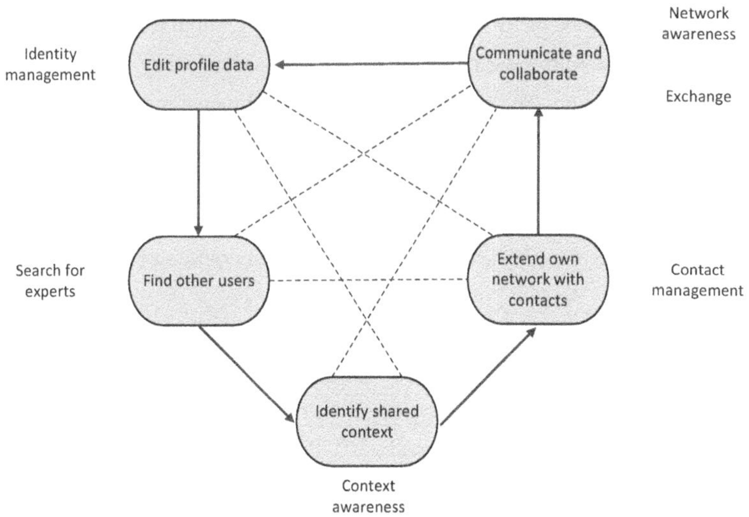

Figure 10: Process model of IT-supported social networking (based on Richter and Koch, 2008)

2.1.2 Towards a framework for the evaluation of social networking aspects in SRNS: related work

On the basis of previous work on enterprise social networking services (Boyd & Ellison, 2007; Koch et al., 2007) and the process model of IT-supported social networking (Richter & Koch, 2008), a framework for the analysis and evaluation of enterprise social networking services was developed by Richter et al. (2009)[20]. This framework builds on the six groups of core functionalities of social networking services (Koch et al., 2007) with two additional areas having been added:

- Supporting functionalities: features and functionalities that cannot directly be associated with a specific activity, but are beneficial as a whole for the platform like support for open APIs, the availability of multiple languages in the interface, etc.
- General properties of the service: factual information about the platform which is helpful and necessary to describe the service as a whole, but not related to the platform's functionalities and features

The eight dimensions of the resulting framework are summarized in table 56 and are explained in the following paragraphs. For every dimension of the framework, there are several criteria. The number of criteria per dimension is given next to the respective dimension. The full framework including the criteria can be found in Richter et al. (2009).

Table 56: Overview of the framework for the analysis of enterprise social networking services (Richter et al., 2009)

Identity management (9)	Search for experts (5)
Context awareness (4)	Contact management (4)
Exchange of information and communication (4)	Network awareness (2)
Supporting functionalities (6)	General properties of the service (8)

Identity management refers to a group of related functionalities to represent one's own person (typically via a profile) in a controlled fashion to a large group of users. In

[20] The author of this thesis is a co-author of the framework proposed by Richter et. al. (2009)

the framework, this area is tested with nine criteria, e.g. the possibility to change privacy settings.

Search for experts deals with the user's ability to identify and to use implicit knowledge. It encompasses both manual search features (e.g. name, university affiliation, research interests, etc.) and the automatic recommendation of potentially interesting contacts by the platform (e.g. researchers working on similar topics). The framework offers five criteria in this area.

Context awareness refers to functionalities of the platform that make the user aware of a shared context with other users (like common contacts, similar research interests, affiliation with the same university or research institute). This functionality is technically often realized with widgets in the platform that visualize the connections between the users. The framework tests this area with four criteria.

Contact management summarizes all functions related to the management of one's own network. The very fundamental concept of a social networking service to *network* with other contacts, radically simplifies contact management, as every user manages and updates his or her own data independently. The task of contact management is thus reduced to managing only one's own contacts or to group them in categories or lists. Functionalities usually associated with this area are to be able to associate tags with users, to visualize contacts and their relationships, and to export contacts for using them with other applications. The framework lists four criteria to evaluate the platform's functionalities regarding contact management.

Network awareness refers to supporting the awareness about activities (or the current status or changes in the status) of the contacts in one's network. Features supporting network awareness can be further divided into push- and pull-based functionalities. Push-based functionalities are providing information about current events in one's personal network automatically, typically upon login into the platform. Pull-based functionalities allow the user to retrieve data based on queries, e.g. contacts who have changed their affiliation with an institute. The framework offers two criteria for network awareness.

Another feature of social networking services is the easiness with which these platforms provide for the *exchange of information and communication*. Regardless of using direct communication with messages between individual users or group discussions in forums, social networking services require no other data (like e-mail addresses of contacts), since everything required for communication is already built-in to the platform and can be consumed after login. The framework offers four criteria to evaluate the features pertaining to this dimension.

Supporting functionalities lists six criteria to test if the platform offers other desirable features like programmability and extensibility with open APIs, and support for multiple languages.

General properties of the service deals with fundamental properties of the platform, like its history, costs (if applicable), number of users, etc. This dimension offers seven criteria.

In a similar vein, Kietzmann et al. (2011) have proposed a framework for the analysis of social media and social networking services based on the widely accepted definition of social networking services by Boyd & Ellison (2007). Their framework differs from the earlier one proposed by Richter et al. (2009) primarily in the naming of the categories. In addition, it makes explicit one area of social media and social networking services – *reputation management* - that has not been accounted for by Richter et al. (2009). As reputation and the attention it entails play an important role in the academic community (Huberman et al, 2009; Franck, 1999; Cronin, 2005), considering it is highly relevant for the analysis of social research networking sites.

2.1.3 A framework for the analysis of social networking related functionalities of SRNS platforms

To be able to analyze the social networking related functionalities of SRNS platforms, a more targeted framework on SRNS is proposed based on the works of Richter et al. (2009) and Kietzmann et al. (2011). The framework has iteratively been refined during the analysis phase and has been specifically adapted towards the needs of a scholarly audience. The categories pertaining to the framework are summarized in table 56 below.

Table 57: Categories of the framework for the analysis of social networking related functionalities of SRNS platforms

Category	Source
Identity management	Identity management (Richter & Koch, 2009); Identity (Kietzmann et al., 2011)
Relationship management	Search for experts (Richter & Koch, 2009); Relationships (Kietzmann et al., 2011)
Communication	Exchange of information and communication (Richter & Koch, 2009); Conversations (Kietzmann et al., 2011)
Network awareness	Network awareness (Richter & Koch, 2009), Presence (Kietzmann et al., 2011)
Reputation	Reputation (Kietzmann et al., 2011)
Sharing	Sharing (Kietzmann et al., 2011), Exchange of information and communication (Richter & Koch, 2009)
Openness	Supporting functions (Richter & Koch, 2009)

In addition, a honeycomb model of social networking related aspects of SRNS has been derived from the categories and is depicted below in figure 11.

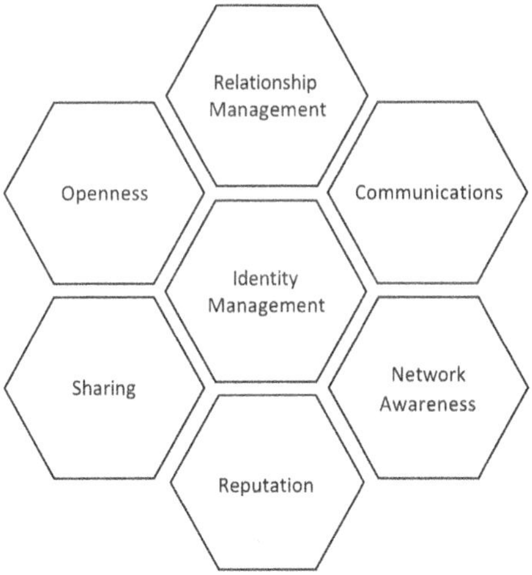

Figure 11: Honeycomb of social networking aspects of social research network sites, own visualization based on Richter et al. (2009) and Kietzmann et al. (2011)

2.2 A Framework for the Analysis of Research Collaboration Related Aspects of SRNS platforms

Since social research network sites go beyond traditional social networking services in that they are focused on a specific audience – scholars – and their needs for support in various stages of research, an additional, more specific framework is needed to assess the affordances and suitability of SRNS to support collaborative and non-collaborative research and research-related tasks in general. Soeldner et al. (2009) have proposed a framework for research support functionalities in social software platforms derived from interviews conducted with experts from the field. Their framework is based on the model of a generic research process that has been conceptualized by Graziano and Raulin (2007), depicted in figure 12.

Figure 12: Generic research process (own visualization, based on Graziano & Raulin, 2007)

This research process model is at the same time comprehensive and generic in its nature and is purported to be applicable to research projects of all domains (Söldner et al., 2009). It conceptualizes research into seven different phases (Graziano & Raulin, 2007; Söldner et al., 2009):

1. The research process starts with the first phase, *idea generation*, which focuses on the identification of relevant research topics – important drivers for this phase are creativity, reviewing the extant literature, and the exchange of ideas with fellow researchers.
2. The ensuing phase of *problem definition* narrows down the fuzzy and broad ideas resulting from step 1 into focused and precise research questions.
3. Following the problem definition, the *procedures design* phase subsumes all necessary activities dealing with the planning and preparation of data collection.
4. The next phase, rather specifically termed *observation*, deals with and summarizes different methods of data collection.

5. The actual analysis of collected data, whether qualitative or quantitative, constitutes the major task of the subsequent phase of *data analysis*.
6. The results of the data analysis are related to the research questions and the contribution to the targeted knowledge basis are identified during the *interpretation phase*.
7. In the final *communication* phase, research results are distributed and shared with the goal to transfer and amplify knowledge; the activities related to this phase are usually publishing via journal papers and presenting at conferences.

Building on the generic model of research phases (Graziano & Raulin, 2007), Yao (2003) and Yao and Tang (2003) identified five supporting functions to facilitate the research process of individual scholars that can be provided by software tools: exploring support, retrieval support, reading support, analyzing support, and writing support. While *exploring support* can help identify relevant extant work of other scholars, the goal of *retrieval support* is to help uncover necessary literature to the topic at hand. *Reading support* can be provided by facilitating the linkage of information fragments and making notes. *Analyzing support* deals with providing suggestions on analysis tools, methods, and their usage. Providing suggestions for possible references, automatic correction, and systems that support citation all fall into the domain of *writing support*.

Based on the results of their empirical study, Söldner et al. (2009) proposed three additional supporting functions on the level of the individual researcher: collection support, interpretation support, and dissemination support. *Collection support* can help transform data collection tasks during the observation phase into a peer-based approach, e.g. by being able to explore data and statistics of other users, thus benefiting the individual researcher. *Interpretation support* can be delivered by technical means that help with enabling and promoting discussions between researchers, implemented via forums or wiki systems. Centrally storing potential interpretations in a wiki system makes these discussions available within a team of researchers and facilitates further discussions. *Dissemination support* refers to technical means that help raise the awareness of one's publications and potentially opens them to a wider audience.

Focusing on the level of team research projects, such collaborative research projects can cover only parts of the research process or can be aligned with the entire process from initial idea generation to the final communication of the results. For comprehensive support of collaborative research processes, activities related to the management of the (virtual) research team need to be taken into account as well. This comprises the coordination of meetings, supporting effective communication, and a variety of other tasks. Based on an empirical, qualitative study, they propose an expanded framework of research support functions (Söldner et al., 2009), depicted in figure 13.

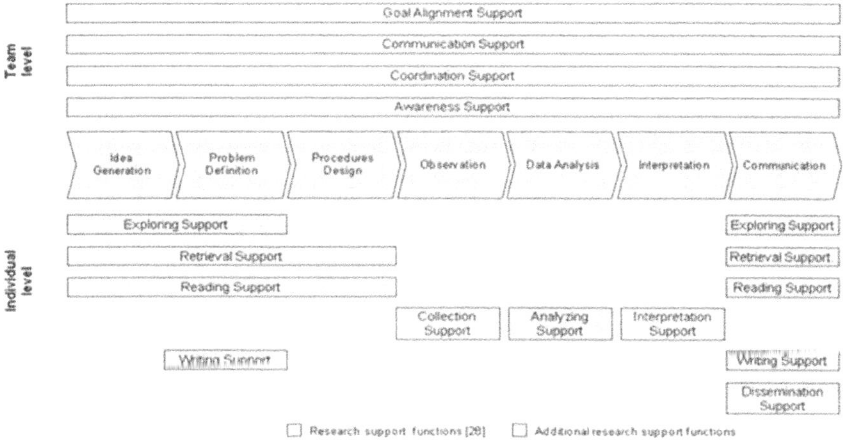

Figure 13: Framework of research support functions (Söldner et al., 2009)

On the team level, the framework suggests four additional support functions that are independent of the individual stages of the research process: goal alignment support, communication support, coordination support, and awareness support. Since social software can facilitate these areas according to Söldner et al. (2009), they are also included in the framework for the analysis of research collaboration related aspects of SRNS platforms.

3 Methodology and Data Collection

The need to perform a thorough analysis of the social research networking sites (SRNS) arises since they constitute new and complex offerings that have not been sufficiently treated and examined in extant literature. Based on the framework presented in the previous chapter of this part, relevant SRNS sites currently existing (and those that have been discontinued) will be analyzed in order to derive a deeper understanding of the features and offerings of SRNS systems, as well of their intended use through in-depth interviews with the founders of the platforms.

This chapter, therefore, presents the research method applied and explains how data was gathered and analyzed. The chapter contains three sections. The first section elucidates why a qualitative research approach, the case study method, was used. The second section presents the details of the data collection. Finally, the third section describes the case analysis in detail.

3.1 Research Design

Since social research network sites represent a new phenomenon, relatively little is known about them and the current state of technology has not been explored systematically. To the author's best knowledge, there is no comprehensive overview of the features, functionalities, and affordances of SRNS and how they can be leveraged to support individual scientists and teams of researchers for research-related tasks and (collaborative) research. Thus, the goal of this study is to explore the current state of the technology in the area of SRNS and to understand how features of these tools might help individual researchers and teams of scholars to become more efficient and effective. In addition, the study also aims to uncover the intended use of the tools by their founders and providers and thus attempts to come up with a classification of these tools.

In order to address this goal, an explorative qualitative research approach is used. In contrast to quantitative research approaches, qualitative data can yield in-depth insights into the phenomenon under study by taking into account causal relationships, complex patterns, and context-specific factors. Overall, qualitative research is helpful in discovering and generating theory in a context when relatively little is known about the underlying object of study (Eisenhardt, 1989; Miles and Huberman, 1994). Following this qualitative research strategy, an exploratory case study with embedded units of analysis was conducted (Eisenhardt, 1989; Yin, 2013).

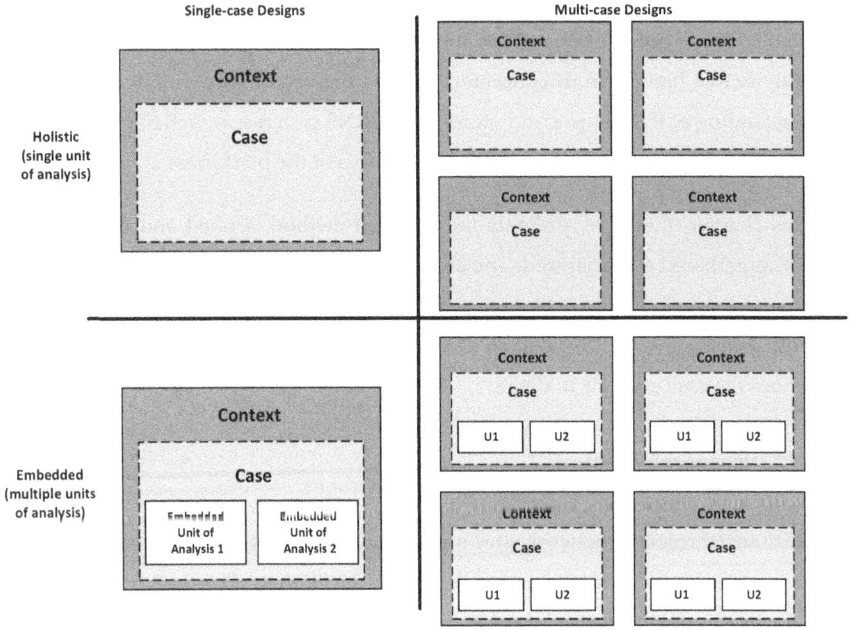

Figure 14: Basic types of case study designs (Yin, 2013)

To further support the resulting conclusions, a comparative case study is applied, i.e. data from multiple cases were collected and examined iteratively (Yin, 2013). The iterative procedure of investigation within-case and cross-case supported the creation of new insights (Eisenhardt, 1989). Figure 14 depicts case-study designs, the design chosen for this research was the multiple-case design in the embedded variant (multiple units of analysis).

3.2 Research Sample, Data Collection, and Data Analysis

In this section, the selection of the research sample, the data collection process, and the subsequent data analysis are described in detail.

3.2.1 Research sample

The sample of SRNS platforms was chosen based on a previous publication by the author of this thesis in which 24 social networking services that address a professional or an academic audience have been identified and analyzed (Möslein, Bullinger, & Söldner, 2009). The initial sample and the functionalities identified is depicted in figure 15.

Network / Criteria	2collab.com	academia.edu	academici.com	biomedexperts.com	centraldesktop.com	collabrx.com	epws.org	escidoc.org	globaledge.msu.edu	labmeeting.com	laboratree.org	lalisio.com	lumifi.com	mendeley.com	mynetresearch.com	network.nature.com	pingtsta.com	researchgate.net	saba.com	scholarz.net	scilife.net	scispace.net	ssrn.com	thoughtleaders.within3.co
Identity and Network																								
Personal Profile	x	x	x	x	x		x		x	x	x	x	x	x	x	x		x	x	x	x	x	x	
Directory of Profiles	x	x	x	x			x			x	x	x	x	x	x	x		x		x	x			
Search for Profiles	x	x	x	x			x			x	x	x	x	x	x	x		x		x	x			
Interaction and Communication																								
Messages		x	x	x			x		x	x	x	x	x	x	x	x		x		x	x			
Instant Mess. Service						x														x				
Information and Content																								
Wiki			x				x	x							x							x		
Group Editor			x		x															x				
Social Tagging	x		x												x			x			x			
Social Rating																	x	x			x			
Data Upload	x	x	x	x	x		x		x	x	x	x	x	x	x			x	x	x	x	x		
Paper Upload	x	x	x	x			x		x	x	x	x	x	x	x			x	x	x	x	x	x	
Commenting	x		x				x			x			x					x	x	x		x	x	
Topical Focus																								
Generic	x	x	x		x		x	x	x	x	x	x	x	x	x	x		x	x	x	x	x	x	
Specific				x		x											x							x
Degree of Openness																								
Free	x	x	x	x	x		x		x	x	x	x	x	x	x	x		x		x	x	x	x	
Commercial			x		x										x		x							
Open for everyone	x	x	x		x		x		x		x	x	x	x	x	x		x	x	x	x	x	x	
By invitation only				x		x											x					x		x

Figure 15: Initial sample of 24 social networking services addressing a professional or an academic audience

As a result, six social networking services from the sample were selected for a closer analysis of features and functionalities, since they were purpose-built to support researchers in collaborative settings and other research-related activities. Two additional networks that were not contained within the initial sample derived from (Möslein et al., 2009) have been added following a pyramiding approach (Von Hippel et al, 2009): CiteULike and Trellis. Trellis is a recently developed social research networking site focusing on supporting collaboration between scientists, founded in 2014 and available to a wider audience starting in 2016.

To allow for a comparison of the different social research networking sites, a sample was chosen based on the following six criteria:

- web-based service
- at least basic social networking functionality
- addressing primarily an academic audience
- representation of target audiences from different disciplinary fields
- openness to a broad public
- constitutes or constituted more than a niche offering

In total, eight cases have been identified and analyzed, thus allowing for a reasonable generalization of insights.

3.2.2 Data collection

Data collection was performed by gathering from multiple sources and through a combination of different techniques (Yin, 2013). The platforms were analyzed alongside the framework outlined in *chapter two* of this *part* by three independent researchers. The analysis focused on the identification of relevant characteristics as standalones, therefore interdependencies and relations have not been explored. In addition, interviews with the founders of the platforms have been performed. The interview transcripts were analyzed in-depth by two independent researchers. Data coding and qualitative content analysis were performed with the help of the qualitative research package MAXQDA. The data coding and analysis was carried out based on content analysis procedures to code data (Mayring, 2002). The coding was performed by two independent researchers and was subsequently compared by following an analyst triangulation approach (Yin, 2013). When data collected from the different sources seemed to be inconsistent, inconclusive, or contradictory, the researchers went back to the interviewee to clarify these issues. The overall research approach used in part III is summarized in figure 16.

Figure 16: Research design of part III

A summary of the cases including the key facts of each case can be found in table 58.

Table 58: Summary of cases including key facts of each case

Social research network site	Description	Years active	Members	Mission statement	Access
Academia.edu	Social research networking site with strong paper sharing and collaboration capabilities	2008 – today (May 2017)	35-49 million (disputed)	Accelerate the world's research	Free and premium (paid)
Mendeley	Mendeley is a reference manager and academic social network that can help organize research, collaborate with others online and discover the latest research	2007 – today (May 2017)	Over 6 million (as of 2017)	Empowering researchers to organize their references, to connect and inspire each other, to store and share their data	Free and premium (paid)
ResearchGate	Social research networking site that allows researchers and scientists to find collaboration partners, share papers, and ask and answer research-related questions	2008 – today (May 2017)	More than 12 million[21]	Connect the world of science and make research open to all	Free
scholarz.net	Integrated online software for scientific work	2008 – January 2013	433 (as of November 2011)	Do better and more efficient research and academic networking	Free
Laboratree.org	Social networking for scientists and a research management tool	2008 – 2013	1000 (as of 2009)	Creating Laboratreee, a Web-Based Platform to Enhance Research Collaboration	Free
MyNetResearch.com	Web 2.0 portal created to enable researchers to engage in global collaborations	2008 – 2015	13,500 (as of April 2010)	Maximizing research productivity through global collaboration	Free and premium (paid)
CiteULike	Online bookmarking service for storing and sharing bibliographic references to academic papers	2004 – today (May 2017)	unknown	CiteULike is a free service for managing and discovering scholarly references	Free and premium (paid)
Trellis	An online communication and collaboration platform for members of the scientific community	2014 – today (May 2017)	unknown	Trellis is a professional network for the scientific community that makes it easy for groups of any size, disciplinary composition, or affiliation to collaborate only	Free (early access)

[21] https://www.researchgate.net/about, retrieved March 25, 2017

3.2.3 Data analysis

The overall analysis of the data was driven by the research questions:

What is the current state of technology regarding social software tools specifically relevant to an academic audience? What is their intended use by their providers and can they further be classified according to their functionalities and intended use?

In all the eight cases described here, an interview with the founder was performed and the platform analysis has been conducted as described above. In select cases, additional questions were discussed in email conversations and skype telephone calls with the platform founder and team members of the respective SRNS platform. Besides, additional secondary resources were analyzed to get a more consistent and comprehensive understanding of the case. These resources include in most cases secondary literature on the platform (academic publications and books wherever available), blogs and newspaper articles that were concerned with the platform under scrutiny, webcasts and training videos published by the platform if available, and webcasts by independent bloggers and researchers. Figure 17 graphically shows the kinds of data sources employed and table 59 lists the data sources used for the eight cases chosen for this study.

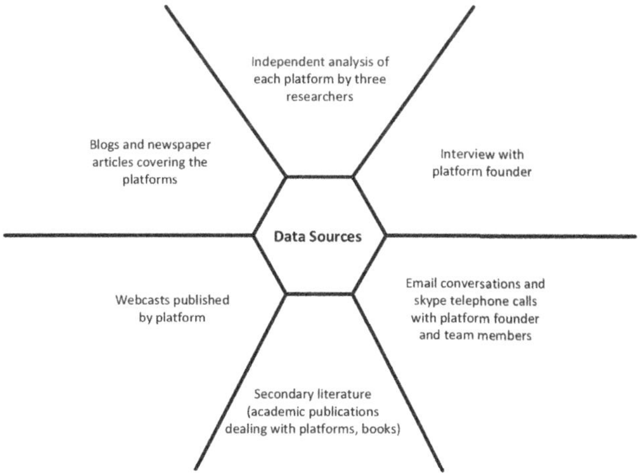

Figure 17: Overview of data sources employed in the case studies

Table 59: Data sources used in the case studies, per case

Case	Data Sources
All cases	• Independent analysis of the platform by three researchers • Interview with founder of the platform
Academia.edu	• Email conversations & skype telephone calls • Secondary literature (academic publications, books) • Blogs and newspaper articles, Twitter profile of founder
Mendeley.edu	• Email conversations & skype telephone calls • Webcasts published by the platform • Secondary literature (academic publications, books) • Blogs and newspaper articles, Twitter profile of founder
researchgate.net	• Email conversations & skype telephone calls • Webcasts published by independent science bloggers • Secondary literature (academic publications, books) • Blogs and newspaper articles, Twitter profile of founder
Scholarz.net	• Secondary literature (academic publications, books) • Blogs and newspaper articles
Laboratree.org	• Blogs and newspaper articles
MyNetResearch.com	• Email conversations & skype telephone calls • Blogs and newspaper articles
CiteULike	• Secondary literature (academic publications, books) • Blogs and newspaper articles
Trellis	• Email conversations & skype telephone calls • Blogs and newspaper articles

Additional information on the interviewees and when the interviews were performed is provided in table 60 below.

Table 60: Overview of the sample including interviewee-related information

SRNS platform	Description of the original platform[22]	Interview Partner (anonymized)	First interview round	Second interview round
Scholarz.net	Management and execution of own or group projects	Manager SN	January 2010	None, platform defunct
Academia.edu	Directory of researchers and overview of organizations	Manager AE	January 2010	Declined[23]
Laboratree.org	Online collaboration and management of research teams	Manager LT	January 2010	None, platform defunct
Mendeley.com	Online and offline management and recommendation of publications	Manager MD	February 2010	November 2016
Mynetresearch.com	Document and project management for research groups	Manager MR	January 2010	None, platform defunct
Researchgate.net	Academic social networking to maintain awareness of a topic or network	Manager RG	February 2010	Declined[24]
Citeulike.org	Reference collection and recommendation	Manager CL	January 2010	Platform unchanged[25]
Trellis.com	Academic social network with focus on communication and collaboration	Manager TL	Platform founded later	April 2017

[22] As of the time of the first round of the interviews. The platforms that still exist today have evolved dramatically since then. The current state of the platform (as of April, 2017) that reflects these changes is described in *chapter 4* of this *part* of this thesis

[23] The interviewee has been contacted again in 2016 and 2017, but has either not responded or declined another interview. In the case of academia.edu, there is an abundance of secondary information, since the platform's founder has given multiple interviews to newspapers and podcasts that have been analyzed as part of this research as well.

[24] The interviewee has been contacted again in 2016 and 2017, but has either not responded or declined another interview. In the case of ResearchGate, there is an abundance of secondary information, since the platform's founder has given multiple interviews to newspapers and podcasts that have been analyzed as part of this research as well.

[25] The platform visibly has not changed since the time the original research was carried out.

4 Cases

In the following, eight cases of social research networking sites will be presented. The details on how social networking and research support are realized within these sites will be described in detail within the subsequent findings chapter. The analysis of the cases was carried out along the lines of the framework presented in *chapter 2* of this *part*.

4.1 Case 1: Academia.edu

Academia.edu is a venture-capital-backed[26] social research networking site launched in 2008 by its founder, Richard Price, together with Andrew Watkins (Stanford University), Jarques Pretorius (Art Institute of California in San Francisco) and Ben Lund from the University of Cambridge (Ortega, 2016). According to its self-presentation, Academia.edu provides a web-based platform on which users can share papers, monitor the impact of their own research, and stay informed about the research of other scholars they follow on the platform. The self-reported mission of Academia.edu is to "accelerate the world's research"[27]. While the platform belonged to the very pioneers of social research networking services due to its first-mover advantage, it starts to face more and more criticism in recent years related to ethical considerations since some users reported having been asked to pay a fee to the platform in exchange for recommendations of their papers[28]. Other researchers fear conflicts of interests and future issues arising out of Academia.edu's profit-oriented business model (Richard Price has raised venture capital for Academia.edu amounting

---

[26] https://www.theatlantic.com/education/archive/2015/12/the-convoluted-profits-of-academic-publishing/421047/, retrieved February 28, 2017

[27] https://www.academia.edu/about, retrieved February 28, 2017

[28] http://blogs.lse.ac.uk/impactofsocialsciences/2016/02/01/should-you-deleteacademiaedu/, retrieved February 28, 2017

to a total of $17.8 million[29], with the latest round of funding closed back in September 2013[30]). Recently, some scholars went even as far as to call out to the researcher community to delete their accounts at Academia.edu.[31], among other reasons because of allegations of "vendor lock-in" due to restrictive terms of service and lack of open and public APIs, and the overall "closed" philosophy being antithetical to the "ethos of academia"[32].

Figure 18: Landing page of Academia.edu advertising a disputed membership number[33]

Finally, others have pointed out[34] that the membership numbers advertised at Academia.edu's website must be grossly incorrect – the website displays a seemingly-random generated number between reloads of the website fluctuating around 49 million current members ("academics"), while other sources report an estimated total

---

[29] https://www.theatlantic.com/education/archive/2015/12/the-convoluted-profits-of-academic-publishing/421047/, retrieved February 28, 2017

[30] https://www.crunchbase.com/organization/academia-edu#/entity, retrieved February 28, 2017

[31] https://www.forbes.com/sites/drsarahbond/2017/01/23/dear-scholars-delete-your-account-at-academia-edu/#37fa905c2d62, retrieved February 28, 2017

[32] http://blogs.lse.ac.uk/impactofsocialsciences/2016/02/01/should-you-deleteacademiaedu/, retrieved February 28, 2017

[33] Screenshot retrieved on March 24, 2017 from www.academia.edu

[34] Private conversation with the founder of a competing platform in 2016

number of 17 million academics worldwide[35]. Figure 19 sheds more light on the highly disputed question of the total number of Academia.edu's users.

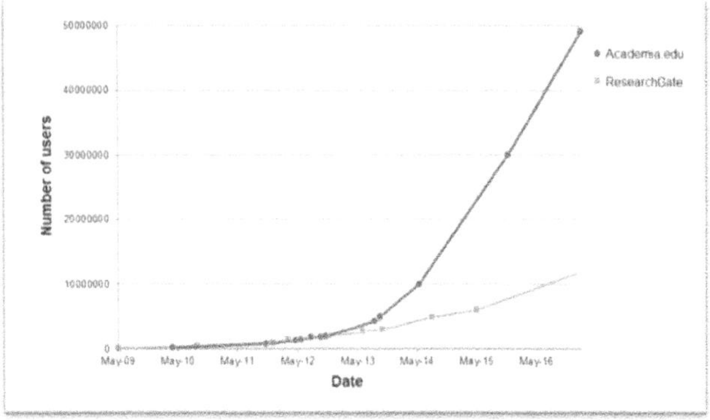

Figure 19: Purported number of users of Academia.edu vs ResearchGate[36]

The key facts on Academia.edu are summarized in table 61.

Table 61: Key facts on the Academia.edu case

Social research networking site	Academia.edu
URL	http://academia.edu
Description	Social research networking site with strong paper sharing and collaboration capabilities
Founded in	2008
Years active	until now (March 2017)
Members	35-49 million (heavily disputed)
Mission statement	Accelerate the world's research
Access	free and premium (paid)

[35] https://techcrunch.com/2013/09/26/academia-edu-2/, retrieved February 28, 2017

[36] https://shiftandrefresh.wordpress.com/2017/03/22/academic-social-networking-sites-over-time-two-useful-figures/, retrieved March 25, 2017

4.2 Case 2: Mendeley

Mendeley, a portmanteau word derived from the surnames of German biologist Gregor Mendel and Russian chemist Dmitri Mendeleev[37], was founded by Victor Henning, Jan Reichelt, and Paul Föckler in 2007[38]. After the first public beta version was made available in August 2008, Mendeley became quickly popular in the academic world and the founders won several start-up and innovation awards in 2009, among them "Best Social Innovation Which Benefits Society 2009"[39], "European Start-up of the Year 2009"[40], and was ranked #6 in "Top 100 tech media companies" by The Guardian[41]. After several years of continued growth and service expansion (among others support for Apple's iPhone and iPad platforms), Mendeley was acquired in 2013 by the Elsevier publishing company for an undisclosed amount, purported to be between $65 million and $100 million[42]. The acquisition of Mendeley by Elsevier triggered an angry outburst of many users, due to a perceived conflict between the open access movement that users associated Mendeley with (Ortega, 2016) and Elsevier's disputed and despised business model[43], that has incited thousands of academics to boycott Elsevier's journals and refraining from performing activities like refereeing and editorial work for Elsevier (see the "Cost of Knowledge" movement[44]).

---

[37] http://blog.mendeley.com/start-up-life/how-our-name-evolved-from-b-movie-monster-to-mendeley/, retrieved March 02, 2017

[38] http://www.doctorpreneurs.com/paul-foeckler-interview/, retrieved March 02, 2017

[39] https://techcrunch.com/2009/07/09/the-europas-the-winners-and-finalists/, retrieved March 03, 2017

[40] https://blog.mendeley.com/2009/03/17/we-won-the-plugg-conference-start-up-rally-heres-how-it-went/, retrieved March 02, 2017

[41] https://blog.mendeley.com/2009/09/11/our-the-guardian-week/, retrieved March 02, 2017

[42] https://www.elsevier.com/about/press-releases/corporate/elsevier-acquires-mendeley,-an-innovative,-cloud-based-research-management-and-social-collaboration-platform, retrieved March 02, 2017

[43] http://www.zephoria.org/thoughts/archives/2013/04/11/mendeley-elsevier.html, retrieved 30 March 2017

[44] http://thecostofknowledge.com/, retrieved 30 Mar 2017

Table 62: Key facts on the Mendeley case

Social research networking site	Mendeley.com
Description	Mendeley is a reference manager and academic social network that can help organize research, collaborate with others online, and discover the latest research[45]
Founded in	2007, acquired by Elsevier in 2013
Years active	2007 until now
Members	Over 6 million
Mission statement	Empowering researchers to organize their references, to connect and inspire each other, to store and share their data
Access	Free and Premium

Mendeley is special within the social research networking sites available in that it constitutes a hybrid offering between a web-based social networking site with the usual functionalities associated with a social networking service. In addition, it is also offered as a literature management application available for the desktop operating systems Windows, Linux, and Mac OS X, as well as for Apple iOS-based tablets and phones[46]. Besides reference management, Mendeley Desktop also comes with a Web Importer that allows to add articles directly to the library from websites like amazon.com, search engines, and academic databases. In addition, Mendeley Desktop features a citation plugin for Microsoft Word, Microsoft Word for Mac, and Libre Office with over 1,000 citation styles and the option to create own styles[47]. This combination makes Mendeley quite unique within social research networking sites, no other SRNS offers this feature set so far until today. Table 62 lists the key facts on Mendeley.

[45] https://www.elsevier.com/solutions/mendeley, retrieved March 02, 2017

[46] https://www.mendeley.com/download-mendeley-desktop/, retrieved March 19, 2017

[47] https://www.mendeley.com/reference-management/reference-manager/, retrieved March 19, 2017

4.3 Case 3: ResearchGate

ResearchGate is a venture-capital-backed social networking service for scientists with pronounced similarities to Facebook and LinkedIn. The platform was launched in 2008 by the physicians Dr. Ijad Madisch and Dr. Sören Hofmayer and computer scientist Horst Fickenscher. The founders met at Harvard University in Boston, Massachusetts, where the platform was initially launched, and then subsequently moved to Berlin shortly after the initial launch. Between 2010 and 2017, the founders collected total equity funding amounting to more than $100 million in four rounds, with the most recent funding (series D) amounting to $52.5 million having been announced on February 28, 2017[48], although the funding was already closed in November 2015[49]. ResearchGate's venture capital backers include Microsoft founder and billionaire Bill Gates.

The platform's mission is to "connect the world of science and make research open to all"[50]. Researchers wishing to join the platform are required to have an email address at a university or similar recognized institution with a scientific background or have to be manually approved as a published researcher in order to get an account on ResearchGate. Once joined, they can leverage the sophisticated social networking functionality offered by ResearchGate as well as collaborate with other researchers on the platform. According to a recent report on ResearchGate published by techcrunch.com, there are 12 million registered members on ResearchGate (as of February 2017)[51]. Membership on the platform is currently provided free, revenue is generated by advertising (primarily for recruitment purposes)[52].

---

[48] https://www.crunchbase.com/organization/researchgate#/entity, retrieved March 25, 2017

[49] https://techcrunch.com/2017/02/28/researchgate-raises-52-6m-for-its-social-research-network-for-scientists/, retrieved March 25, 2017

[50] https://www.researchgate.net/about, retrieved March 25, 2017

[51] https://techcrunch.com/2017/02/28/researchgate-raises-52-6m-for-its-social-research-network-for-scientists/, retrieved March 25, 2017

[52] http://www.businessinsider.de/researchgate-ads-network-11-million-scientists-researchers-2016-12, retrieved March 25, 2017

Table 63: Key facts on the ResearchGate case

Social research networking site	ResearchGate
URL	researchgate.net
Description	Social research networking site that allows researchers and scientists to find collaboration partners, share papers, and ask and answer research-related questions
Founded in	2008
Years active	until now (March 2017)
Members	more than 12 million[53]
Mission statement	"Our mission is to connect the world of science and make research open to all."[54]
Access	Free (only users with a valid university or research institution email address are accepted)

In the past, ResearchGate had to face criticism for emailing invitations to the platforms in an unsolicited way to coauthors of users. A study investigating the email notification behavior of ResearchGate found that in some cases a user received up to 980 email messages from the platform during the course of a year (Murray, 2014). ResearchGate claims to have changed the unsolicited email invitation practice as stated in their online help system[55].

The social networking and research support functionalities of ResearchGate will be described in more detail in the next sections. Table 63 lists the key facts on the ResearchGate case.

[53] https://www.researchgate.net/about, retrieved March 25, 2017

[54] https://www.researchgate.net/about, retrieved March 25, 2017

[55] https://explore.researchgate.net/display/support/Inviting+colleagues+to+ResearchGate, retrieved March 25, 2017

4.4 Case 4: Scholarz.net

Scholarz.net was a social research network site with a focus on social networking in an academic setting, knowledge, and reference management. It was founded as a spin-off of the interdisciplinary research project "Scientific Work in the Web" at the University of Würzburg in 2008 by Dr. Daniel Koch[56], back then a PhD student in economics, and Marc Willwacher. At the same time of the launch of scholarz.net, the developers of scholarz.net founded the company "KnowledgeWorkz GmbH" to provide support and help with further development and marketing of their platform[57][58]. scholarz.net's mission statement was to enable researchers to be able to do research more efficiently and help with academic social networking – finding interesting contacts, exchange knowledge, and collaborate and organize project groups[59]. Unfortunately, despite its unique collaborative feature set, scholarz.net did not take off and was taken over at the end of 2012 by the competing social research site researchgate.net[60] which entailed discontinuation of scholarz.net's service and no re-use of scholarz.net's technology by ResearchGate:

> *"Scholarz.net will be discontinuing its services come January 10, 2013. The platform's users are requested to back-up all files they have stored on scholarz.net and to open a new account at ResearchGate. A simple to use export tool has been provided."*[61]

The key facts on scholarz.net are provided in table 64.

---

[56] https://idw-online.de/de/news280821, retrieved March 10, 2017

[57] https://digiversity.net/2009/scholarz-net-virtuelle-plattform-fur-forscher/, retrieved March 09, 2017

[58] https://www.researchgate.net/blog/post/researchgate-takes-over-scholarz-net, retrieved March 09, 2017

[59] http://upload-magazin.de/blog/2279-5-fragen-an-scholarznet-die-wissenschaftsplattform/, retrieved March 10, 2017

[60] http://theheureka.com/researchgate-scholarz, retrieved March 10, 2017

[61] http://connectedresearchers.com/researchgate-takes-over-scholarz/, retrieved March 10, 2017

Table 64: Key facts on the scholarz.net case

Social research networking site	scholarz.net
URL	https://www.scholarz.net (now redirects to researchgate.net)
Description	Providing integrated online software for scientific work
Founded in	2008
Years active	until January 2013
Employees	Unknown
Members	433 (as of November 2011)[62]
Mission statement	"Do better and more efficient research and academic networking"[63][64]
Access	free

62 According to Nentwich and König (2012)

63 https://digiversity.net/2009/scholarz-net-virtuelle-plattform-fur-forscher/, retrieved March 10, 2017, translated by the author

64 http://upload-magazin.de/blog/2279-5-fragen-an-scholarznet-die-wissenschaftsplattform/, retrieved March 10, 2017, translated by the author

4.5 Case 5: Laboratree.org

Laboratree was a web-based research management and collaboration tool for scientists built upon a social network platform. It was founded by Sean Mooney, PhD, back then an assistant professor of medical and molecular genetics at the School of Medicine of the University of Indiana[65]. The development of Laboratree was organized by Selican Technologies, Inc., whose now-defunct website described Laboratree as follows:

"We are developing Laboratree, a web-based platform that will enhance research collaboration by facilitating communication and information sharing among laboratory research project teams. Laboratree was created by scientists to overcome structural roadblocks encountered in laboratory research projects."[66]

Laboratree allowed its users to create a simple profile encompassing basic attributes and including a feed as part of the profile (see figure 34). Networking with other users of the platform was possible via messages and communication in groups and projects within the system. Awareness of the status of other users, whether they were online or offline in the system, was incorporated into the profile.

Apart from its rather basic social networking functionalities (also due to Laboratree officially being a "work in progress" that never left the stage of minimum viable product), the platform's focus was on providing support in managing research and collaborating online with other researchers:

"It is designed to help team members jointly develop research proposals or plans, manage documents, review experimental results, and ease project communication."[67]

---

[65] http://www.buckinstitute.org/buck-news/sean-mooney-phd-joins-buck-faculty, retrieved March 10, 2017

[66] http://web.archive.org/web/20130615161531/http://selican.com/, archived version of selican.com of Jun 15, 2013, retrieved March 11, 2017

[67] http://web.archive.org/web/20130615161531/http://selican.com/, archived version of selican.com of Jun 15, 2013, retrieved March 11, 2017

Unfortunately, despite some good initial ideas and seed funding[68], Laboratree did not make it beyond the beta stadium and was finally discontinued in 2013.

Table 65 summarizes the key facts on Laboratree.org

Table 65: Key facts on the Laboratree case

Social research networking site	Laboratree.org
URL	http://laboratree.org (defunct)
Description	Social networking tool for scientists and a research management tool
Founded in	2008
Years active	until 2013
Employees	unknown
Members	1000 (in the year 2009)
Mission statement	Creating Laboratree, a Web-Based Platform to Enhance Research Collaboration
Access	free test drive of alpha version was available back in 2013, beta version was under development

[68] https://www.sbir.gov/sbirsearch/detail/134315, retrieved March 11, 2017

4.6 Case 6: MyNetResearch.com

MyNetResearch.com was a Web 2.0 portal created with the goal of enabling researchers to engage in global collaborations. Founded in 2008 by management information systems researcher Dr. Bay Arinze of Drexel University and developed by Venice Consulting Group, MyNetResearch offered a collaborative space in a social networking environment. Membership in the platform was free with an optional premium membership that provided additional storage capacity and additional features like project statistics, archival functions, and blogging within the platform[69]. The website allowed researchers to find each other, follow news and discussions in discipline-specific forums, collaborate on projects, and get access to specialist tools to aid them in their research. Unfortunately, due to a lack of market success, the platform was discontinued in 2015 (Jordan, 2017). A summary of the key facts on MyNetResearch is provided in table 66.

Table 66: Key facts on the MyNetResearch.com case

Social research networking site	MyNetResearch.com
URL	http://mynetresearch.com (defunct)
Description	Web 2.0 portal created to enable researchers to engage in global collaborations
Founded in	2008
Years active	until 2015
Members	13,500[70]
Mission statement	Maximizing research productivity through global collaboration[71]
Access	free and premium membership

[69] http://www.veniceconsulting.com/portfolio/mynetresearch, retrieved March 10, 2017

[70] As of April 2010 according to a tweet by Dr. Bay Arinze, http://archive.fo/E5KD1, retrieved March 11, 2017

[71] http://www.veniceconsulting.com/portfolio/mynetresearch, retrieved March 11, 2017

4.7 Case 7: CiteULike

CiteULike is a web-based offering that provides an online bookmarking service for storing and sharing bibliographic references to academic papers. It includes features commonly associated with social networking services, like maintaining a profile to represent one's own identity in the service, getting in contact with other users of the system, and exchanging messages. However, the features related to social networking are not very highly developed in the CiteULike, the focus of the platform rests more on the social bookmarking functionality. CiteULike was founded in 2004 by Richard Cameron, who initially ran the service privately. In December 2006, Richard founded Oversity Ltd. together with Chris Hall, Kevin Emamy, and James Caddy for the continued development and support of CiteULike[72]. In 2009, Mendeley and CiteULike announced a collaboration to allow data synchronization between a user's accounts in the two services[73]. The integration went live in June 2009, roughly three months after the initial announcement[74], but was then discontinued in February 2013, when Mendeley ceased to support the integration.

Since 2009, CiteULike has been suffering from a decline with a slowdown of new registrations and less active users in general. CiteULike is considered in danger of disappearing entirely, due to varied reasons, among other its limited usefulness as a reference management tool. This drawback might have even become more evident with the integration agreement with Mendeley (Ortega, 2015). Table 67 summarizes the key facts on CiteULike.

[72] http://www.citeulike.org/faq/faq.adp, retrieved March 08, 2017

[73] https://blog.mendeley.com/2009/02/16/citeulike-and-mendeley-collaborate/, retrieved March 08, 2017

[74] https://blog.mendeley.com/2009/06/02/citeulike-and-mendeley-collaborate-its-live/, retrieved March 08, 2017

Table 67: Key facts on the CiteULike case

Social research networking site	citeulike
Description	an online bookmarking service for storing and sharing bibliographic references to academic papers
Founded in	2004
Years active	until now (March 2017)
Members	Unknown
Mission statement	"CiteULike is a free service for managing and discovering scholarly references"[75]
Access	Free and Premium ("Gold")

[75] www.citeulike.org, last accessed 08 Mar 2017

4.8 Case 8: Trellis

Trellis is offered by the American Association for the Advancement of Science (AAAS), an international non-profit organization dedicated to the advancement of science, as an online communication and collaboration platform for researchers. Following a survey of AAAS members, in which 80% of the respondents remarked that connecting and communicating with other scientists in an online fashion needs improvement, AAAS launched the Trellis platform in December 2014 in a private beta[76]. According to the AAAS, in May 2016, Trellis had more than 7,000 users coming from various disciplines and countries, organized in more than 450 groups. By September 2016, the AAAS expected to have a user base of roundabout 100,000 AAAS members within the platform[77]. According to Trellis's founder and general manager, Joshua Freeman, the goal in creating Trellis was:

"We wanted to set up an easy-to-use common platform that enables members of the STEM community to come together online and collaborate. Trellis allows them to set up groups of any size and regardless of institutional affiliation, disciplinary focus, or geographic location and come together and start to collaborate."

In addition, Joshua Freeman highlighted the comprehensive nature of the platform:

"[…] without going off to a fragmented set of communities or collaboration tools. […] a platform where any scientific association can set up groups to enable engagement with and among their members, not on a siloed platform, but as part of the broader community, making engagement efficient (and rewarding) for their members."

Table 68 summarizes the key facts of the Trellis case.

---

[76] https://www.aaas.org/news/stpf/trellis-puts-science-community-at-fingertips, retrieved May 08, 2017

[77] https://www.aaas.org/news/stpf/trellis-puts-science-community-at-fingertips, retrieved May 08, 2017

Table 68: Key facts on the Trellis case

Social research networking site	Trellis
Description	An online communication and collaboration platform for members of the scientific community
Founded in	2014
Years active	until now (May 2017)
Members	139,000 (9th of May, 2017)
Mission statement	Trellis is a professional network for the scientific community that makes it easy for groups of any size, disciplinary composition, or affiliation to collaborate online
Access	Free (early access version)

5 Findings

This chapter presents the results of the in-depth cross-case analysis of the data gained from the eight case studies including the data gained from the interviews with the founders of the SRNS platforms. In total, the findings help further the understanding of these novel research tools, in line with the goals of this study. First, key functionalities of these research tools have been identified that distinguish them from standard social networking services. Second, these functionalities and further features of the platforms analyzed in the eight cases have been investigated under the lens of the framework presented in *chapter 2* of this *part* regarding research support functions. After a thorough comparison in the cross-case analysis, it becomes evident that the social research networking sites analyzed here vary considerably from each other in terms of their key functionalities regarding academic social networking and how they can provide support for individual and collaborative research processes. The findings from the cross-case analysis, presented in the next sections, help establish the current[78] state-of-technology of social research networking sites. Furthermore, a typology that classifies SRNS platforms according to their main functionality and the intended use by their founders is proposed.

The following three *sections* discuss the findings regarding social networking characteristics and research support functions on the individual and the team level of SRNS platforms. The final *section* in this *chapter* presents a typology of SRNS platforms that is intended to help understand their main use case seen from the perspective of their founders.

[78] as of September 2017

5.1 Social Networking Features in SRNS Platforms

This section will discuss the findings regarding the social networking features of the SRNS platforms identified by a thorough cross-study analysis of the case studies including the interviews of the platform founders. The discussion of the findings will follow the structure of the honeycomb model of the social networking related aspects of SRNS that was presented in the discussion of the analysis framework in chapter 2.1 of this part and is depicted for purposes of readability again in figure 20 below.

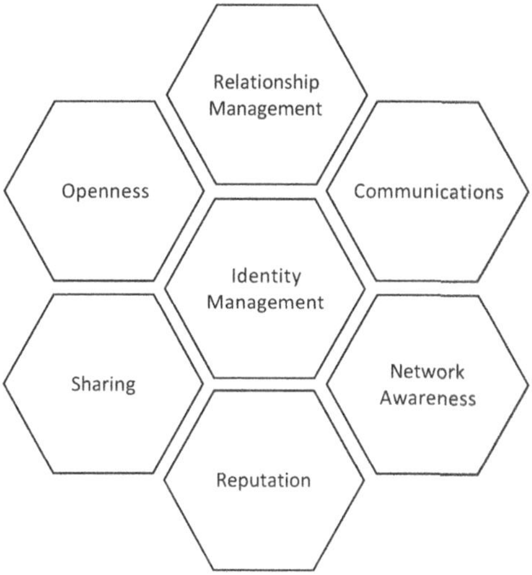

Figure 20: Honeycomb model of social networking related aspects of SRNS platforms

The following subsections, therefore, discuss the eight cases under the lens of the framework depicted in figure 20 and will include quotations from the founders where appropriate.

5.1.1 Identity management

All the eight platforms analyzed as part of the case studies offer identity management functionalities, as can be normally expected from social networking services. However, not all of the platform founders conceived their SRNS system as a classical social networking service, as one of the founders stated:

> *"Users didn't actually want facebook.com, because facebook.com was already there and they could have used it if they wanted to." (Manager MR)*

Another interviewee corroborated the idea that their creation was not actually a social networking service in the traditional sense:

> *"We don't like to call it a social network, even if it uses the same kind of technology. [...] because the objective is not only socializing. That's not why [researchers] are coming online. The reason they are coming online is to do work". (Manager LT)*

On the other hand, another founder saw it entirely differently and emphasized the importance of identity and network management in his statement:

> *"Some sort of facebook.com for researchers, that's what's needed, helping one to quickly find people with specific competencies and qualifications." (Manager RG)*

Consequently, following the original intentions of the founders, the degree of sophistication of the identity management functionalities varies considerably between the platforms. All eight platforms, even the now-defunct ones like scholarz.net, Laboratree.org, MyNetResearch.com, allowed its users to construct a basic profile, sometimes including the possibility to link to the Scopus author ID or the ORCID ID, as is the case with Mendeley. ResearchGate is offering the most highly sophisticated profile management features within the sample of SRNS platforms, as depicted in figure 21.

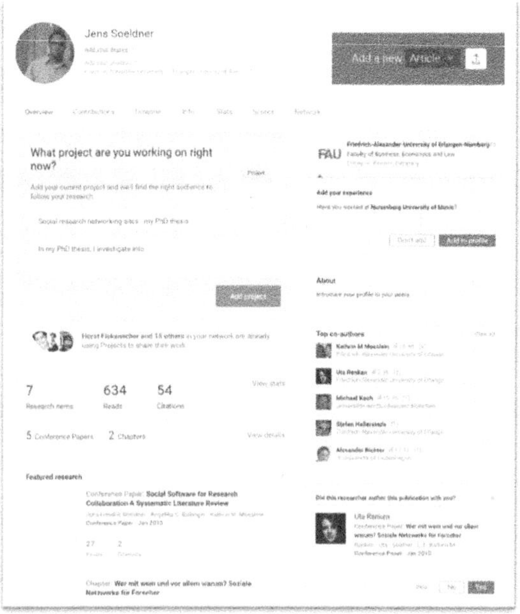

Figure 21: Screenshot depicting ResearchGate's profile editor[79]

Providing relevant information about researchers to facilitate is crucial in helping identify potential and suitable partners for research collaborations, as the following statement by a platform's founder emphasizes:

"The most important thing for these sites is how much information is collected and not just how much, but the quality of the information that is collected for each new member, because that is what enables you to have very sophisticated searches to actually identify the specific skills for the persons you want to work with." (Manager RG)

ResearchGate allows it users to create a very comprehensive profile on which they can articulate their academic achievements and showcase the achievements and their person in a way that is on par with other successful professional or hedonic social networking services like LinkedIn, Facebook, or Xing.

---

[79] https://www.researchgate.net/profile/Jens_Soeldner, retrieved March 26, 2017

In a similar vein, Mendeley offers its users to maintain a slightly simpler profile with fields relevant to an academic audience that can be used to search for other profiles: institution, research interests, publications, editorships, professional experience, and education history. In addition, linking to a Scopus author ID or an ORCID ID[80] (Open Research Contributor ID[81]) is directly possible within the profile. Mendeley's profile editor is partially depicted in figure 24.

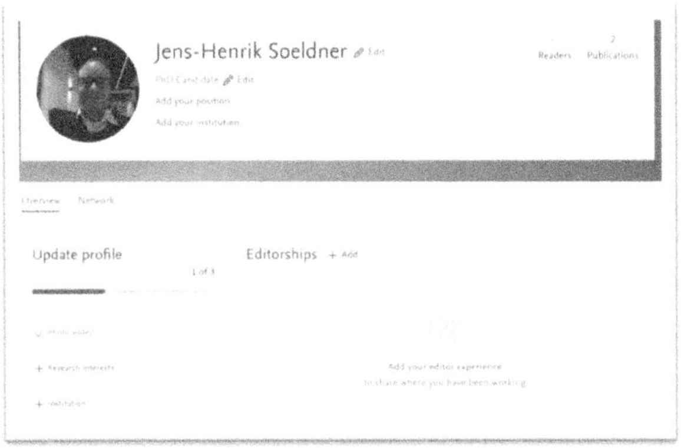

Figure 22: Screenshot of Mendeley's profile editor

In comparison, Academia.edu offers very basic features in terms of identity management. While the construction of a public profile is possible, the social features remain at a relatively shallow level, and more sophisticated features that would encourage regular use of the platform are lacking. However, Academia.edu offers one feature only found in few social networking services – an analytics module, that lets a user see usage statistics related to his profile or papers for a period of the past 60 days. The analytics module is related to getting notifications by the system when one's profile has been accessed e.g. via google (see figure 23) and constitutes a feature that can aid in developing one's profile and reputation (He & Jeng, 2016).

---

[80] https://blog.mendeley.com/2016/11/30/mendeley-integrates-with-orcid-uniquely-identify-your-research/, retrieved March 19, 2017

[81] https://orcid.org/, retrieved March 19, 2017

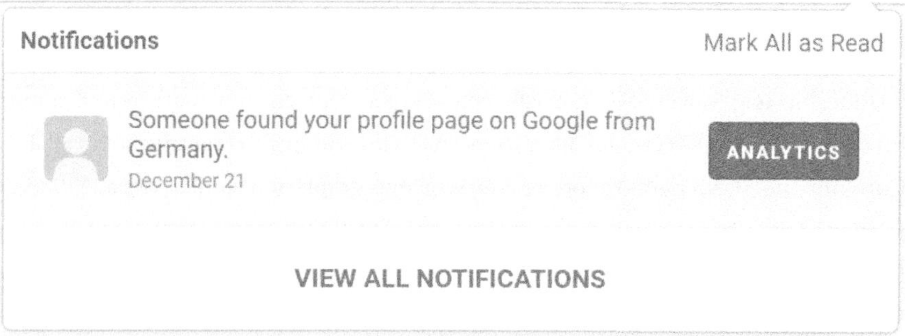

Figure 23: Academia.edu notifies the user of profile accesses via google's search engine

In addition, subscribing to an Academia.edu premium membership will unlock two additional columns in the analytics module further describing the visitor by revealing the visitor's home university and role[82]. Academia.edu's premium membership has been made available on March 8th, 2017[83].

5.1.2 Relationship management

Relationship management features of the SRNS platforms are closely connected to the aforementioned identity management functionality. Identifying other users that would be worthwhile partners for collaboration was a driver for some of the platform founders to create their SRNS system, as the following statement of an interviewee illustrates:

> *"But the reality is that the best person to work with you on a particular subject may not be your colleague, may not be your PhD chair, may not be your friend. There are people in other countries who you can collaborate with who may be better fits for you." (Manager MR)*

---

[82] http://support.academia.edu/customer/en/portal/articles/2313235-analytics-overview, retrieved February 28, 2017

[83] https://medium.com/academia/academia-introduces-a-premium-account-1181aa8405a3#.a7e69bln5, retrieved March 25, 2017

Most platforms, however, offer only very basic functionalities in this area, typically implemented via a following functionality, additional metadata describing the relationship (e.g. since when it exists, notes on the contact, etc.) apart from a simple list of one's own followers and other users one follows in turn is typically not available. Currently, no SRNS platform offers a relationship graph or a similar visualization of relationships between users, as some professional SNS platforms like Xing or LinkedIn feature. On the other hand, Mendeley integrates the 'following' feature in a clever fashion with the reference management functionality also found in the system. Figure 24 depicts the relationship management functionality in Mendeley. As can be seen in the screenshot, if a potential contact is also the author of a document already found within a user's library, the system highlights the fact, in addition to the information if other people the user follows have the same contact.

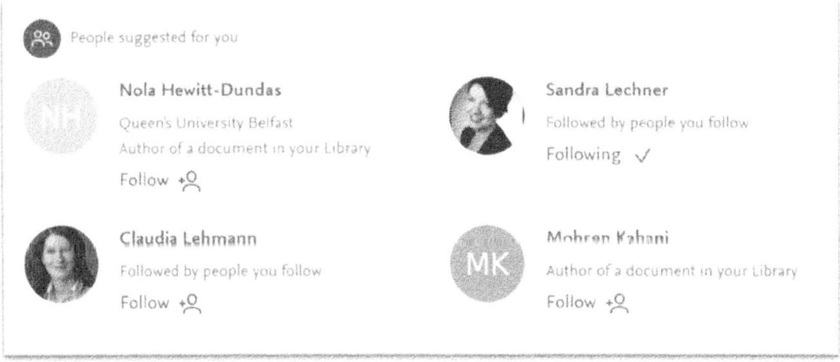

Figure 24: Following functionality on Mendeley allows for basic relationship management

5.1.3 Communication

Similarly to identity and relationship management, features supporting communication are on a relatively primitive level in most SRNS platforms, although facilitating communication was indicated as a reason for the platform creation by several interviewees as the following statement illustrates:

"We had issues to communicate with certain project members, for example, when a new person joined a project and needed to collaborate with colleagues. [...] We wanted a

simple way to set up e-mail lists that directly corresponded to the structure of groups and projects." (Manager SN)

According to several interviewees, traditional ICT technology was not providing for adequate forms of communication. Thus, the interviewees stated a desire for functionalities that would facilitate the communication with project partners and team members or mitigate the weaknesses of traditional email communication. Thus, some facility to enable communication within the platform is present in almost all SRNS platforms under scrutiny, as one interviewee exemplifies in his statement:

"For example, built into the site, there is a sort of an internal messaging tool, which is basically internal e-mail." (Manager RG)

Still, most platforms offer only the sending of simple messages within the system, with more advanced functionalities like sending one message to a group or attaching files lacking in almost all platforms. Trellis, for instance, has implemented communication with one's contacts in a less straightforward way than found within other systems. Instead of offering a communication feature directly from a contact's profile page, the user of Trellis needs to find the "My Discussion" functionality within the platform in order to communicate with other users, as depicted in figure 25.

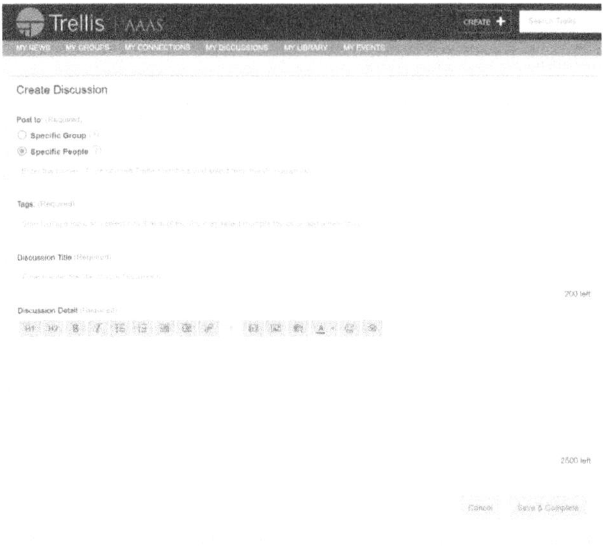

Figure 25: Screenshot depicting the communication feature within Trellis

ResearchGate offers the most comfortable messaging functionality within the sample of SRNS platforms, however limited to composing messages to a single user at a time. Sending a message to multiple contacts is currently not implemented in the system.

5.1.4 Network Awareness

Being aware of activities within one's field or network and discovering who else is active in a research field can be of crucial importance for researchers. One founder emphasizes this issue with his interview statement, leading to the development of what is one of the leading SRNS platforms:

> *"The second big thing that happened was when I finished my PhD, I discovered two other doctoral students who worked on the same problem for three years and we had never discovered or heard about each other. That struck me as crazy that there wasn't a database where we were listed, every researcher listed, what they are working one, what their research interest was. You should at least be able to find who is in your area." (Manager MD)*

The three wide-reaching platforms Academia.edu, Mendeley, and ResearchGate all offer relatively advanced network awareness functionalities, implemented via their news feed. While none of the platforms currently display the online/offline status of one's contacts within the system, the news feed allows the users to see what one's contacts are up to and currently researching on. The following interview statement by a founder illustrates the importance of network awareness as follows:

"You have a profile, you have to update your profile with new papers and conferences you are going to, whatever it is and then people who are following you can see your updates and similarly you have your own newsfeed and you can follow more people. You know, you can see what Stephen Hawking is thinking about, for instance. He posted an update on the site yesterday." (Manager RG)

ResearchGate is the most advanced platform as well in this respect, but Academia.edu and Mendeley still offer good network awareness features. Mendeley integrates its news feed directly with the strong reference management functionalities of the platform, as depicted in figure 26.

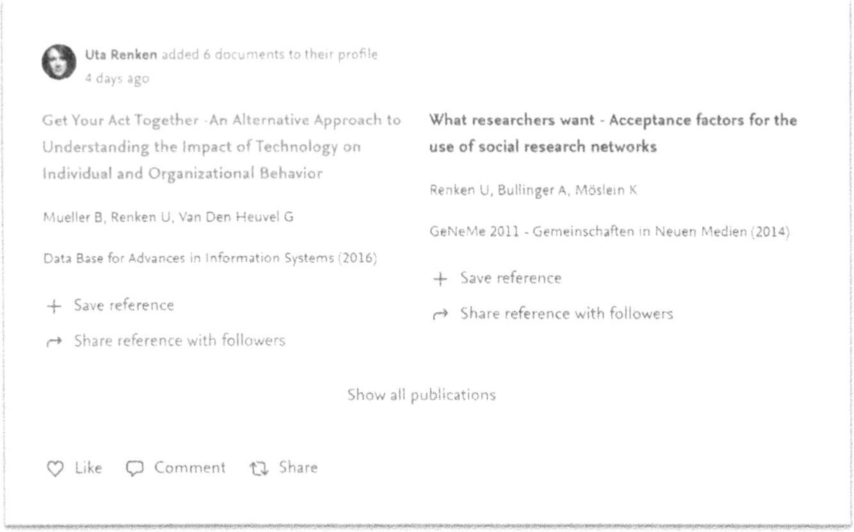

Figure 26: Mendeley displays updates of activities of contacts in its news feed, thus allowing for network awareness

5.1.5 Reputation

The three dominant SRNS platforms Academia.edu, Mendeley, and ResearchGate offers features related to reputation management. Managing and gauging one's reputation within the academic community is an important distinction from regular social networking services due to the importance of attention and visibility within the academic field for promotions and making a career in academia (Huberman et al., 2009; Franck, 1999; Cronin, 2005), reputation management is a highly relevant functionality of SRNS platforms in order to be valuable for their target audience. Within the sample of SRNS platforms, the reputation management functionalities of ResearchGate are standing out. ResearchGate offers dedicated functionalities in this area called "RG Score" and "RG Reach" (see figure 27).

Figure 27: Screenshot showing ResearchGate's reputation management features, the RG Score[84] and RG Reach

ResearchGate presents its scoring system as a "new way to measure scientific reputation", aiming for a more comprehensive metric that "is calculated based on how all of your research is received by your peers, not just the work you've published". The platform claims that the algorithm measures scientific reputation "based on how all of your research is received by your peers"[85], also taking into account unpublished research and how one's contributions are perceived on ResearchGate by one's peers, taking into account the ResearchGate scores of the users interacting with one's contributions on the platform.

The sum of the RG Score of the members of a research institution is then shown on the institution's profile within the platform, as depicted in figure 28.

[84] https://www.researchgate.net/profile/Ijad_Madisch/reputation, retrieved March 26, 2017

[85] https://www.researchgate.net/RGScore/FAQ, retrieved March 26, 2017

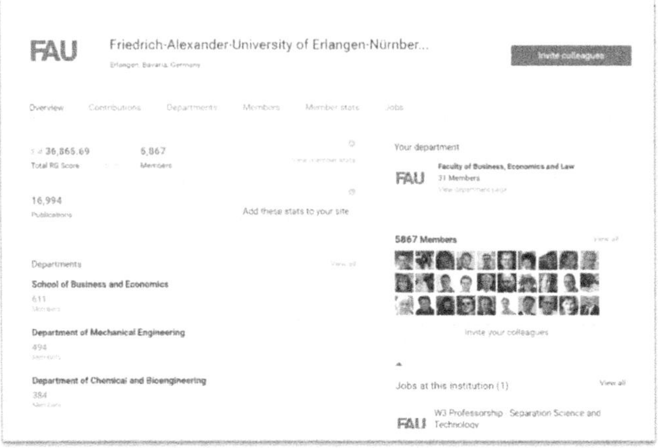

Figure 28: The profile of a research institution features the sum of its members' 'RG Scores'

While providing more meaningful academic reputation scoring systems is an important endeavor, and some aspects of the RG Score have been called a "step into the right direction"[86], overall ResearchGate has been criticized for being intransparent and irreproducible over time, and only taking into account activities that take place on ResearchGate – Kraker et al. (2015) called ResearchGate's reputation management system a "good example of a bad metric" in an online review of the RG Score[87].

5.1.6 Sharing

Sharing of information and publications is one of the most salient features in almost all of the platforms, and constitutes a major reason for their creation by their founders, as one interviewee stated:

> *"Furthermore, we wanted to provide a way for the folks at the university and people at my group to disseminate documents and datasets among each other." (Manager MR)*

---

[86] http://www.socialsciencespace.com/2015/12/researchgate-score-good-example-of-a-bad-metric/, retrieved March 26, 2017

[87] http://www.socialsciencespace.com/2015/12/researchgate-score-good-example-of-a-bad-metric/, retrieved March 26, 2017

Several other interviewees mentioned the wish for facilitated sharing of information, data, and references, as the following statement illustrates:

"It all started with a need for technological support during working on my PhD thesis. I was looking for tools to be able to handle my data more efficiently. When I saw that the tool I was thinking about did not exist, I just started to develop it on my own … as easy as that." (Manager AE))

Another founder voiced a similar desire to help with managing and sharing of information as a trigger for the creation of their SRNS system:

"The idea was born originally, as said, that we were just looking for some tools to make our lives as PhD students easier. Having to type everything manually or send stuff over via e-mail or to format references manually, that should not be the way you have to do it nowadays." (Manager MD)

In general, strong sharing capabilities are a major influencing factor for the adoption of SRNS platforms and their regular use, as will be discussed in detail within part IV of this thesis. With the exception of CiteULike, they all exhibit strong sharing capabilities, with Mendeley and Trellis standing out. In the case of Mendeley, this is expected, since the platform is primarily being known and used as a reference management and literature sharing platform and has been developed with this use case in mind, as the following statement by one of its founders illustrates:

"We were primarily looking to create a tool that allowed us to share papers and references in an easy-to-use manner. And also an intelligent tool, that would recommend papers to read, back then we wanted to create some sort of last.fm for research papers with strong built-in sharing capabilities." (Manager MD)

Trellis, a SRNS platform that emerged relatively recently, is offering the most sophisticated sharing capabilities within the sample of SRNS platforms analyzed herein. Trellis allows its user to upload documents and to organize them conveniently within a document library, similar to the functionality exposed by Microsoft's enterprise collaboration platform SharePoint, as depicted in figure 29.

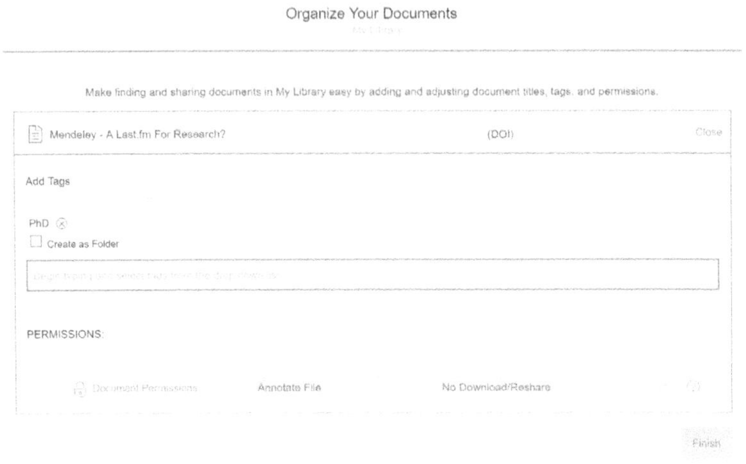

Figure 29: Trellis offers sophisticated document sharing capabilities

5.1.7 Openness

One very important aspect lacking in all platforms except Mendeley is openness and the possibility to export data. Mendeley is the only platform in the sample that currently provides an open API allowing its users to build research tools of their own that make use of the data contained within Mendeley. According to Techcrunch, the Mendeley API, as of 2013, is used by around 300 apps and will be kept free and open to use, even after the Mendeley acquisition by Elsevier[88]:

"Additionally, as has always been our policy, Mendeley will continue to offer you private and secure access to your data via our Open API, which means that you will never be tied to Mendeley's tools and interfaces exclusively."[89] (Manager MD)

The social networking related features of the platforms are summarized in table 69.

---

[88] https://techcrunch.com/2013/04/08/confirmed-elsevier-has-bought-mendeley-for-69m-100m-to-expand-open-social-education-data-efforts/, retrieved March 30, 2017

[89] https://blog.mendeley.com/2013/04/09/qa-team-mendeley-joins-elsevier/, retrieved March 30, 2017

Table 69: Social networking features of the SRNS platforms per case

Social research network site	Identity management	Relationship management	Communication	Network Awareness	Reputation	Sharing	Openness
Academia.edu	Basic, good analytics with statistics related to profile and publications	Basic (via following), Search for other users is very simple	Very basic messaging, no groups or communities	Good network awareness (via news feed)	Monitoring of impact	Strong sharing capabilities	no open API
Mendeley	Basic profile, link to Scopus author ID or ORCID iD possible	Basic (via following), integrated with reference management	Very basic messaging, no group communication	Good network awareness (via news feed)	via stats: h-index, citations, readers, views	Strong sharing capabilities, separate desktop app for reference management	Only platform providing an open API
ResearchGate	very sophisticated	strong (via following)	Good messaging features including sending attachments	Strong network awareness (via news feed)	RG Score, RG Reach, various other stats	Strong sharing capabilities	no open API
scholarz.net	Very basic	very basic (via contacts)	very basic	none	none	Strong sharing capabilities	No open API
Laboratree.org	Very basic	Very basic	Very basic	Some, online/offline status integrated into profile	none	Strong sharing capabilities	No open API
MyNetResearch.com	Very basic	Very basic	Integrated messaging widget	none	none	Some sharing capabilities	No open API
CiteULike	Extremely basic	none	Extremely basic	Very basic	none	none	No open APIs
Trellis	Very basic	Very basic (via contacts), cumbersome	Basic, no straightforward implementation	Basic, via home feed	none	Very strong sharing capabilities	No open APIs

5.2 Research Support Functions in SRNS Platforms on the Individual Level

This section will discuss the findings regarding the features of the SRNS platforms concerning research support on the level of the individual researcher. The findings have been elaborated by the in-depth cross-case analysis of the platforms including data gained from the interviews of the platform founders. The discussion of the findings is structured along the lines of the framework of research support functions (Söldner et al., 2009), which is depicted for enhanced readability again within this section in figure 30. The illustration below depicts the whole framework including support functions on the individual level, as well as on the team level. The team level perspective will be investigated in section 5.3, while the focus in this section is on support functions on the level of the individual researcher.

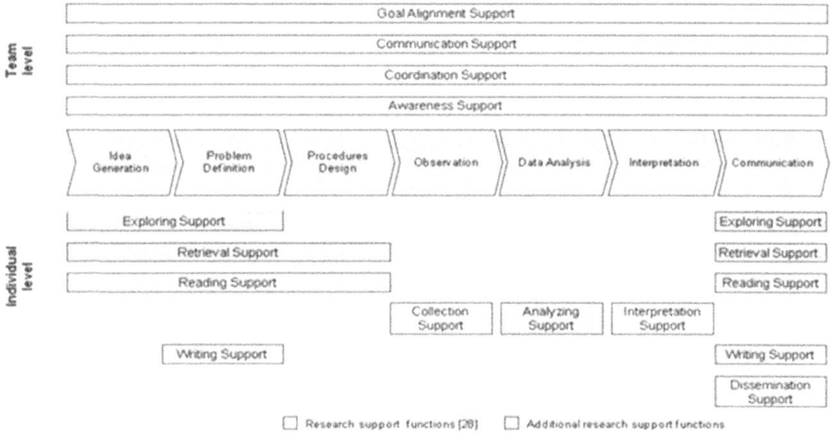

Figure 30: Framework of research support functions (Söldner et al., 2009)

While all eight platforms at least provide a basic set of features expected from social networking services with some of the platforms under scrutiny being quite advanced and sophisticated in this respect, functionalities related to research support functions vary more widely between the individual platforms. The following subsections investigate the findings from the eight cases including the interviews with the platform founders structured along the support functions on the individual level in order to shed light on the strengths and weaknesses and the suitability for research support of the SRNS platforms.

5.2.1 Exploring support

Exploring support refers to facilitating to find and identify relevant existing work of other scholars or other scientists to engage in collaborative research with. Almost all SRNS systems with the exception of the now defunct Laboratree, were or are offering features conducive to exploring support. This is typically implemented by features like a direct search for papers, people, research interests, or universities and the ability to browse within the structure that the SRNS platform presents. ResearchGate is particularly sophisticated in this respect and allows 'browsing' the academic world, due to comfortable and easy-to-use search functionalities. This of course depends on the quality of the information that is provided by these sites, as the statement of one platform founder underlines:

"The most important thing for these sites is how much information is collected and not just how much, but the quality of the information that is collected for each new member, because that is what enables you to have very sophisticated searches to actually identify the specific skills for the persons you want to work with." (Manager RG)

If the platform has a sufficient user base and the quality of the data exposed by the platform is of a high quality, this can be very helpful in exploring the data set on the lookout for research partners, as illustrated in the following interview statement:

"But the reality is that the best person to work with you on a particular subject may not be your colleague, may not be your PhD chair, may not be your friend. There are people in other countries who you can collaborate with who may be better fits for you." (Manager MR)

Academia.edu also helps in discovering relevant collaboration partners and research publications via a search and paper recommendation function. However, full text search within several million academic papers (according to the platform) is restricted to the paying customers of the newly introduced premium edition (currently available for EUR 89 per year or EUR 8.99 in a monthly subscription model[90]). The premium-only advanced search advertises full text search capabilities of over 15 million and 17 million papers within the same screenshot (see figure 31).

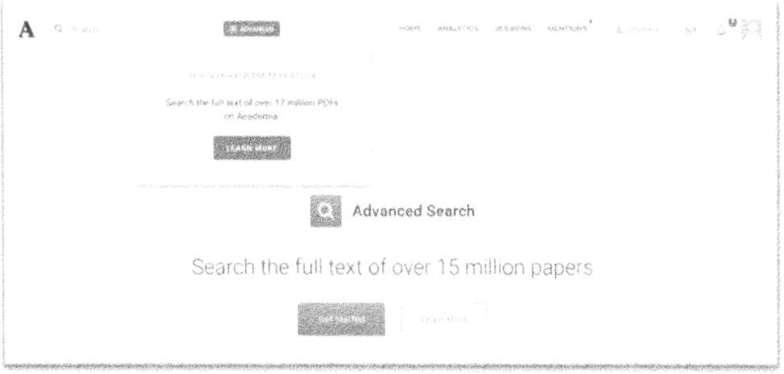

Figure 31: Academia.edu is promoting premium features like full-text search

This inconsistency is in line with dubious membership numbers published by the platform, as discussed in chapter 4 of this part. After upgrading to the premium edition, four additional features were made available: insights into readers of one's publication, full text search, finding mentions, and using the analytics module (see figure 24). However, a test drive of the full-text search failed – searching for the term "academic social network" did not yield any results within three minutes and displayed no hits. After several attempts, the search finally yielded results[91].

5.2.2 Retrieval support

Retrieval support deals with helping uncover and download necessary literature to the topic at hand. Several SRNS platforms provide strong functionalities in this area, for instance, Mendeley, which constitutes an interesting case of a hybrid solution between a social network for scientists and a desktop (and mobile) software for

[90] Pricing information retrieved online from https://www.academia.edu/upgrade?feature=search&trigger=search-popover, retrieved March 25, 2017

[91] Several searches were tried on March 25, 2017. Due to the errors, Academia.edu's support was contacted via Twitter afterwards.

literature sharing, annotation, and reference management that is also available as an app for mobile devices. The desktop version of Mendeley is a full-featured literature management platform that allows its users to create a database of bibliographic references and share them with other Mendeley users including PDF files of academic publications. It also provides a bookmarking service similar to CiteULike with which users can sab bibliographic references directly from publishers' websites by virtue of a webbrowser plug-in. By combining a social networking service for scientists with a reference management platform, Mendeley provides a strong feature set encompassing retrieval support.

While ResearchGate is not offering the same feature set as Mendeley, it is also heavily used for retrieval support, as the subsequent part IV of this thesis will show. In the case of ResearchGate, it is customary that users write to the authors of papers that are not directly available, e.g. due to publishers' embargoes, and to ask for a copy of a paper – a wish that is typically fulfilled by the users on the platforms. Thus, while not being a reference management platform per se, ResearchGate also offers retrieval support through social interaction with the original authors primarily.

5.2.3 Reading support

Reading support refers to facilitating the linkage of information fragments and making and sharing annotations. Within the sample, only Mendeley via its desktop or mobile apps, is currently offering a significant functionality that contributes to reading support, by allowing its users to annotate papers and share these annotations with collaborators they are connected with within the system. The now defunct scholarz.net also offered some functionalities in this area, but the platform has been discontinued in January 2013, after they have been acquired by ResearchGate. As the manager of scholarz.net was stating, the core strength of the platform was to provide help with the organization of notes and literature:

"Our software is specially tailored to the needs of the individual researcher"[92] *(Manager SN)*

5.2.4 Collection support

According to Söldner et al. (2009), collection support refers to transforming data collection tasks occurring in the observation phase of the research process (Graziano & Raulin, 2007) into a peer-based approach. This can manifest in being able to explore data and statistics gathered and generated by other users, thus benefiting the individual researcher. Two now defunct platforms were offering rudimentary collection support: Laboratree allowed for the sharing of datasets, as the manager of Laboratree stated:

"We wanted a simple way for the folks at the university and people at my lab to disseminate documents and datasets that were important for collaboration, irrespective of whether that would be at the same department or at the other side of the world. And we also wanted to have a platform to also develop applications that we could then host that would take advantage of the professional relationship between researchers that are in the system to help with research collaboration." (Manager LT)

Laboratree was designed to mirror the structure of collaborative research projects and aimed to provide a virtual workspace for geographically dispersed teams, with the goal of sharing data, apart from improving collaboration and communication, thus reducing disconnection in the research teams that leads to poor project outcomes[93].

MyNetResearch was offering an online survey manager that was intended to help in collecting data, according to a press release issued while the platform was still

---

[92] Dr. Daniel Koch, as quoted by https://digiversity.net/2009/scholarz-net-virtuelle-plattform-fur-forscher/, retrieved March 09, 2017, quote translated by the author

[93] https://tstkdemo.westat.com/public/TSResourceTool.aspx?tid=1&rid=548, retrieved March 11, 2017

operational: "Online Survey Manager: helps to create and manage on-line surveys, offering 15 types of questions, survey templates, and summary reports."[94]

Among the major active platforms, only Mendeley currently offers features related to this specific type of research support. Mendeley Data, launched in November 2015[95], allows for collection support, and also dissemination support. Mendeley Data enables researchers to upload raw data from their scientific projects, and assign the data a unique identifier (a DOI). In collaboration with a few journal websites (e.g. ScienceDirect, an offering that also belongs to Elsevier, Mendeley's parent company), the linkage of academic publications on these partnering journals to the research dataset hosted on Mendeley Data is possible. Figure 32 shows the creation of a new dataset on Mendeley Data.

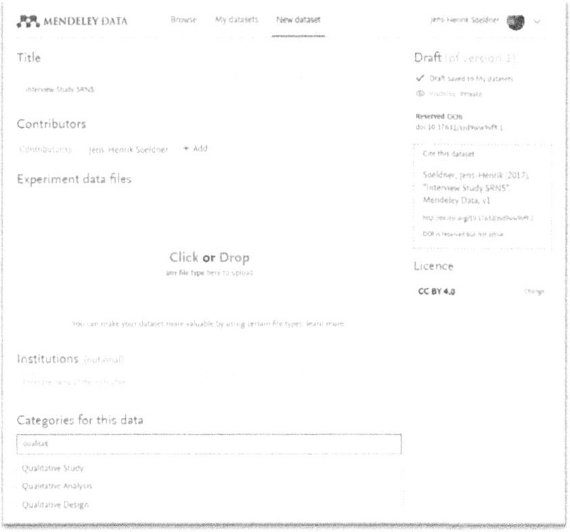

Figure 32: Screenshot depicting the creation of a new dataset in Mendeley Data

---

[94] http://www.prweb.com/releases/mynetresearch/collaborative_research/prweb991374.htm, retrieved March 11, 2017

[95] https://blog.mendeley.com/2015/11/09/put-your-research-data-online-with-mendeley-data/, retrieved March 30, 2017

Mendeley Data's functionality is also exposed via Mendeley's publicly available and accessible API, so developers are enabled to create apps that leverage that functionality and data stored within the service[96].

5.2.5 Analyzing support

Providing suggestions on analysis tools, methods, and their usage is the intended purpose of analyzing support (Söldner et al., 2009). Apart from being able to ask related questions in the forums or Q&A sections of SRNS platforms that offer this functionality, no existing SRNS platform currently offers analyzing support. Only the defunct and discontinued platform MyNetResearch offered a tool called "Research Methods Adviser" and was advertised as "Research Methods Adviser: help the scholar in selecting a research design, sampling techniques, and statistical methods" by the platform[97]. A screenshot of the discontinued system (dating back to 2009) is depicted in figure 33.

---

[96] http://dev.mendeley.com/, retrieved March 30, 2017

[97] http://www.prweb.com/releases/mynetresearch/collaborative_research/prweb991374.htm, retrieved March 11, 2017

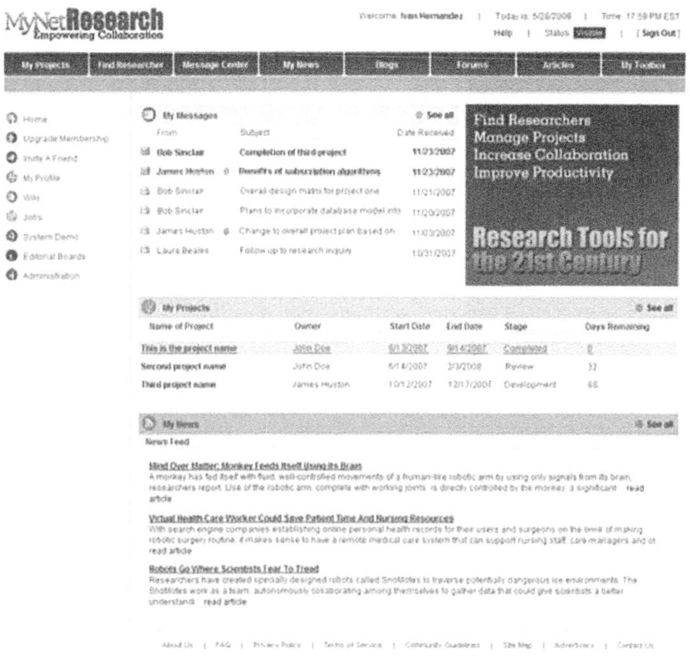

Figure 33: Screenshot showing the start screen of MyNetResearch.com

5.2.6 Interpretation support

Interpretation support, defined as technical means that help with enabling and promoting discussions between researchers (Söldner et al., 2009), and typically implemented via forums or wiki systems can be found in a couple of SRNS platforms. However, the forum-like implementation that is used in all SRNS platforms for interpretation support is cumbersome and can be seen as rather unsatisfactory due to spam and irrelevant questions asked within these forums. Figure 34 shows a typical contribution to the generic "Questions" forum within ResearchGate.

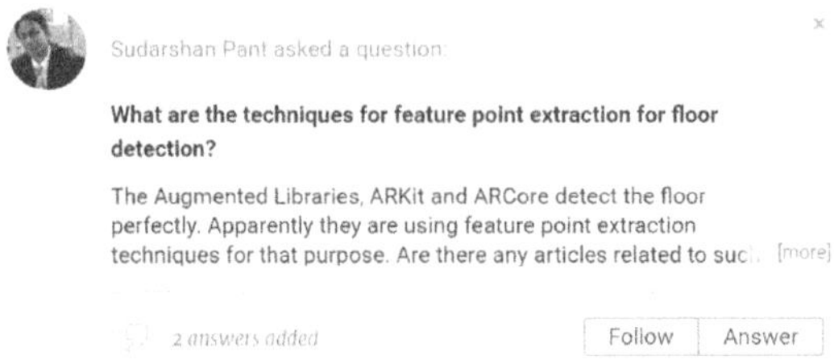

Figure 34: ResearchGate's generic "questions" functionality

5.2.7 Writing support

Providing suggestions for possible references, automatic correction, and systems that support citations are all related to writing support. Several systems within the sample offer widely varying functionalities that can be regarded as providing writing support. The most advanced form of writing support was provided by the now defunct platform scholarz.net. The online text editing functionality provided by scholarz.net offered some collaborative writing features, further enriched with the possibility to add annotations or notes to shared texts with the option to export them to a Microsoft Word document. This intention to support the user in collaboratively managing notes and text fragments can still be seen in a screenshot of the platform that reminds of current content management systems or the popular text editing software 'Scrivener' (see figure 35).

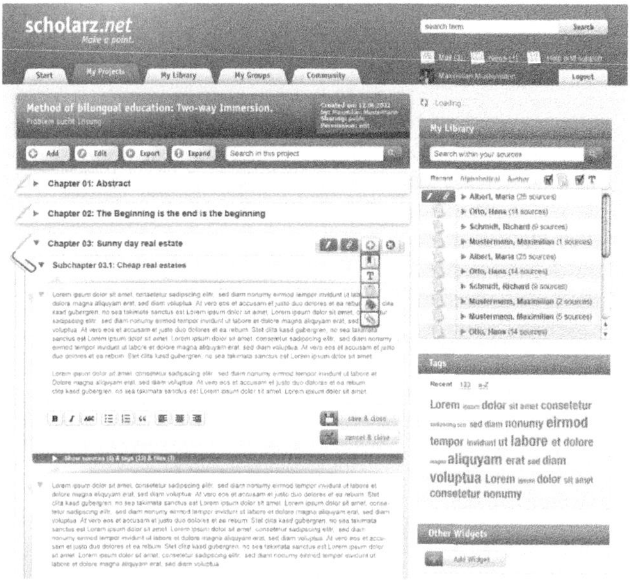

Figure 35: The collaborative writing ('project') editor of scholarz.net[98]

More recently, Academia.edu introduced its "session" functionality. Co-production of research papers in a team of researchers, thus providing writing and also coordination support, is the goal of Academia.edu's session functionality. A user can open a paper he or she is working on to comments by peers and colleagues. According to Richard Price, Academia.edu's founder and CEO, six thousand such sessions take place daily. The typical amount of comments on a paper is about 15 to 20, with some papers getting several hundreds of comments, allowing them to go "viral", according to Price[99]. Since Academia.edu's self-proclaimed user numbers are heavily disputed, these numbers should also be regarded with care and caution. Academia.edu's collaborative writing support feature is depicted in figure 36.

---

98 https://digiversity.net/2009/scholarz-net-virtuelle-plattform-fur-forscher/, retrieved March 09, 2017

99 https://www.theatlantic.com/education/archive/2015/12/the-convoluted-profits-of-academic-publishing/421047/, retrieved March 25, 2017

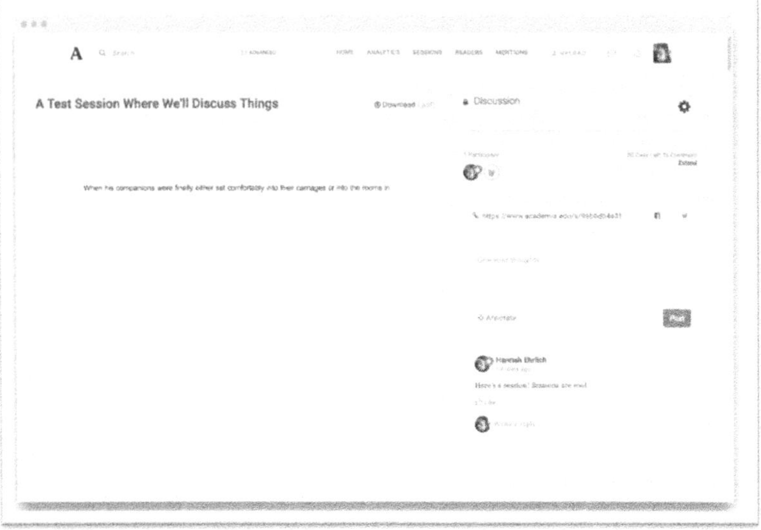

Figure 36: Academia.edu's session feature allows getting feedback on paper drafts

5.2.8 Dissemination support

Dissemination support refers to technical means that help raise the visibility and awareness of one's own publications and potentially make them available to a wider audience (Söldner et al., 2009). Several platforms provide dissemination support, a support function that is inherently social in its nature, thus profiting from the social networking character of the platforms. All three major platforms, Academia.edu, Mendeley, and ResearchGate, as well as the more recently emerged collaborative platform Trellis allow for uploading one's own publications and partially also monitoring the impact and readership numbers of these publications. Table 70 provides a summarizing evaluation of the individual-level research support functions for all the eight cases.

Table 70: Evaluation of individual-level research support functions per case

Social research network site	Exploring Support	Retrieval Support	Reading Support	Collection Support	Analyzing Support	Interpretation Support	Writing Support	Dissemination Support
Academia.edu	Search for papers, people, research interests, universities	Download of documents; paper recommendation	none	none	none	none	Collaborative writing via "sessions"	Uploading of own publications, monitoring impact of publications
Mendeley	Search for papers, people	Download of documents; paper recommendations	via the Mendeley desktop or mobile app	via Mendeley Data	none	none	Strong reference management	Uploading of own publications, monitoring impact of publications
ResearchGate	Search for papers, people, notification via feed	Download of documents; paper recommendations	none	none	none	Via forums ("Questions")	none	Uploading of own publications, monitoring impact of publications
scholarz.net	Search for people	Download of documents available within the platform	none	via projects	none	via projects	Collaborative writing editor	none
Laboratree.org	none	none	none	Document upload and sharing	none	Via projects	none	none
MyNetResearch.com	Literature search and citation analysis	none	none	Online survey manager	Research methods adviser	Via forums	Journal selection guide; bibliography creator	none
CiteULike	Search for papers	Download of citations	Some	none	none	none	none	none
Trellis	Search for papers within the library	Download of documents	none	none	none	Via groups	none	Uploading of own publications

5.3 Research Support Functions in SRNS Platforms on the Team Level

The framework of research support functions (Söldner et al., 2009) suggests the desirability of four support functions independent of individual stages of the research process (Graziano & Raulin, 2007): *goal alignment support, communication support, coordination support*, and *awareness support*. These four support functions on the team level are relevant throughout the entire research project (as depicted in figure 30 in *section 5.2* of this *part*). These functions are present in some of the SRNS platforms, however to a much lesser extent than the support functions on the individual level, as discussed in the previous section.

5.3.1 Goal alignment support

Support for the alignment of the goals of the individual participants within a collaborative research project throughout the entire research process constitutes a crucial support function in order to facilitate long-running projects (Söldner et al., 2009). As they point out, a continuous and iterative alignment of researchers' goals is an antecedent of successful collaborative research projects. Söldner et al. (2009) suggest technical solutions, e.g. wiki systems, as a central information base within a project. Unfortunately, none of the three 'big' SRNS platforms Academia.edu, Mendeley, and ResearchGate offer relevant features in this area. Only the discontinued platforms scholarz.net and Laboratree offered basic goal alignment support via their projects functionality, and the more recent Trellis platform can be used to provide goal alignment support via its 'groups' functionality.

5.3.2 Communication support

According to Söldner et al. (2009), communication support within collaborative research projects refers to facilitating the exchanging of information within research projects that are carried out by teams of scholars. Since all the platforms in the sample with the exception of CiteULike offer support, albeit basic, for communication through their properties being a social networking service at their core, very basic technological support for 1:1 communication is provided. However, the functionality exhibited by the platforms in this area can be regarded as relatively weak and insufficient to make the SRNSs a suitable basis for maintaining conversations between team members, so resorting to an external system for communication is inevitable. Within the sample of SRNS platforms, Trellis offers the best support for communication within teams, but still not up to the level of dedicated systems.

5.3.3 Coordination support

Similarly, coordination support refers to supporting teams engaged in collaborative research in setting up meetings and managing appointments (Söldner et al., 2009). They find that typically dedicated and specialized tools like "doodle" are being used within larger teams to facilitate coordination. Within the sample of SRNS platforms, coordination support can be achieved to a certain degree within Trellis, as well as within the discontinued platforms scholarz.net and Laboratree.

5.3.4 Awareness support

Finally, while most of the platforms provide awareness within one's network of contacts on the individual level (typically implemented as a news feed), awareness support on the team level, e.g. seeing what one's collaborators are actively working on within the project (Söldner et al., 2009), is available only in the platform Trellis via its groups feature within the sample of the analyzed SRNS platforms. A comprehensive summary of the research support functionalities on the team level is provided in table 71.

Table 71: Evaluation of team-level research support functions per case

Social research network site	Goal alignment support	Communication support	Coordination support	Awareness support
Academia.edu	none	weak	none	Some on the individual level
Mendeley	none	weak	none	none
ResearchGate	none	weak	none	Some on the individual-level
scholarz.net	Some via projects	Some via projects	Some via projects	None
Laboratree.org	Some via projects	weak	Some via projects	None
MyNetResearch.com	none	weak	none	none
CiteULike	none	none	none	none
Trellis	Some via groups	Strong within groups	Some via groups	Some via groups

5.4 Towards a Typology of SRNS Platforms

This *section* holistically integrates the findings derived from the in-depth analysis of the platforms and the iterative comparison of the data gained from the interviews with the founders of the SRNS platforms. In total, several critical aspects that contribute to a better understanding of these novel systems, how they differ from traditional social networking services and how they can be grouped into types and functionality clusters as well as strategic implications that could help in their further development have been identified. The following subsections discuss and integrate these findings. First, basic functionalities are highlighted and differences between these novel SRNS platforms and traditional social networking services are identified. Second, four typical configurations of basic functionalities that give rise to a typology of SRNS platforms are presented. Third, strategic implications for the providers of SRNS are derived.

5.4.1 Basic functionalities of SRNS and how they differ from traditional SNS

Data from the interviews reveal that the founders and developers of the social research networking services are convinced that their platforms *differ significantly from existing social network sites* which they consider insufficient for the needs of researchers. As one interviewee representatively stated:

"Users didn't actually want facebook.com, because facebook.com was already there and they could have used it if they wanted to." (Manager MR)

In the following, these differences will be presented along with the framework for social software presented by Koch and Richter (2007), depicted in figure 37.

According to the classification scheme for social software (Koch and Richter, 2007), *information management* tools allow for data structuring making wikis a prominent example. This need is mirrored with one SRNS platform having been explicitly developed to support *information management*, as one interviewee describes:

"It all started due to a personal need when I was doing my PhD. I am doing my PhD in economics and was on the lookout for a tool to manage my data efficiently". (Manager SN)

Figure 37: Basic functionalities of social software (Koch and Richter, 2007)

Beyond the scope of the individual researcher, SRNS platforms can support *information management* within a group of researchers, as one interviewee explains:

"Furthermore, we wanted to provide a way for the folks at the university and people at my group to disseminate documents and datasets among each other." (Manager MR)

Identity and network management is another main functionality of social software which is primarily represented within social networking services, with Facebook or LinkedIn as the most widely used and well-known examples. This functionality allows for the representation of oneself and the management of one's contacts and is also found in social research networking sites. One interviewee emphasized the importance of *identity and network management*:

"Some sort of facebook.com for researchers, that's what's needed, helping one to quickly find people with specific competencies and qualifications." (Manager MR)

However, profile details are designed to display the scientist's experience with certain research methods or show the publications of a user. Another issue which can be addressed by *identity and network management* functionality is gaining an overview about actors in the same research field, as one interviewee stated:

"The second big thing that happened was when I finished my PhD, I discovered two other doctoral students who worked on the same problem for three years and we had never discovered or heard about each other." (Manager MD)

The basic functionality *communication* is represented within the social networking services most prominently by instant messaging tools within the service. This feature is also present in almost all SRNS platforms under scrutiny. An interviewee exemplifies this as follows:

"For example, built into the site, there is a sort of an internal messaging tool, which is basically internal e-mail." (Manager SN)

In addition to three basic functionalities of social software (Koch and Richter, 2007), some of the SRNS platforms in the sample also offer new tools to support researchers, exceeding the offerings present in hedonic social networking services. Multiple research-specific features, like knowledge management tools, citation and reference management, and paper recommendation engines have been implemented and are typically combined within a platform. These tools enable researchers to collaboratively structure, coordinate, and conduct their work online within the platform. One interviewee stresses the importance of the collaborative features within his – by now discontinued - platform:

> *"We don't like to call it a social network, [...] because the objective is not only socializing. That's not why [researchers] are coming online. The reason they are coming online is to do work." (Manager LT)*

Based on the data gained through the interviews and the case studies, a definition on what constitutes a SRNS platform and how they differ from traditional social networking services was proposed by Bullinger et al. (2010):

> *"Social research network sites (SRNS) are a web-based service that allows individual researchers to (1) construct a public or semi-public profile within a bounded system (identity management), (2) articulate a list of other researchers (network management) with whom they share a connection and communicate (communication), (3) share information with other researchers within the system (information management), and (3) collaborate with other researchers within the system (collaboration)."*

This definition elaborated based on the research presented here found widespread acceptance in academic publications dealing with social research network sites (e.g. Ortega, 2016; Jordan, 2017).

5.4.2 From four types of SRNS to functionality clusters

In addition to the basic functionalities described above, the interviews reveal that the purposes and actual research support functionalities of the sites differ according to the usage intentions by their developers and founders. This difference also has a pronounced influence on the functionalities provided by the respective platforms. Hence, in order to derive a taxonomy of SRNS platforms, the sites were clustered according to their purpose and functionalities in a final step of the data analysis phase. An in-depth and integrated analysis of the interviews and the platforms at a time close to the initial launch of the platforms (Bullinger et al., 2010)[100] revealed four different types of SRNS platforms which are discussed below.

The first type, *research directory sites,* focuses on the identification of researchers according to certain criteria, e.g. the scholar's research agenda or special competencies in a field, theory or method as well as they facilitate the first contact between users. As one interviewee stated:

> *"The most important thing for these sites is how much information is collected and not just how much, but the quality of the information that is collected for each new member, because that is what enables you to have very sophisticated searches to actually identify the specific skills for the persons you want to work with." (Manager RG)*

To populate the directory, sites that offer this functionality type allow a researcher to present his or her comprehensive profile to the scientific world. In this type, functionalities supporting *identity management* and *communication* are hence very well established. Initially, at the time of its inception, Academia.edu was a typical representative of this type, but this kind of functionality is now a mainstay in all relevant and active SRNS platforms on the market.

---

[100] The author of this thesis is a co-author of this publication and has contributed significantly in the identification of relevant theory, the research design, the collection and analysis of data, and the interpretation of the results

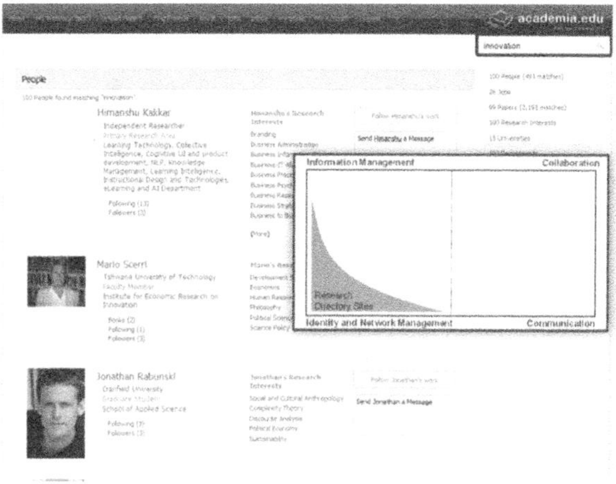

Figure 38: Academia.edu (historic screenshot as of 2010) was a prototypical research directory site and has since its initial launch incorporated other functionality groups

The second initially discovered type supported researchers in staying aware of their network or a field of a research. Termed *research awareness sites*, these services allowed researchers to maintain their profile, supply detailed information on their current work and interests as well as follow other users they are interested in to keep track of their activities. One interviewee summed it up as follows:

> *"You have a profile, you have to update your profile with new papers and conferences you are going to, whatever it is and then people who are following you can see your updates and similarly you have your own newsfeed and you can follow more people. You know, you can see what Stephen Hawking is thinking about, for instance. He posted an update on the site yesterday." (Manager RG)*

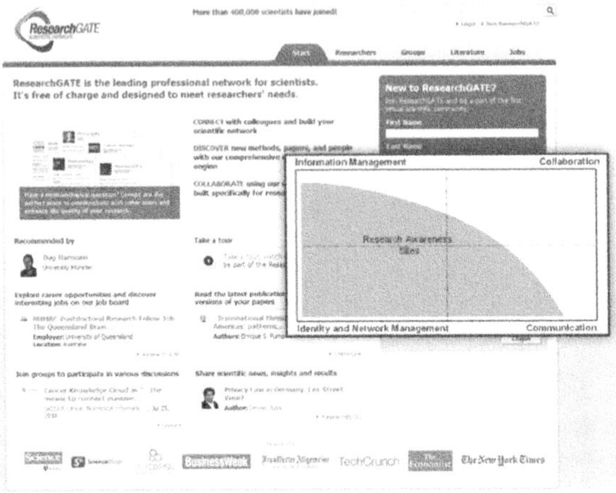

Figure 39: ResearchGate (historic screenshot as of 2010) was and still is the SRNS platform offering the most advanced research awareness functionality

Tools that were accounting primarily for the functionalities *identity and network management* as well as *information management* were well developed within this type. In its initial form, ResearchGate fell into this category and allowed its users to create a single point of awareness for information on topics and people they were interested in. As things moved on with the SRNS platforms, this functionality cluster is now also found within all relevant SRNS platforms, with ResearchGate still offering the most advanced functionality of this cluster up to date in 2017.

Sites focusing on the support of a researcher's daily work are named *research management sites*. They for instance provide tools to collect and manage references or propose references to a researcher. Another possible application is the improved management of research e.g. by tools to structure ideas. One interviewee put it as following:

"the feature range and main benefit is more on the productivity-tool side" (Manager SN)

A SRNS platform that fell primarily into that type classification, supported individuals and teams in carrying out their research by providing supportive tools. Accordingly, their main focus was on providing *information management* functionalities. Mendeley, in its original form, was a typical representative, has since then been enhanced with the other functionalities described above, but remains still the most prominent and advanced *information management* SRNS platform until today.

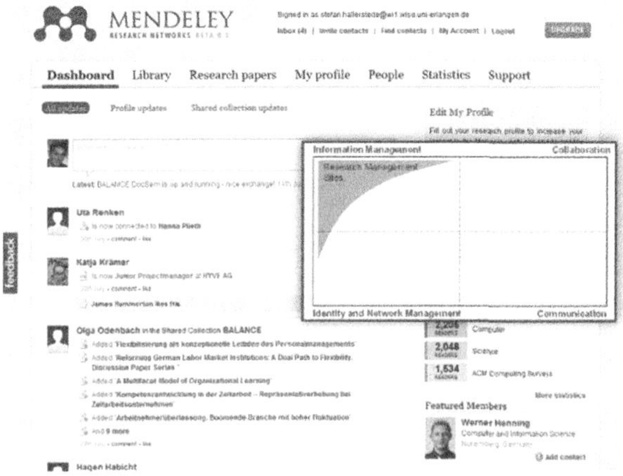

Figure 40: Research management sites (screenshot of Mendeley Beta 0.9 as of 2010) capitalize on network effects by recommending potentially relevant literature on the basis of other users' preferences

As the fourth type, *research collaboration sites* were identified. Platforms that fall into this type focus on the support of (virtual) research collaboration by facilitating a joint research process, as one interviewee explains:

"We believe that we're focusing on trying to enable the collaboration to happen. Not the development of the collaboration itself. [...]. Whether [collaboration] would be at the university, whether that would be at the same department, whether that would be at the other side of the world." (Manager LT)

To achieve this goal, sites of this type (e.g. MyNetResearch) focus on tools to support online collaboration functionalities. This implies opportunities to work synchronously on a shared scientific dataset and to collaborative develop data analysis scripts, which can be executed on the site. As of September 2017, some of the extant SRNS platform now offer these kind of collaborative features to a differing degree (see *sections* 5.2 of this *chapter*), like Academia.edu with its 'sessions' feature, or Mendeley with Mendeley Data.

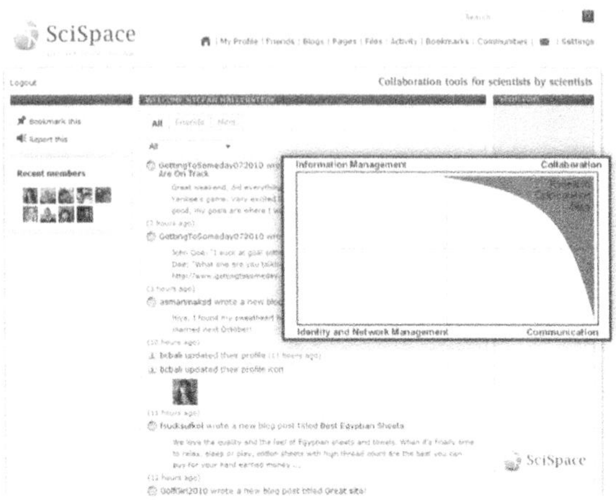

Figure 41: Research collaboration sites (screenshot of SciSpace as of 2010, now defunct) provide collaborative tools for teams of researchers

The initially proposed typology of SRNS platforms (Bullinger et al., 2010) is shown in figure 42. It characterizes the four prototypical types of SRNS platforms along the four basic functionalities. As the figure shows, the four types exhibit an overlap in the basic functionalities *identity and network management, communication, information management,* and *collaboration*. Additionally, sites cannot exclusively be assigned to only one type, but rather have a dominant type.

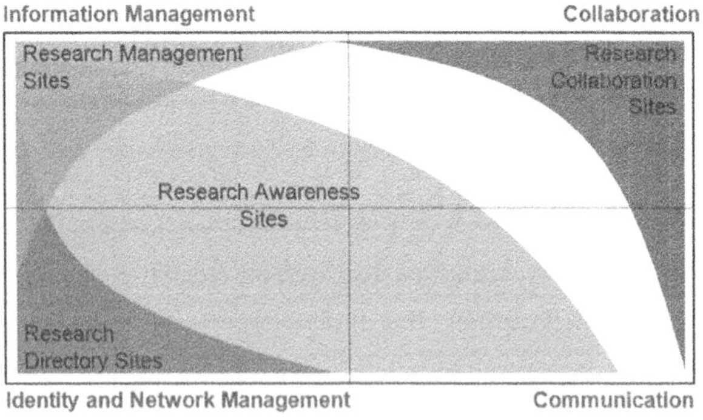

Figure 42: Typology for SRNS platforms (Bullinger et al., 2010)

This typology and the functionality it refers to is still current even today, but the three major SRNS platforms are now more complete in their functionality spectrum than at the time of this initial typology, covering a larger area of functionality. However, research collaboration features have not seen the same degree of continued use and improvement in SRNS platforms today as have research directory, research awareness, and research management related functionalities that have greatly evolved since the original inception of the platforms.

5.4.3 Implications on the further development of SRNS platforms

Given the four original types of social research networking sites as described in Bullinger et al. (2010), data analysis revealed possible future pathways for each type. As the further development of these sites up to now has shown (and unfortunately also the discontinuation of several platforms in the sample), the predictions made by Bullinger et al. (2010) turned real to the most part.

Research directory sites are outstanding in the simplicity they offer to their users. Entry barriers are hence extremely low. Additionally, *research directory sites* exhibit a viable business model by offering details of registered researchers to institutions seeking for academic personnel. These advantages might protect research directory sites from a hostile takeover by *research awareness sites*. Such takeovers can be expected as the two types share a major set of functionalities, while *research awareness sites* typically hold a larger user base.

Concerning *research awareness sites*, a need was visible in the early stages of their existence to improve identity management by (1) improving profile information and (2) providing powerful search tools. This might enable them to take over *research directory sites*. Furthermore, the data indicated the potential to integrate research management tools, e.g. reference management and advanced recommender systems. One interviewee stated this as follows:

> *"Up to now, we never played the same game. Twelve or fourteen weeks ago, we put the reference repository online. Now we move towards their [research directory site] strategic direction." (Manager MD)*

Research management sites capitalize on network effects, e.g. by recommending relevant literature on the basis of other users' preferences. To fulfill their potential, an increase in the number of members was necessary. The interviewees showed an interest to develop the *research management sites* towards a *research awareness site*:

"We intend to integrate more functionalities for the community." (Manager MR)

However, a second possible pathway was visible by a merger with a *research awareness site* to combine a large user base and the capacity to capitalize on network effects[101].

The most focused type of the four are *research collaboration sites* that provide particular collaboration tools for highly specific groups of researchers. This leads to a strong usage pattern of registered members, but limits possibilities to capitalize on network effects. Accordingly, data analysis indicates potential advantages if *research collaboration sites* are integrated as sub-communities within larger *research awareness sites* or *research management sites*[102].

On a more general level, there were also business opportunities visible for each type of the SRNS platform to address the privacy needs of specific organizations (e.g. industrial research or universities). A business model would have been to offer such institutions that do not want to make their research visible, e.g. due to intellectual property concerns, a dedicated private instance of the SRNS platform. This was in line with a development back then when several of the social research network sites experimented with offering sub-communities as isolated silos or in a protected environment with a transparent passage from the protected sub-community to the global, open network. As one interviewee stated:

"We noticed that a lot of institutions implemented Web 2.0 platforms, which were not really being used due to the abundance of different platforms. Thus, we had the idea of

[101] This prediction turned out true with the takeover of Scholarz.net by ReseachGate, see the presentation of the cases in *chapter 4* of this *part*

[102] This prediction also turned out true – Academia.edu, ResearchGate and Mendeley now contain such functionalities as features within the platforms

creating these sub-communities and to integrate them with the global platform. Data are stored on a different platform, behind the firewalls of the universities, but it's essentially the same system with a separate area. It also brings increased awareness to the university from the global system … we get a lot of requests for such sub-communities." (Manager RG)

Strategic considerations of future pathways were very relevant given the strong increase in new registrations on some of the sites after their initial offering. This indicated a change from prototypical realizations used by early adopters to a more established application for research collaboration, as one interviewee aptly put it:

"The research productivity gains are too great to not use this technology. So right now, I would say that we are just passing the early adopter stage … way past the early adopter stage, we're now beginning to see a faster rate of adoption, more users in different countries." (Manager MD)

As the considerable commercial success of some of the platforms (ResearchGate, Mendeley, and Academia.edu) has shown[103], the strategic implications outlined above were highly relevant. Other platforms that were not able to attract a significant user base and evolve their offering into the right direction have discontinued the offering and are now extinct or have been taken over, just to be discontinued (as was the case for Scholarz.net).

[103] see the presentation of the cases in *chapter 4* of this *part*

6 Discussion and Reflection

As research regarding features and affordances of social research networking services is still scarce, this empirical study contributes to an understanding of this novel class of social software tools. Based on a framework specifically developed for the analysis of these novel platforms building on previous publications of the author (Söldner et al., 2009; Richter et al., 2009), eight social research networking services have been analyzed in-depth regarding their features and affordances concerning social networking and research support. By the inclusion of interviews with the founders of all of the analyzed platforms the case studies were enriched with data, thus enabling the study presented in this *part* to provide a holistic view of this novel class of social software applications.

As the findings suggested, all of the still existing platforms provide at least a basic level of social networking (with some platforms offering a very sophisticated social networking experience), thus allowing to initiate new contacts with other researchers, follow their research-related updates and possibly even to initiate new collaborations. As far as research support is concerned, the findings show that the platforms vary widely in their focus and thus in the affordances they provide to researchers looking for support in their individual research tasks and processes. On the team level of research support functionality (Söldner et al., 2009), most of the platforms still offer only little functionalities to effectively and efficiently steer and support complex team research. Apart from a discussion of actual features and affordances for research support, this study raises questions regarding the openness of the platforms and the possibility to export one's data from the platform. Only one platform in the sample offers an open API and allows for export of data. Hence, there is a high risk of *vendor lock-in*, when using these platforms. In addition, other areas of conflict have been made visible in the study. In general, questions regarding the viability and sustainability of the business models of the platforms come up. Some of the platforms have exhibited marketing-related activities that have been considered unethical by some critics. The reputation scores offered by some of the more advanced platforms are also under dispute regarding their validity and meaningfulness. Moreover, there is an underlying tension between the open access philosophy generally promoted and taken advantage of by the platforms, which is necessary to make them fully useful despite potential copyright issues with papers uploaded to the platform, and the lack of openness exhibited by most of the platforms. It is still unclear how this underlying conflict between an open access to publications and lack of openness in the platform can be resolved. To a certain degree, one could venture to say that social research networking services make existing tensions and internal contradictions in the academic system more visible. Regarding the academic reputation system, the reputation models found in some of the platforms could help spark a discussion around the academic recognition system and whether it needs to be reorganized and reformed.

This *part* also presented a definition of the then evolving software application *social research network sites* along with their four basic functionalities – *identity and network management, communication, information management,* and *collaboration.* In addition, it suggested a taxonomy of social research network sites according to the purpose their founders had in mind back at the time of the initial launch and the starting phase of these services. While the three 'big' SRNS platforms Academia.edu, Mendeley, and ResearchGate offer strong features as research directory, research awareness or research management sites, none of the extant platforms is currently suitable to support truly collaborative research or to really solve the variety of problems typically accompanying scientific collaborations: "*problems of coordination and misunderstandings and problems of culture and information security*" (Walsh and Maloney, 2007, p. 11).

Since this study was largely dominated by the perspective of providers of the platforms – as interviews with the founders of the SRNS platforms analyzed herein provided the basis for this inquiry, the results need to be counterbalanced with insights from actual users of these platforms. Thus, in order to provide a more holistic understanding of SRNS platforms, the following part IV sets out investigate how and why these SRNS platforms are actually being used within the context of management research.

Part IV

Empirical Study 2:

How and Why Do Management Researchers Use Social Research Networking Sites?

J.-H. Soeldner, *Understanding Social Research Networking Sites*,
Markt- und Unternehmensentwicklung Markets and Organisations,
https://doi.org/10.1007/978-3-658-31575-7_4

1 Needs and Goals

In the preceding *part III*, a feature-based state-of-the-art description of social research networking sites was elaborated using a framework based on previous publications by the author of this thesis. This framework took into account both social networking related aspects as well as the support potential of the SRNS platforms for individual and collaborative research activities. In essence, four types of SRNS platforms have been identified: research directory sites, research awareness sites, research management sites, and research collaboration sites (see figure 43).

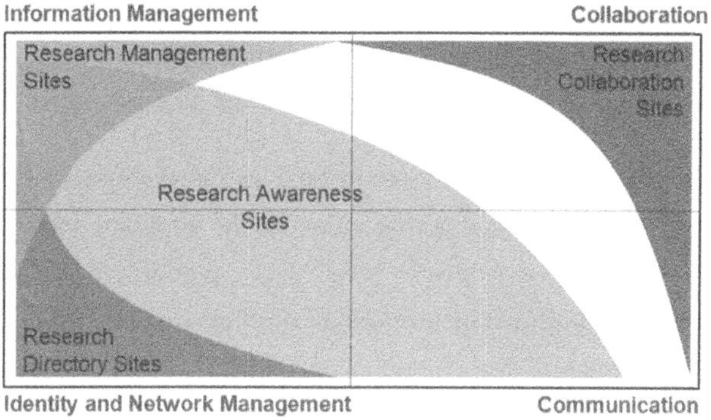

Figure 43: Typology for SRNS platforms derived in part III of this thesis

This typology was elaborated from case studies involving interviews with the platform providers and a thorough investigation of the feature sets of the platforms. As part of the analysis, two frameworks were leveraged to analyze the social networking-related aspects of the SRNS platforms as well as aspects related to supporting individual and team-level research collaboration. Since this study focused on features and the perspective of the platform providers, actual usage patterns, and how and why scholars leverage these platforms for social networking with their peers and for supporting research tasks and collaborative research were not yet investigated as part of the study presented in the preceding part.

Hence, this *part* aims to fill this research gap by conducting a thorough investigation into the question of how and why researchers use SRNSs. Since there are considerable disciplinary differences in how scientists make use of computer-mediated communication tools (Heimeriks et al., 2008), this study focuses on researchers stemming from a single field (management research) within a single scientific discipline (business research). This research is part of the larger body of research on adoption and continuance of SNSs platforms that is summarized in sections 4.2.6 and 4.3.3 of the literature review presented in *part II* of this thesis.

To date, the understanding of the primary antecedents of members' intention to adopt and to continue to use SNSs, in general, is limited (Shi et al., 2010; Shin & Hall, 2012), and even more limited in the case of SRNSs on which currently only a single study exists that was solely based on the descriptive analysis of data collected within a small population in a single country (Meishar-Tal & Pieterse, 2017).

Therefore, this study intends to contribute to the understanding of SRNSs by shedding light on the key aspects that influence the adoption and continued use of SRNS platforms. This knowledge can help existing platform providers conceive and develop strategies to improve their offerings and thus promote the use of SRNSs and can serve as a guidance for emerging and future platform providers to fill in functionality gaps not currently satisfied by already existing offerings. To enrich the understanding of the phenomenon at hand, it is crucial to analyze user behavior through appropriate theoretical underpinnings (Benbasat & Barki, 2007). Hence, this study leverages the theoretical lens of the Uses and Gratifications Theory (UGT), a theoretical framework that has been applied successfully to explain how traditional SNSs fulfill users' gratification needs (Ku et al., 2013; Ifinedo, 2016; Dolan, 2015).

Based on UGT, this study thus exploratively investigates the details of the use and the perceived utility of these sites and the gratifications derived from using them by scholars whose professional career depends on their research and publication performance and also on their visibility in the academic marketplace. Since professional social networks (like LinkedIn or Xing), web-based search engines for academics (like Google Scholar), citation management tools (like EndNote or Citavi) and generic collaboration tools (such as Dropbox, Skype, and many others) already abound, these dedicated SRNSs platforms need to offer a unique and attractive feature set for scholars to incite their adoption and continued usage (Meishar-Tal & Pieterse, 2017). These factors that influence members' adoption of SRNS and their continuance intention, however, have not been satisfactorily investigated up to now. To further the understanding of these factors, this exploratory qualitative study attempts to identify members' primary gratifications derived from using SRNSs. While a prior study (Meishar-Tal & Pieterse, 2017) has uncovered different types of gratifications, new, broader, and more in-depth studies are needed to validate these findings and further identify other types of gratification that academic users can derive from using SRNSs. This leads to the main research question of this study:

How and why do management researchers use social research networking services?

Answering this question can also help to shed more light on the findings of part III, that were largely dominated by the perspective of the platform providers, and thus provide a more holistic view of SRNSs platforms by exploring the perspective of users and investigating the actual use (versus the envisioned or intended use from the perspective of the platform providers, as elaborated in *part III* of the thesis) of these platforms through the theoretical lens of UGT.

Thus, this study extends the work carried out by Meishar-Tal & Pieterse (2017) by conducting a thorough investigation of the antecedents of the use of SRNS platforms through case studies comprising structured interviews with 19 experienced users from the field of management research stemming from several countries and continents (including Germany, the Netherlands, the United States of America, the United Kingdom, Iran, India, and Nigeria) and working on different levels in their academic career (professor, post-doc, and PhD student levels) to overcome any biases, to provide a holistic picture of the dynamics involved in it, with an assumption that the successful outcome can then be generalized to represent the whole scientific community of management researchers, if not the whole scientific world in general. By doing so, this study also overcomes the limitation of the study by Meishar-Tal & Pieterse (2017), which was solely based on the descriptive analysis of the data collected through a small population in a single country.

The remainder of this empirical study is organized as follows. Chapter 2 presents the theoretical underpinnings of this study. The following chapter 3 describes the research methodology, data collection, and data analysis. Next, chapter 4 presents the findings derived from the analysis of the data. Subsequently, chapter 5 provides a discussion and reflection of the findings and the final chapter 6 concludes this study by summarizing the study and providing an outlook for future research.

2 Theoretical Underpinnings

Individual and organizational adoption and continuance of use of generic social networking services is a research topic that has been explored within numerous studies (for an in-depth overview see sections 4.2.6 and 4.3.3 of the literature review presented in *part II* of this thesis). Since the focus of this study is on fostering an understanding of usage patterns of SRNSs by academic researchers, a topic that extant research has not yet sufficiently investigated (Meishar-Tal & Pieterse, 2017), applying a suitable theory that is able to explain the media choice of individuals is crucial (Ifinedo, 2016). Individual and social needs, varying drastically from one person to another, are the primary reasons why individuals use traditional SNSs (Ifinedo, 2016; Kang et al., 2013; Ryan et al., 2014; Park, 2014). In order to understand the factors underlying scholars' adoption, use, and usage continuance of SRNSs, it is apt to acknowledge the crucial role of individual user needs, gratifications, and social influence in the discourse.

Two theoretical underpinnings (i.e. uses and gratification theory (UGT) and social influence (SI) processes framework) are deemed particularly suitable in this situation since they emphasize individual needs, gratifications, and also social imperatives (Ifinedo, 2016). Combining these two theoretical lenses should be helpful in uncovering useful information regarding academics' usage patterns of SRNS and the underlying needs and gratifications influencing adoption and continued use of these platforms. This chapter, therefore, introduces the uses and gratifications theory (UGT) and the social influence (SI) processes framework in the next two sections.

2.1 Uses and gratifications theory

Uses and gratifications theory (UGT) constitutes an influential sociological theory or approach to help explain and understand why and how individuals actively seek out and select specific media outlets to satisfy specific gratification needs (Blumler, 1979; Katz & Foulkes, 1962; Katz, Blumler, & Gurevitch, 1974). The term gratifications was initially used by Herzog (1944) to refer to specific types or dimensions of satisfaction that members of the audience of radio programs were experiencing according to their reports (Dolan et al., 2015). UGT operates under several assumptions: individuals are conscious of their needs and use media in a goal-oriented fashion, media consumers are able to assess and evaluate value judgments of media content and actively link their needs and gratifications leading to the choice of a specific medium (Ifinedo, 2016; West & Turner, 2007; Katz et al., 1974).

Initially, UGT has been applied to study needs and gratifications in the context of traditional media, such as television, radio, and newspapers (Ifinedo, 2016; Luo, Chea, & Chen, 2011; West & Turner, 2007). More recent studies have leveraged UGT to analyze needs and gratifications in the context of computer-mediated communication (CMC) technologies, which social networking services are a part of (Cheung & Lee, 2009; Cheung et al., 2011; Dholakia et al, 2004; Ifinedo, 2016; Dolan et al., 2015). Typically, the needs and gratifications that UGT refers to, are related to entertainment and relaxation, social interaction and communication, remuneration or reward, and enhancement of one's knowledge, skills, and abilities (Dolan et al., 2015; Ko, Cho, & Roberts, 2005). In a study on social media engagement behavior in the marketing field, Dolan et al. (2015) posit that content on (sales- and marketing-related) social media can be divided into four major groups, depending on if the content provided is primarily related to *information*, *entertainment*, *remuneration*, or *relational needs*. According to Dolan et al. (2015), the delivery of suitable content in these areas will help in gratifying the needs of social media users and therefore result in the stimulation of positively valenced social media engagement behavior (SMEB), propelling adoption and continuance of these platforms.

UGT itself does not mandate a categorization of needs and gratifications, most recent studies leveraging UGT in the context of social media and social networking services typically divide needs and gratifications into three, four or five main groups (e.g. Dolan et al., 2015; Ifinedo, 2016; Meishar-Tal & Pieterse, 2017). In their previous study concerning academics' use of social networking services, Meishar-Tal and Pieterse (2017) propose five major types of needs that academic social networking services could offer related gratifications to: (1) cognitive needs – consuming information and building knowledge, (2) affective needs – generating excitement and pleasure, (3) social needs – interacting with others and creating a sense of belonging to a group, (4) individual needs – promoting one's self, enhancing one's confidence and self-esteem, and (5) escapist needs – creating a virtual and imaginary environment that one can use to escape reality. This study will leverage the same categories as proposed by Meishar-Tal and Pieterse (2017), they are summarized in table 72.

Table 72: Types of needs that social media responds to by providing gratifications

Need	Gratifications	Exemplary Studies
Cognitive needs	Consumption of information and knowledge	Shao, 2009; Chen, Clifford, & Wells, 2002; Maddox, 1998; Chen et al., 2002
Affective needs	Enjoyment, entertainment, excitement, pleasure	Eighmey & McCord, 1998; Taylor et al., 2011; Raney & Janicke, 2013
Social needs	Social interaction, sense of belonging, seeking support, connecting with friends and colleagues	Stafford, Stafford, & Schkade, 2004; Hennig-Thurau, Gwinner, Walsh, & Gemler, 2004; Muntinga et al., 2011; Leung, 2009; Park et al., 2009
Individual needs	Remuneration, personal gain, self-promotion, enhancement of self-esteem and personal confidence	Dunne et al., 2010; Muntinga et al., 2011; Füller, 2006
Escapist needs	Avoiding reality, fleeing to an alternative virtual and imagined reality	Kaye, 1998; McQuail, 1983; Meishar-Tal & Pieterse, 2017; Quan-Haase & Young, 2010

2.2 Social influence processes

Adoption of a particular technology like SRNSs is not only triggered by an individual's own personal needs or persuasions but is very often also the result of the influence exerted by others and their views (Cheung & Lee, 2009; Ifinedo, 2016; Bagozzi & Dholakia, 2002; Malhotra & Galletta, 1999). This phenomenon has been termed "social influence processes".

Social influence (SI) processes take place when the opinions and behaviors of others affect an individual's actions and views (Chiu et al., 2013; Aronson, Timothy, & Akert, 2010). According to Kelman (1974, 1958), three major types of SI can be distinguished: compliance, identification, and internalization. Table 73 provides a description of these three types of social influence processes together with relevant sources.

Table 73: Description of social influence processes

Social influence process	**Description**	**Sources**
Compliance	Taking over others' opinions, agreeing to comply with implicit or explicit requests made by others; agreeing with other people's positions	Aronson et al. (2010); Kelman (1974; 1958)
Identification	Being influenced by other individuals in the same social group	Cheung et al. (2011); Kelman (1974); Kelman (1958)
Internalization	Accepting a belief or behaviour because it is consistent with one's value system	Cheung & Lee (2010); Kelman (1974); Kelman (1958); Malhotra & Galletta (1999)

3 Method and Data

This *chapter* introduces the reader to the research approach undertaken in this study, the research method used, and how data was gathered and how data analysis was performed. These aspects are presented in the following three *sections* in detail.

The first section explains why the qualitative case study method has been employed. The second section describes the research approach including how data was collected and analyzed. Finally, the third section deals with the data.

3.1 Research Design

In order to investigate the question of '*How and why do management researchers use social research networking services?*', a multiple-case study approach has been applied. Due to the explorative nature of the research question, applying a qualitative research method is appropriate (Yin, 2013; Hammersley, 2012; Siggelkow, 2007; Edmondson and McManus, 2007). In addition, social research networking services and their adoption constitute still a relatively new phenomenon (Meishar-Tal & Pieterse, 2017; Ortega, 2016; He & Jeng, 2016). This lack of comprehensive empirical material and the fact that the research regarding this topic is still in an incipient phase, especially concerning the rationales and reasons for adoption and continued use of social research networking services motivates the choice of the case study methodology (Benbasat, Goldstein, & Mead, 1987). Under such circumstances, it is appropriate to create new assumptions or to refine existing theoretical constructs (Eisenhardt & Graebner, 2007; Eisenhardt, 1989; Edmundson and McManus, 2007; Hammersley, 2012). Since case study research allows for investigating complex interactions between technology, organizations, and people (Dubé & Paré, 2003), it is suitable to obtain a holistic understanding of the topic at hand.

A multiple-case study approach has been adopted since it provides the possibility for comparisons within-case and cross-case. Therefore, the internal validity of the research results is higher than compared to a single-case study approach (Eisenhardt & Graebner, 2007; Eisenhardt, 1989).

3.2 Research Approach

Data for the case studies were collected through a combination of techniques (Yin, 2013). Since the aim of the study was to gain a holistic understanding of the adoption of SRNS platforms by experienced power users and their usage rationales, a purposive sampling strategy was adopted (Marshall, 1996; Seawright & Gerring, 2008; Silverman, 2013). The purposive sampling strategy involves selecting cases or units on the basis of a specific purpose rather than randomly (Tashakkori & Teddlie, 2010).

To examine the adoption of SRNS platforms by experienced or even power users of these platforms, first, data was collected from the major three SRNS platforms ResearchGate, Mendeley, and Academia.edu. As a starting point, all profiles linked to the University of Erlangen-Nürnberg where the profile owner belonged to the faculty of the business school and was identified as a management researcher were manually scanned in these three platforms. Then, their profiles were analyzed in order to determine their suitability for the purpose of this research (Tashakkori & Teddlie, 2010; Seawright & Gerring, 2008), i.e. the profile owners needed to have a fully completed profile within the platform including a portrait of their person, display regular activity on the platform, and also leveraging more advanced features within the platform as discernible from the profile. The overall goal was to identify (power) users, "posters", instead of "lurkers" (Nonnecke, Preece, & Andrews, 2004) [104]that use the platforms regularly instead of maintaining a mostly passive profile. In total, fifteen candidates from the University of Erlangen-Nürnberg were identified and contacted if they were willing to participate in the study by being interviewed. Four candidates declined due to time constraints or other concerns, eleven researchers agreed to participate in the study and face-to-face interviews were scheduled. In addition, 50 management researchers who had profiles on more than one platform and who displayed a high level of activity on these platforms were contacted via ResearchGate and were invited to participate in the study. Of these, eight researchers responded and agreed to participate in the study, the others did either not reply or declined to participate.

---

[104] Nonnecke, B., Preece, J. and Andrews, D., What lurkers and posters think of each other. in 37th Hawaii International Conference on System Sciences, (Hawaii, 2004), IEEE., paper 14

Step 1. Initial Case Selection & Purposive Sampling
- Identification of suitable profiles of management researchers on ResearchGate, Mendeley and Academia.edu: fully completed profile on the platforms, regular activity within the systems, and usage of advanced functions instead of maintaining a passive profile

Step 2. Invitation of Identified Candidates to Participate in the Study
-Eleven researchers working at the University of Erlangen-Nürnberg and eight external researchers from a variety of institutions agreed to participate in the research

Step 3. Data Collection with Semi-Structured Interviews
- In total, 19 interviews were conducted utilizing a tripartite guideline consisting of open-ended questions and potential queries. All interviews were recorded and taped.

Step 4. Transcription and Analysis of Interviews
- The taped interviews were given to an outsourced transcription service for verbatim transcription. After transcription, the transcripts were coded and analysed with MAXQDA12 following a thematic analysis process

Step 5. Case Writing & Finalization
- Results from the interview analysis were compared with the profiles of the interview candidates. A write-up of the results was performed along the lines of UGT theory and SI processes framework

Figure 44: Research design of part IV

Interview data were collected by means of semi-structured interviews prepared with a guideline consisting of open-ended questions and potential queries (Clifford et al., 2016). The guideline comprised three sections: the first section contained primarily questions concerning the demography of the interviewee and the perceived, self-assessed usage profile of the interviewee and questions regarding the platforms that were being employed. The second section aimed to obtain insights regarding the uses that the platforms were employed for, and how the interviewees normally interacted with the platforms, what they liked or did not like about each particular platform, and any concerns they had regarding platform use, e.g. privacy, data security, etc. The questions in the last part focused on exploring the gratifications that the interviewees derived from using the SRNS platforms.

Ten interviews were held face-to-face, nine interviews were conducted via Skype. Each interview lasted between 25 and 45 minutes. Since all participants agreed to a recording of the interview, each interview was recorded on tape. The interviews were concluded by asking the interviewees if they had additional thoughts that could enrich the case studies and help reaching the research goals. All interviews were conducted in the English language, even if the interviewees were German native speakers in order to facilitate transcription by an outsourced transcription service. The interviews were subsequently transcribed by an external party and checked for plausibility by the researcher. In case of gaps or mis-transcriptions, the researcher corrected the transcription by resorting to the recording files. After verbatim transcription, the resulting transcripts were coded and analyzed with the help of MAXQDA 12 software following a thematic analysis process (Braun & Clarke, 2006). The thematic analysis helped the researcher to identify, analyze, and report patterns or themes (Braun & Clarke, 2006). A combination of deductive and inductive thematic analysis was applied during the data analysis phase. This combination was necessary to gain in-depth explanations about what influences researchers to adopt and leverage SRNS platforms. In addition, the inductive approach allowed new themes to emerge from the data. The overall research design underlying this study is depicted in figure 44.

3.3 Case Studies

The selection of a suitable sample of relevant cases for an in-depth analysis constitutes a crucial aspect of the study at hand. The rationale in selecting the case studies was to help generate a first and holistic understanding of why management researchers adopt and use SRNS platforms and how they actually leverage the platforms for research-related activities. Given the millions of registered users within ResearchGate, Mendeley, or Academia.edu, a multi-criteria filtering approach was applied for purposive sampling (Tashakkori & Teddlie, 2010; Marshall, 1996; Seawright & Gerring, 2008; Silverman, 2013) after their profiles within the platforms were surveyed with the aim of determining how long they were using the systems and how intensely was the use – in so far as this could be estimated from an analysis of the profiles alone. Thus, during the interviews, it turned out that some researchers displayed a higher or lower level of activity on the platform as initially estimated and expected during the analysis of the researchers' profiles.

The demographics of the interviewees (e.g. age group, academic level, country, SRNS usage profile, and platforms used) are shown in table 74 below. All the interviewees have been using the SRNS platforms for more than two years. The frequency of the interviewees' visits to the SRNS platforms varied from one to four times per month (indicated in table 74 as a usage profile of "moderately low"), to several times per week (SRNS usage profile indicated as "high") up to daily use of the platform ("very high").

Table 74: Participant demographics

Interviewee Code Name	Age Group	Academic level	Country	SRNS usage profile[105]	Platforms used[106]
I01	35-44	PostDoc	Germany	Very High	RG/M
I02	25-34	PostDoc	Germany	Moderately Low	RG
I03	25-34	PhD Student	Germany	High	RG/M
I04	25-34	PhD Student	Germany	High	RG/M
I05	25-34	PhD Student	Germany	Very High	RG/M
I06	35-44	Professor	Germany	Very High	RG/M
I07	35-44	Professor	USA	Very High	RG/M
I08	25-34	PhD Student	Germany	Moderately Low	RG
I09	25-34	PhD Student	UK	Moderately Low	RG
I10	35-44	PostDoc	Germany	Very High	RG/M/A
I11	25-34	PhD Student	Nigeria	Very High	RG/M/A
I12	35-44	Professor	Netherlands	High	RG/M/A
I13	25-34	PostDoc	Germany	Very High	RG/M
I14	35-44	Professor	Germany	Very High	RG/M/A
I15	45-54	Professor	UK	Very High	RG/M/A
I16	25-34	PostDoc	Netherlands	High	RG
I17	35-44	Professor	Germany	Very High	RG/M
I18	35-44	Professor	Iran	High	RG/-/A
I19	35-44	PostDoc	India	Very High	RG/M/A

Detailed findings derived from the analysis of the case studies are presented in the next chapter.

[105] Very High = Daily use of at least one of the platforms, High = several times a week, Moderately Low = 1-4 times a month

[106] RG = ResearchGate, M = Mendeley, A=Academia.edu

4 Findings

This chapter presents the results of the analysis and iterative comparison of the data gathered in the case studies. The in-depth cross-case analysis of the case studies sheds light on the goals of this study. First, it describes which platforms are used and how often they are used by the interviewees, thus, SRNS usage profiles of the interviewees have been derived both from the interview data and the surveyance of the interviewee's profiles in the platforms. Second, it demonstrates that researchers employ these platforms to satisfy a variety of different needs and derive various gratifications from their use, thus shedding light on the research question underlying this study:

How and why do management researchers use social research networking services?

The two following sections discuss these aspects in depth.

4.1 Research Platform Usage and Frequency

All interviewees actively maintain a profile in at least one social research networking service, with ResearchGate standing out, as all interviewees are users of ResearchGate. This is in line with findings by Meishar-Tal and Pieterse (2017), where ResearchGate was also identified as the preferred platform within their sample. The second most prevalent platform is Mendeley, with 14 out of 19 interviewees identifying themselves as active users on the platform. Researchers using Academia.edu are rarer, most interviewees indicated that the platform is either totally unknown to them or they discontinued use of Academia.edu a long time ago. No single interviewee was aware of the emerging platform Trellis that focuses on more collaborative functionalities. The demographics of the interviewees (e.g. age group, academic level, country, SRNS usage profile, and platforms used) were summarized in table 74 in the preceding chapter. All the interviewees have been using the SRNS platforms for more than two years. The frequency of the interviewees' visits to the SRNS platforms varied from one to four times per month (indicated in table 74 as a usage profile of "moderately low"), to several times per week (SRNS usage profile indicated as "high") up to daily use of the platform ("very high"). One interviewee's statement serves as an example of a user that has been qualified to show a usage profile that can be characterized as "very high":

"I would say I use the platforms every day, as I'm always logged in and anyway I use it constantly. I don't have a regular schedule to say 'okay, now I'm going to go on ResearchGate', because sometimes when you do a search on Google Scholar and then then the PDF appears on your ResearchGate so you click and you find yourself already in ResearchGate reading a paper. [...] Every time, for example, I read a paper that I find interesting or I think 'okay, this person could belong to my community', I follow him on ResearchGate" (I05)

The other end of the spectrum regarding the SRNS usage profile of the interviewees – an example of infrequent, but still regular usage, characterized by "moderately low", has been referred to by an interviewee as follows:

"So, I am not very active there, I use it like once a week or something. I have posted there some papers, but they do not actually inform the users about my ongoing projects. I use it more for visibility, for publicity for the papers that I already have." (I02)

Analysis of the interviews also revealed a shift by several users to consolidate their activities on one or two platforms only. As one researcher representatively stated who identified himself as an early adopter of both ResearchGate, Mendeley, and Academia.edu:

"I was using Academia.edu right after they became available – I think I was among the first users within our university - but I discontinued using their platform since I found them far too pushy and aggressive with their constant notifications and asking to become a premium member. I've also stopped using Mendeley after they've been acquired by Elsevier – since then I found them to be too Elsevier-minded. I wanted a really independent platform. I only wanted to use a single platform – since using multiple platforms is too time-consuming for my taste. ResearchGate seems to me to be the one big player to turn to, in addition, it's a German platform." (I14)

Other interviewees confirmed this tendency to consolidate the number of platforms being used:

"At the beginning when these platforms first came up, that is like several years ago, I was quite active on Academia.edu, I also liked how they represented the scientific family in an older version of the platform. But I must say that I've more or less stopped using them as most of the functionalities are now hidden behind a paywall and I think the activity of most researchers has shifted to ResearchGate. So, I still have a now passive profile on Academia.edu, I am sometimes active on Mendeley when it comes to sharing papers with students or colleagues, but now I mainly use ResearchGate." (I12)

Analysis of the researchers' profiles on the platforms and their statements during the interviews also revealed that ResearchGate and Mendeley are used for very different purposes, while Academia.edu seems to suffer a drying out of user activity and increasing discontinuation in general. Although ResearchGate by now offers functionality for collaboration, these are hardly used by the interviewees within the sample. Interviewees consistently indicated that they are using ResearchGate primarily for exchanging papers, and staying aware of what is happening in their scientific field:

"On the one hand I use it for exchanging papers – I'm aware of sites like Scihub – but I'm too cautious to use it since I think it's quite illegal – and on the other hand I use ResearchGate to stay informed. Since I've uploaded a lot and I've indicated a lot of interests, I get recommended many projects and papers on the site – which is good, since I don't really have time to actively inform myself, since so much is being published in so many journals [...]. I'm also constantly inviting other people all the time so they start using the platform as well, so, yes, I'm very active on the ResearchGate." (I14)

Mendeley is quite different when it comes to the usage of its members. Interviewees indicated they do not really use the social network functionalities of the platform, but either use it as a citation tool (competing with Endnote or Citavi) or to share papers with peers and students or to monitor the progress of students, as one interviewee stated:

"I don't really use Mendeley in the sense of a social network, but more as a practical tool for managing my students and assigning a paper to them. For example, if I come across a relevant paper for one of my Master students, I tag it in Mendeley with the name of the student, for example 'Slash for Chris', and then it gets automatically assigned to him. Also, I use the annotation function quite a lot, when I work with fellow colleagues together on a publication" (I01)

Another interviewee stated that he is using ResearchGate to gauge the right moment to apply for tenure:

"As I am currently employed at a university in the US, the timing of the application for tenure is quite critical. There is no fixed time when you need to apply, you can do it like either after four or five years. So, with ResearchGate I have some visibility into what my competing colleagues at the same university are doing and what they have published, and then it can help me decide to go for the optimal timing." (I07)

Another point that became evident from the interviews is that actually no interviewee was using any SRNS platform for actual research collaboration. Instead, interviewees mentioned other tools not directly dedicated to researchers like Dropbox or Skype. One interviewee stated:

"No, at my department no one is using these platforms for actual collaboration. What was that bug tracking system called again? Ah, it was Mantis – we use that sometimes when we write a paper together in a team – any issue that comes up is being entered in Mantis and can then be followed up. That worked quite well so far." (I16)

4.2 Usage Patterns of SRNS Users under the Lenses of UGT and SI

Uses and gratifications theory (UGT) suggests that media selection is an active process carried out by individuals to match specific media outlets to satisfy specific uses, needs, and gratifications (Katz et al., 1974; Ifinedo, 2016). In addition to this view of the active role of the user in the media selection process, the social influence (SI) processes theory posits that individuals' technology and media adoption is also driven and influenced by the views of others (Ifinedo, 2016; Bagozzi & Dholakia, 2002; Cheung & Lee, 2009; Chiu et al., 2013; Aronson et al., 2010). The following subsections will discuss the findings from the interviews utilizing the theoretical lenses of UGT and SI.

4.2.1 Consumption of information and knowledge

Getting access to and consuming knowledge and information is referred to by UGT as gratification to satisfy cognitive needs (Shao, 2009; Chen et al, 2002; Maddox, 1998). As the in-depth cross interview analysis shows, this is one of the main drivers why scholars adopt and use a particular SRNS platform. Almost all interviewees mentioned that they use ResearchGate for getting access to publications their own university library does not have access to, either because the library did not subscribe to that particular publication outlet or the publication cannot be accessed yet due to embargo. As one German interviewee stated:

"So basically I use ResearchGate very often to access papers that I cannot access via a library and many times I got similar requests for my own papers from other researchers, too." (I01)

The problem of getting access to publications is not surprisingly even more salient in African countries, as one interviewee from Nigeria put it:

"My university does not really offer comfortable access to many publications due to budget limitations. So, I help myself by making extensive use of these platforms, I try to find the paper on Academia.edu or write to the author directly via ResearchGate." (I11)

Apart from getting access to otherwise hard-to-get or restricted publications, researchers use these platforms to be exposed to new research trends for inspiration and idea generation.

> *"I check almost every day on ResearchGate what my peer researchers who I follow are doing – I think it really helps me stay up-to-date on current developments within my field." (I06)*

Being aware of what others are doing who are active in the same field or pursuing a similar line of research is another topic that emerged in several of the interviews, as an interviewee mentioned:

> *"It's really hard to keep on top of your research field – since when I am using Mendeley and ResearchGate with their paper recommendations, staying aware of what's currently hot got so much easier." (I19)*

Keeping abreast of new articles in the field can be facilitated greatly by following the leading researchers, as another interviewee stated:

> *"Every time for example I read a paper that I find interesting or I think 'okay, this person could belong to my community', I follow him on ResearchGate. And from the moment I follow him I start receiving the notification about the activity ... so basically that's how I do it. Then I find it quite useful to be notified if that particular researcher has published some new article, typically closely related to my field, so that's really very helpful in keeping track of what's going on in the field." (I05)*

4.2.2 Enjoyment and entertainment

Social media are known to be used extensively for hedonic purposes, i.e. for enjoyment, entertainment, excitement, or pleasure (Berger et al., 2014). The needs underlying hedonic use of social media are referred to as *affective needs* by UGT (Eighmey & McCord, 1998; Taylor et al., 2011; Raney et al., 2013). While using academic social networking services can help with promoting one's self and enhancing confidence and self-esteem, a use that can also contribute to one's enjoyment, but is distinguished as constituting a separate need within the UGT theory and is discussed in section 4.2.4 of this chapter, no single interviewed researcher was really inclined to use SRNS platforms out of this motive. As one interviewee put it:

"No, I don't think reading hundreds of papers is as entertaining as watching hundreds of photos of your friends on Facebook." (I10)

However, some researchers mentioned that they genuinely enjoy that their articles are of interest to other researchers and help others in their research:

"One aspect I really do enjoy about these platforms is that I get notified if someone reads my publications – I find this actually quite gratifying that my papers are not write-only but you can see that they are actually downloaded and read." (I15)

Another interviewee corroborates this view:

"On the other hand, I like the stats on ResearchGate – lately for example I published in a conference proceeding and then you start receiving these stats about who reads it. And then your interest definitely grows into like you know I don't care but as soon as you get a new read, you want to see who or from which area it came from ... so that's the entertaining part I would say" (I05)

4.2.3 Social interaction and belonging to a professional community

A key feature of social networking services is facilitating communication and social interaction between users of the platform and helping build communities, thus gratifying needs like connecting with colleagues, building a sense of belonging, and seeking support, collectively referred to as *social needs* by UGT (Leung, 2009; Stafford et al., 2004; Hennig-Thurau et al., 2004; Park et al., 2009; Muntiga et al., 2011). In addition, social influence (SI) processes are also playing a role in users' adoption of a particular media outlet, even when using the media is not triggered in the first place by an individual's need or personal persuasion, but rather by the influence exerted by colleagues (Cheung & Lee, 2009; Ifinedo, 2016; Bagozzi & Dholakia, 2002; Malhotra & Galletta, 1999). Literature names three major types of social influence processes: compliance with others' opinions, views or requests, identification with other individuals within the same group or community, and internalization of others' beliefs or behaviors (Kelman, 1974; Kelman, 1958; Cheung & Lee, 2010; Malhotra & Galletta, 1999).

A cross-analysis of the interviews revealed that gratifying social needs and complying with expectations is another major driver why researchers, in the end, do use professional academic platforms, even if they are normally rather reticent with engaging in (hedonic) social networking services:

"In the beginning, I did not want to create a profile on ResearchGate, but since I'm back from maternity leave and want to become a professor in the long run, I've finally signed up for the platform and started to use it on a regular basis. [...] I think it's more like social pressure. So in the end you also do what the others do." (I02)

Another motif that came up during the analysis of the interviews is wanting to show presence when colleagues are also active and being part of the research community in one's discipline and be noticed within that discipline or community:

"Yes, so a lot of people in my field of management research use this network, so I use the platform as well. For my future career plans, it's quite important that I'm visible within the community." (I13)

Other interviewees have mentioned that they seek professional recognition within their community:

"First thing in the morning, I log in to Academia.edu and ResearchGate to check on my readership and stats. In my personal environment here where I live, I have little support for what I do, so using these networks provides me with the recognition I need to keep myself motivated and going." (I11)

Another interviewee stated:

"The stats generated on the platform and the scores are really motivating for me ... I like to see how I make my progress within the academic community in my field." (I01)

Wanting to share research within one's community is also a pervasive motif that came up several times within the interviews. In addition, several interviewees from Germany mentioned self-archiving as a use case for their activity in ResearchGate:

"I started to use ResearchGate as some sort of archive for my publications. Yes, I would even say, self-archival is probably one of the main reasons why I use the system." (I10)

Self-archiving is a topic that has garnered considerable debate and confusion within the research community. As the same interviewee stated:

"Actually, the self-archival rules are quite confusing, so they really depend on the publisher or the outlet. We had a lot of discussions within our chair and our academic community around it and everybody is kind of confused. ResearchGate provides some information on its website on how to correctly do self-archival." (I10)

Another aspect of belonging to a professional community is building new academic collaborations and expanding one's relations with other scholars. Although social networking services are supposed to facilitate new connections, none of the interviewees indicated that they used any SRNS platform to initiate new connections. Instead, the platforms proved to be useful once personal contact had been established at a conference, as several interviewees indicated:

"I've never contacted anyone I didn't know from real-life on ResearchGate ... but once I've met people at conferences, I start to follow them, and then you kind of stay in touch via the platform." (I12)

4.2.4 Self-promotion and enhancement of confidence and self-esteem

Using SRNS platforms for self-promotion and enhancement of self-esteem and personal confidence was a theme that most of the interviewees mentioned as a major gratification derived from the use of the platforms, in particular referring to ResearchGate. UGT associates usage motives related to self-promotion and ego-bolstering (as well as other motives like remuneration or personal gain) with individual needs (Dunne et al., 2010; Muntinga et al., 2011; Füller, 2006).

Several interviewees indicated – in particular, those whose usage patterns of the platforms exhibit near-daily or daily usage that a driving force for their platform use is wanting to know how often their publications are read, as one interviewee stated:

"First thing in the morning, I log in to Academia.edu and ResearchGate to check on my readership and stats. In my personal environment here where I live, I have little support for what I do, so using these networks provides me with the recognition I need to keep myself motivated and going." (I11)

Several other interviewees have expressed similar views regarding the gratifications derived. For instance, one of the researchers stated:

"I particularly like ResearchGate as it provides me with constant feedback and encouragement as I am presented with the number of reads and citations. Checking these stats almost on a daily basis is quite enjoyable and motivating for me I think." (I15)

Another management researcher had similar views and stated:

"These gamification elements related to reputation scores and similar features in ResearchGate is something I genuinely like about the platform and I think it's probably the main reason why I'm using it. I also find it quite nice to see that my publications have a real-world impact and are used and cited. And I have to admit there's almost an addictive quality to these stats and badges – like your article reached this and this number of citations – it's like the badges you earn in nowadays' computer games. Quite addictive actually." (I17)

However, there is also a downside to the scoring system implemented by ResearchGate, as one management researcher has remarked:

"Their scoring system can be tricked easily … there was this clever graduate student who had almost no publications but he found out that ResearchGate rewards some random activity on the platform like following and recommending, so his ResearchGate score was soon way higher than those of the researchers at our university who were really actively publishing papers. The ResearchGate score is not something that should be taken too seriously or should be trusted, as you can very easily trick it. It can definitely not be considered to be a mature academic measurement instrument." (I06)

In sum, a thorough cross-analysis of the interviews indicated that self-promotion is probably the number one driver underlying the adoption and (daily) use of the platforms by many researchers. In particular, ResearchGate is particularly strong in appealing to scholars' personal egos, something that other more utilitarian platforms like Mendeley did not achieve. However, as several interviewees indicated, the reputation system exposed by ResearchGate should by no means taken as a serious academic measurement instrument, as it has major flaws that allow for easy exploitation of the system and to increase one's reputation score on the platform far beyond one's real academic achievements.

4.2.5 Escapism

One key aspect of hedonic social networking services like Facebook is to provide a technology-mediated outlet for avoiding reality, procrastinating, or fleeing to alternative virtual or imagined realities. UGT refers to this complex of motives as escapist needs (Kaye, 1998; McQuail, 1983; Meishar-Tal & Pieterse, 2017; Quan-Haase & Young, 2010). During the interviews conducted for this study, this topic was also explored with the interviewees. However, none of the interviewees indicated that they were using any of the SRNS platforms for motives that can be linked to escapist needs. As one interviewee stated representatively:

> *"Of course, these systems, in particular, ResearchGate provide some sort of fun when seeing one's progress reflected in stats and scores, but hey, the appeal of the platform to while away time is totally like zero – when I want some entertainment or interact with my friends, I go to Facebook or have a coffee with my colleagues, but definitely not to ResearchGate or even less Academia.edu or Mendeley." (I10)*

This finding is in line with previous research done by Meishar-Tal and Pieterse (2017), where escapist needs also did not register with anyone in their sample. Thus, gratifying needs related to escapism can be regarded as irrelevant when it comes to currently available SRNS platforms.

5 Discussion and Reflection

In general, this explorative study explores adoption and use of SRNS platforms by management researchers under the theoretical lens of the uses and gratifications theory (Katz et al., 1974) which has been successfully applied in previous studies investigating adoption and usage continuance of social media (Ifinedo, 2016; Cheung and Lee, 2009; Cheung et al., 2011; Dholakia et al., 2004; Dolan et al., 2015; Meishar-Tal and Pieterse, 2017). In addition, the social influence (SI) processes framework has been leveraged in order to help better understand adoption and usage of SRNS platforms not triggered by an individual's own personal needs, but due to the influence exerted by colleagues and peer pressure (Chiu et al., 2013; Aronson et al., 2010). This study extends the previous research carried out by Meishar-Tal & Pieterse (2017) by conducting a thorough investigation into the antecedents of use of SRNS platforms through structured interviews with a carefully selected international group of power users from the field of management research to overcome any biases, to provide a holistic picture of the dynamics involved in it, working under the assumption that the successful outcome and the insights gained can then be generalized to represent the whole scientific community. By doing so this explorative study also overcomes the limitation of the study by Meishar-Tal & Pieterse (2017), which was solely based on the descriptive analysis of the data collected within a small population in a single country. The findings of this study offer both theoretical and practical implications for platform providers and users alike, as well as contributing to the overall academic discussion in the fields of social software and research collaboration. The following subsections provide a discussion and reflection of the findings.

5.1 Insights into Usage Patterns and Gratifications Driving Adoption and Use of SRNS Platforms

The findings of the study offer first insights into why academics coming from the field of management research are using SRNS platforms in the way they do it. The following subsections will discuss these insights from the perspectives of usage patterns identified and from a gratifications perspective.

5.1.1 Usage patterns of SRNS platforms

Results from an in-depth cross-analysis of the interviews show that the platforms are mainly used for consumption of information (like getting access to publications not available via one's own local university library and staying informed about what other researchers in the same field are working on) and to a similar degree for the sharing of information, which is in turn motivated by a variety of gratifications, as has been shown in the previous chapter and will be discussed below more holistically.

Unlike traditional social networking services like Facebook, where interaction with other users is considered to be the main use case (Boyd & Ellison, 2007), this does not seem to hold true for SRNS platforms. Instead, interviewees indicated that they turn to other social networking services like LinkedIn or Facebook or messaging services like Skype in order to stay in touch and interact with peers and academic friends. This indicates that SRNS platforms seem to function differently from other social networking services and need to be seen in a different light.

Very few researchers in the sample leveraged the collaborative features offered by the platform. Only one interviewee indicated that she is using one particular platform, Mendeley, intensively to collaborate with her peers and also with students writing their theses for purposes of progress monitoring and collaboration. This might be due to the specifics of the academic field of management research, that demands less collaboration from its actors than other academic fields like physics or biology where researchers have to work together more intensively in order to bring about significant academic results. Future research might shed more light on discipline-specific usage patterns within SRNS platforms.

5.1.2 Gratifications behind adoption and use of SRNS platforms

Looking at the findings from a gratification perspective underlying the actual use of the platforms, only three out of five gratification types discussed within this study proved to be significant in triggering academics to visit and use SRNS platforms. The most pronounced gratification identified in the cross-analysis of the interviews is self-promotion and enhancement of confidence and self-esteem. Almost all the interviewees mentioned self-promotion within the academic field as a major motivation to visit an SRNS platform, in particular, ResearchGate and to a much lesser degree Academia.edu. This can also help explain the comparatively lesser popularity of Mendeley within the sample of the interviewees, as it offers only very little features that can help with self-promotion and thus does not really appeal to this type of gratification.

Other gratifications underlying the adoption and use of SRNS platforms were the consumption of information and knowledge, and social interaction and belonging to a professional community. Enjoyment and entertainment and providing an outlet for escapism, gratifications that regular social networking services cater to (Quan-Haase & Young, 2010) seemed irrelevant in the case of SRNS platforms, which is in line with the findings presented by Meishar-Tal & Pieterse (2017).

5.2 Theoretical Insights

On a theoretical level, this study contributes to the existing literature in various ways. A combination of uses and gratifications theory (UGT) and the social influences (SI) processes framework were used to analyze management researchers' adoption and use of the SRNS platform. The combination of these two theoretical frameworks is a novelty in the investigation of academics' adoption of SRNS, a research field that is still in a very early phase due to the relative newness of these platforms and needs to be further explored. The results of the study suggest that UGT and SI processes are suitable theoretical frameworks to study the phenomenon of SNS adoption which is in line with Ifinedo (2016).

Tying back to the wider field of research collaboration, that has been extensively discussed within *part II* of this thesis regarding the state of the literature, the results indicate of this study indicate that the currently available SRNS platforms still seem to be lacking in providing relevant features that would encourage academics to use these platforms for collaboration. An alternative explanation for the apparent lack of interaction and collaboration within these platforms could be that those platforms that offer more collaborative features (like Mendeley or Trellis) do not sufficiently cater to gratifications like self-promotion. Future research should also explore the influence of the academic discipline on adoption and usage patterns of SRNS platforms, thus contributing both to the literature on research collaboration and social software.

5.3 Practical Insights

This study also offers important implications for practitioners. On a practical level, the findings of the study indicated that platform providers that want their SRNS platform to attract widespread adoption need to take the gratifications that users can derive from platform use more into focus. Platform providers should not only focus on providing more and more features within their offerings but need to understand the "whys" and "hows" of user adoption. While more collaboration-oriented platforms like Mendeley or Trellis provide a strong feature set that could be used to help researchers carry out certain aspects of collaborative research in an easier fashion, If these platforms do not sufficiently appeal to gratifications like self-promotion or enhancement of confidence and self-esteem of their users, they might see less adoption or could lose out to competitors that have found ways to appeal to these gratifications.

5.4 Opportunities for Future Research

The findings of this study present ample opportunities for future research with the potential of providing significant contributions to various research streams. Regarding the field of research collaboration, running future similar studies in research fields and scientific disciplines other than management research could shed more light on disciplinary differences related to collaborative behavior and discipline-dependent usage patterns of SRNS platforms. SRNS platforms could also provide an empirical field to further study scientists' collaboration strategies or scientific productivity and collaboration patterns, thus previous research, e.g. by Ponomariov & Boardman (2009) could be further extended.

In addition, it might be useful to leverage these first findings gained in this explorative qualitative study by extending and widening the empirical field and further refining the methodological approach to come up with a taxonomy of scientists' communication and collaborative strategies, similar to Bozeman & Corley (2004). Preliminary results suggest that archetypical user types could be identified based on applying uses and gratifications theory (UGT) and social influence (SI) processes framework to a wider empirical field. A cross-analysis of the findings gained from the interviews conducted in this study indicates that there could be user archetypes like "The Information Seeker", "The Self-Archiver", "The Networker", "The Academic Narcissist", or "The Follower", similar as suggested by Bozeman & Corley (2004) in their study on scientists' collaboration strategies. Thus, SRNS platforms might prove to be both a valuable empirical field and study object to further inform scientific research both on research collaboration and social software.

6 Conclusion

Developing an understanding of extrinsic and intrinsic factors that have an impact on academics' adoption and continued use of SRNS platforms constitutes an important scientific undertaking for both researchers' and practitioners' communities within two distinct academic fields – research collaboration and social software. This empirical study further investigated social research network sites by investigating the adoption and usage of these platforms through a combination of the theoretical lenses of the uses and gratifications theory and the social influence processes framework. Due to the exploratory nature of the research presented herein, this study does not claim to provide final insights on the topic; clearly, more studies are needed to extend the borders of knowledge on this topic. Researchers should continue to explore the impact of social influence processes and different categories of uses and gratifications on scientists' adoption of the relatively novel class of SRNS platforms given the applicability of these theoretical models in furthering the discourse. Future studies in this field should seek to broaden insights by extending the empirical field to other academic disciplines and to include perspectives from various cultural contexts.

Current and future providers of SRNS platforms can profit from a deepened understanding of uses, gratifications, and the impact of social influence in order to improve their platforms by focusing on providing features that cater to these uses and gratifications to help drive adoption and increase the value proposition of their platform. The findings can also help individual researchers and research organizations pick the right tools and platforms by understanding how these platforms can help with certain use cases like facilitating information consumption or building new relationships and strengthening existing ones within scientific communities. Lastly, understanding the gratifications that can be derived from leveraging these platforms, researchers can make a more informed decision regarding the adoption and use of platforms that fulfill their individual needs.

Part V

Discussion and Conclusion

J.-H. Soeldner, *Understanding Social Research Networking Sites*,
Markt- und Unternehmensentwicklung Markets and Organisations,
https://doi.org/10.1007/978-3-658-31575-7_5

1 Summary of Studies and Contribution

This dissertation deals with social research networking sites, a novel kind of web-based platforms that can help support scholars in their tasks within individual research processes and collaborative research in various ways. The need for supporting individual and team-based research processes is outlined in *part I*, the introduction. In the introduction, the suitability of social software, the latest generation of tools in the development of the CSCW field, for supporting collaborative processes, is also established.

In a broad and comprehensive overview of research on both collaborative research and social software in *part II*, a systematic literature review that covers a timeframe from 2000 to 2016, the need for further research on the characteristics and properties of *social research networking sites (SRNS)*, a subclass of social software-based applications that started to emerge around the year 2008, is identified.

The subsequent *part III* shows by a thorough and framework-guided analysis of eight SRNS platforms including interviews with their founders (encompassing well-known and widely used platforms like *Academia.edu, ResearchGate, and Mendeley*, platforms that were discontinued due to lack of success, as well as a recently emerged collaborative platform named *Trellis*) that there are many unique ways in which scholars can be supported in various aspects of their research-related work. In addition, *part III* also presents a typology of SRNS platforms developed in this dissertation. It is shown that in the first phase around the initial launch of these SRNS platforms, it was possible to make a clear association between an SRNS platform and a certain type. In the course of the further development of those platforms that survived and prospered, they took on additional functionalities from the other functionality clusters, while still continuing to exhibit a main type.

However, merely looking at the features and affordances of SRNS platforms as well as at the use their founders intended for their platforms is not sufficient to fully understand these novel services. A more holistic view on these platforms is required to shed light on how they are actually being used by scholars, their target audience, and to understand the reasons why researchers adopt and continue to use these platforms. Therefore, *part IV* takes the perspective of the users of these SRNS platforms by an in-depth case study with 19 researchers stemming from the field of management research in order to provide a more holistic understanding of these platforms by taking the users into account as well.

This final *part V* of this dissertation is organized as follows. This chapter provides a summary along with the contributions of *parts I* to *IV*. Chapter 2 presents a holistic view of the practical implications for five different groups of addressees – research policymakers and funding agencies, research managers, doctoral students and advisors, individual scholars and academic research teams, and providers of SRNS platforms. Finally, directions for future research in the fields of research collaboration, social software, particularly on social research networking sites, are presented in chapter 3.

1.1 Summary of Part I

In part I, first the critical importance of *research collaboration* for producing scientific advancement in today's knowledge and information societies was systematically derived based on a broad foundation of supporting publications and statements made by science policy organizations. In addition, the challenges associated with increased collaboration in research are also elucidated. These challenges encompass many different activities like setting up research collaborations, finding the right partners, dividing labor between researchers, monitoring and coordinating progress within virtual teams, and many more tasks that also pose difficult issues related to communication, coordination, and collaboration. As a result, virtual teams of researchers can greatly benefit from state-of-the-art collaboration technology to mitigate the negative effects of non-colocation and distance (Arinze, 2012; Walsh & Maloney, 2007; Cummings & Kiesler, 2007). There is an abundance of research regarding the use of collaboration technology in a corporate environment. Leveraging collaboration technology to support individual scholars and virtual teams of researchers working in academia is far less researched, apart from studies investigating basic communication and collaboration technologies like e-Mail

(Vasileiadou & Vliegenthart, 2009), the impact of which on collaboration productivity is furthermore disputed. Therefore, the need for further research on how to support researchers is recognized and research questions that lead the process of inquiry within this thesis are established.

1.2 Summary of Part II

In part II, a state-of-the-literature report on research results both on *research collaboration* and *social software* was provided. This was necessary, since extant research in the field is heavily fragmented, due to various factors. The substantial and long-standing body of research addressing research collaboration is extremely scattered and split into various strands due to the multi-leveled, interdisciplinary, and complex nature of the phenomenon *research collaboration*. As far as *social software* is concerned, the literature base on this new generation of CSCW tools evolved very fast in recent years since the emergence of the technology approximately ten years ago[107], making it difficult for researchers trying to get a comprehensive overview of the field. To bring together findings from these two fields in a comprehensive fashion within one document, this literature review systematically identified 92 publication in the area of research collaboration and 511 papers in the field of social software resulting from a *manual screening* of 51 journals and conferences within the timeframe of 2000 to 2016. The 92 publications related to research collaboration were classified into four broad categories: (1) the *macro-level perspective*, (2) the *meso-level perspective*, (3) the *micro-level perspective*, and (4) the *technological perspective*. The *technological perspective* showed some overlap with the second research field, *social software*[108]. The 511 publications that were affiliated with *social software* were classified into seven major categories: (1) *theoretical view*, (2) *social and behavioural view*, (3) *organizational view*, (4) *design view*, (5) *business view*, (6) *political view*, and (7) *academic use view*. Research in each of these categories was summarized and based on thematic fields, links, and interactions, a fine-grained sub-categorization of the two fields was developed and presented.

[107] see section 2.4 of part II on the occurrences of the first publications on *social software*

[108] Publications that showed up in both fields were classified within the research field they exhibited a stronger affiliation to

Furthermore, a discussion and reflection on the findings were presented with respect to the research methods used and the pervasiveness of literature. The systematic literature review concluded with the identification of dominant research gaps within the two areas of *research collaboration* and *social software* and directions for future research were provided. The literature review concluded that a call for more research on the structure of scientific collaborations and the beneficial role of collaboration and communication technologies in reducing the challenges with collaborative research (Walsh and Maloney, 2007), remains largely unanswered up to now. In parallel to the academic discussion calling for more research on how to support collaborative research, several enthusiastic researchers and individuals have created platforms built on social software and social networking technology, a development that happened largely unnoticed by academia and was underrepresented in the traditional publication channels like journals and conferences. Thus, the research questions

> *What is the current state of technology regarding social software tools specifically relevant to an academic audience? What is their intended use by their providers and can they further be classified according to their functionalities and intended use?*

are investigated in detail in the following part. A summary of the systematic literature conducted within part II of this thesis is provided in table 75.

Table 75: Summary of part II

Study	Part II – Systematic Literature Review: Research Collaboration and Social Software
Research questions	• What is the current state-of-the-art regarding collaborative research and social software? • Are these fields interlinked? • What are research gaps and directions for future research?
Method used	• Systematic literature review
Sample	• 92 publications in the area of *research collaboration* and 511 publications in the area of *social software* identified in a process of manual screening of 51 journals and conferences within the timeframe of the years 2000 - 2016
Results	• Development of a fine-grained subcategorization of the two fields • Social software and social networking services facilitate collaboration and communication in a corporate environment • Call for more research on the structure of scientific collaborations and the beneficial role of collaboration and communication technologies in reducing the challenges with collaborative research remains largely unanswered up to now

Research framework

Implications	• Research in both areas is heavily fragmented, literature review can help contribute to bridging the gaps • Key features of an emerging class of social software and social networking based tools need to be researched in what way they make these platforms relevant to an academic audience and how they can support researchers in research-related tasks, whether they occur within collaborative research projects or in research processes carried out by individual scientists

1.3 Summary of Part III

Part III focused on answering the research questions resulting from the fact that the emergence of a novel kind of platform intended to support researchers in various research-related tasks occurred largely unnoticed by research and was consequently largely underrepresented in scientific publications:

What is the current state of technology regarding social software tools specifically relevant to an academic audience? What is their intended use by their providers and can they further be classified according to their functionalities and intended use?

To achieve this, first, a framework for the analysis of the characteristics and features of social research networking sites was established. This basis for the analysis builds on previous publications by the author of this dissertation and combines independent work into a framework to analyze both the social networking-related and the research (collaboration) support-related aspects of these research tools. This framework is then subsequently used to analyze eight academic social networking platforms in a case study following a multi-case design with embedded units of analysis which are the social networking-related aspects and the research support-related aspects and the intended use of the platforms according to their founders. An in-depth cross-case analysis of the eight cases demonstrates that a considerable variation among the platforms exists. While some of the platforms have become quite mature and also have become quite successful from a business viewpoint, it also becomes evident that taking only features and intended use into account is not sufficient to provide a holistic and comprehensive understanding of these platforms. It is therefore necessary to study the question of how and why these platforms are actually being used by researchers, a purpose the subsequent part is dedicated to. A summary of part III is provided in table 76.

Table 76: Summary of part III

Study	Part III – Empirical Study 1: Social Research Networking Services – Market Overview, Features, and Functions
Research question	• What is the current state of technology regarding social software tools specifically relevant to an academic audience? What is their intended use by their providers and can they further be classified according to their functionalities and intended use?
Method used	• Exploratory qualitative case study design
Sample	• Eight social research networking sites (SRNS), drawing on a multitude of data including interviews with the founders of the platforms (among other secondary sources)
Results	• Identification of key functionalities of the platforms in two areas (academic social networking and support for (collaborative) research on the individual and the team level • Platforms vary considerably from each other in their social networking features as well as in their functionalities regarding research support • Collaborative features are the least developed aspect in most of the platforms • A typology for SRNS platforms has been elaborated
Research framework	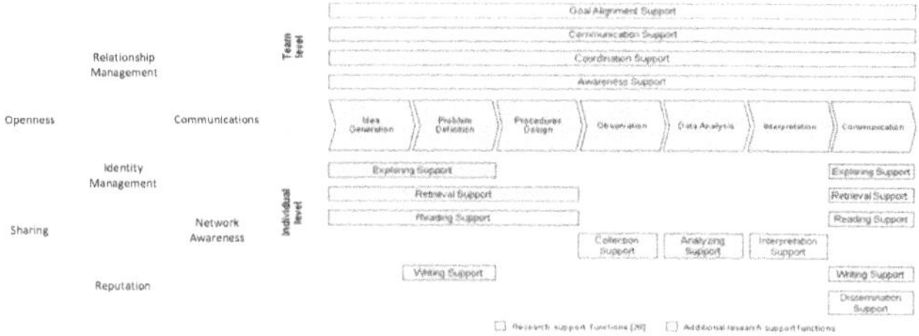
Implications	• Openness of the platform is critical, as well as a holistic understanding of how and why researchers adopt and use these platforms

1.4 Summary of Part IV

Part IV deals with answering the research gaps that the case study analysis of part III gave rise to. It is motivated by the fact that looking only at the feature-related aspects and the intended use as envisioned by the founders and providers of the SRNS platforms is not sufficient to provide a holistic and comprehensive understanding of this novel class of tools. Instead, the perspective of users also needs to be taken into account. Therefore, part IV is led by the research question:

How and why do management researchers use social research networking services?

In order to answer this question, part IV resorts to two influential theoretical frameworks that have been applied successfully in previous studies investigating the adoption and usage continuance of social media: uses and gratifications theory (UGT) and social influence (SI) processes framework. Since the research presented in part IV is of an explorative nature due to the newness of the phenomenon of social research networking services and their adoption, a qualitative research method is adopted. Due to a lack of comprehensive empirical material and the research concerning this topic being in an incipient phase, the case study methodology is chosen. In total, 19 semi-structured interviews with scholars from the field of management research stemming from different institutions, countries, and continents were conducted. The findings from an in-depth analysis of the interviews were combined with an investigation of the profiles of the interviewees within the research platforms to enrich the data collection. Analysis and iterative comparison of the data yielded several distinct and interesting findings regarding why academics coming from the field of management research are using platforms in the way they do it. The main use cases uncovered during the analysis phase were consumption and sharing of information. Actual research collaboration was relatively rare and has only been identified in a few cases. The findings also shed light on the gratifications underlying the adoption and use of SRNS platforms. Apart from the previously mentioned consumption of information, the main gratifications identified were self-promotion within the platform and one's academic community, and social interaction and increasing the feeling of belonging to a professional community. Other types of gratifications like using the platform for enjoyment or as an outlet for escapism proved to be largely irrelevant, which is in line with previous research on the topic. Theoretical, as well as practical insights, were derived and opportunities for future research were also established in part IV. Table 77 provides a summary of part IV.

Table 77: Summary of part IV

Study	Part IV – Empirical Study 2: How and Why Do Management Researchers Use Social Research Networking Sites?
Research question	• How and why do management researchers use social research networking services?
Method used	• Exploratory qualitative case study design
Sample	• Nineteen case studies comprised of semi-structured interviews with experienced users of social research networking sites (SRNS) platforms coming with an academic background as management researchers and an analysis of their profiles within one or several SRNS platforms
Results	• The main use cases are consumption and sharing of information • Actual research collaboration within the platform is rare • Apart from information consumption, further identified gratifications that influence adoption and use are self-promotion within the platform and the academic community, and social interaction and increasing a feeling of belonging to a professional community
Theory used	• Uses and Gratifications Theory (UGT) • Social Influence (SI) Processes Framework
Implications	• Currently available SRNS platforms partially lack features to encourage academics to use these platforms for collaboration • Some platforms do not sufficiently cater to important gratifications that could help propel further adoption of the platforms

Part V concludes this dissertation by providing a summary of contributions. In addition, it provides a comprehensive view of the implications for practice for five different groups of addressees and directions for future research based on the results of the three research studies (part II – part IV). These are presented in the following two chapters.

2 Implications for Practice

This thesis has focused on shedding light on a new class of social software-based collaborative systems called *social research networking sites*. These services were created out of the need for further and additional support in research-related processes and tasks of individual researchers and (virtual) teams of researchers working together in collaborative research projects. Based on the results of the preceding systematic literature review and two empirical studies, this chapter presents implications derived from these studies for different audiences.

2.1 Implications for Research Policy Makers and Funding Agencies

Performing research has recently become a highly social and collaborative endeavor due to several factors like the growing interdisciplinarity of research projects, enormous resource requirements in certain disciplines, and the necessary increase in specialization of researchers (Haeussler and Sauermann, 2013; Katz and Martin, 1997; Laudel, 2002). In addition to changes in the scope and size of collaborative research projects, the traditional organization of science is undergoing changes as well and a growing share of research is performed in an open collaborative fashion (Möslein et al., 2009; Franzoni and Sauermann, 2014). Research policy agencies like the "European Research Council" (ERC) or similar organizations have been established for or tasked with supporting collaborative research (Nedeva, 2013). Policymakers and funding agencies should look into the affordances provided by the SRNS platforms to investigate if these affordances can help contribute to their missions and goals. Due to the far-reaching effects of policy-level decisions and the high complexity of the phenomenon *research collaboration*, further research is surely warranted.

2.2 Implications for Research Managers

It is important for research managers to understand what social research networking sites are able to offer to make collaboration and exchange within their research group more efficient and effective. To help research managers get a grasp of what these platforms can offer in terms of functionality, four clusters of functionalities have been empirically identified from an in-depth analysis of interviews and case studies. Table 78 briefly sums up these functionality clusters together with their key value proposition.

Table 78: Functionality clusters of social research networking sites and their key value propositions

Primary functionality manifestation	**Key value proposition**
Research directory	Identifying other researchers, e.g. as potential partners in collaborative research, or applying for grants
Research awareness	Staying aware of developments in one's field and about activities of scholarly peers
Research management	Management of routine research tasks, e.g. references, structuring research
Research collaboration	Supporting virtual teams in research collaboration, facilitating a joint overarching research process

After having gained an overview of tools suitable for their needs, the next step is to find out whether a specific tool is the right one for a particular project. According to recommendations given by Salustri and Weerasinghe (2010), mandating the usage of the tool is the next step. However, the adoption and oftentimes non-adoption of software systems presents a complex problem. According to Renken (2012), several steps can help mitigate the non-acceptance of technology and ultimately drive adoption. Research managers need to develop an implementation strategy, inform their users about the benefits of the tool, and provide introductory trainings if an SRNS platform should become a mandatory part of conducting research activities (Renken, 2012).

In addition to implementing such tools within one's own research group to improve the efficiency and effectiveness of group processes, they can also be of help in various other tasks that research managers are typically involved with. One potential application of these tools can be to facilitate securing funding within the competitive academic grant system, by implementing a more efficient and effective way of identifying grants and winning them. This includes new possibilities to help identify opportunities, provide new interconnections with other researchers, and leverage a low-cost research infrastructure (Duffy, 2010).

2.3 Implications for Doctoral Students and Doctoral Advisors

Implementing and using an SRNS platform can be an enabler for process improvements in many research-related tasks and areas. One aspect that can profit from new affordances and facilitation through technology is managing a doctoral program and the ongoing development and supervision of doctoral students (Zaman, 2010). SRNS platforms and even basic social software tools like a blog can help doctoral students to accelerate and professionalize their research process by creating a community of peer reviewers, interacting with other researchers by getting comments on draft work published on the platform and using these results in creating their dissertation (Willard & Leffingwell, 2010). According to Zaman (2010), the management of doctoral programs can profit from the use of SRNS platforms in several ways: doctoral advisors can gain increased awareness of what their PhD students are working on and the progress they are making, and doctoral students can find research partners by creating a network and build social capital (which can be also helpful later on in their career). In addition, an SRNS platform that supports research management and research collaboration, e.g. by providing wiki-like functionalities, can help in systematically documenting unstructured information like ideas generated during the PhD process.

2.4 Implications for Individual Scholars and Academic Research Teams

Conducting research facilitated by SRNS platforms holds several benefits for individual scholars and (virtual) teams of researchers. Several research-related tasks are facilitated due to the rich set of features exposed by these platforms and new possibilities and affordances that did not exist before the advent of these tools have been created. Specifically, connecting with other researchers, communicating with one's researcher partners, and engaging in collaborative research are greatly facilitated (Brunvand & Duran, 2010). However, since the affordances differ greatly from tool to tool as has been shown in part III of this thesis, researchers have to choose which tool(s) they will use in their own research and within their research group. As has been pointed out in the previous parts, factors like open APIs, exportability, and interoperability should definitely be taken into account. Committing on a single platform as a "one-stop-shop" that seemingly offers most or all of the desired functionalities can come at the high price of vendor lock-in and create issues later on as highlighted by den Besten et al. (2010). After having committed to an SRNS platform considering the afore-mentioned caveats, research teams can profit from having an experienced user on their team that can help colleagues with using the new technology and facilitating the transition to a new way of conducting research, thus helping to mitigate user resistance to new technology (Renken, 2012).

2.5 Implications for SRNS Platform Providers

The SRNS platforms under scrutiny within this thesis offer a wide and fascinating range of affordances not available before the advent of this technology. Since the first platforms came up around the year 2008, there has been a consolidation among the SRNS platforms with some promising platforms having been discontinued and disappearing from the field. While the still-existing major platforms have reached a sophisticated level of maturity, the functionality cluster least developed is the actual support of ongoing collaborative research. This is particularly surprising, since previously existing (and now discontinued) platforms, already showed good initial ideas and displayed promising affordances in that area. Existing SRNS providers should strive to address this functionality gap in their platforms. Due to the already developed and rather mature market of SRNS platforms, it might be difficult for new market entrants to establish a broad user base. In addition, since all the major platforms have been criticized publicly for several reasons like a business model that contradicts open-access philosophy, unethical behavior in trying to attract new users, the providers of SRNS platforms need to find a suitable long-term business model that does not repel researchers and institutions and establish a level of credibility to ensure trust. Becoming more transparent regarding their internal mechanisms (like reputation scores), and providing open APIs and exportability of data stored within the platform seem suitable steps to establish a higher level of trust and dispel existing criticism.

Establishing a sense of confidence and trust into their platform as a safe repository of sensitive data and knowledge is of paramount importance to the providers, as scientists need to be assured that the data they put into the platforms are secured, and the exchanges they conduct within the system will stay accessible (Brunvand & Duran, 2010). The next priority should be expanding on the affordances exposed by the platform, especially regarding the support of collaborative research processes, since there is great usage potential to be harvested in mitigating the detrimental effects of distance and non-colocation on virtual teams of researchers (Cummings & Kiesler, 2007; Walsh & Maloney, 2007). In addition, building on the results elaborated in part IV of this thesis, taking potential gratifications into account should be a priority for SRNS providers, since failing to cater to these gratifications might very likely lead to an insufficient adoption within the target audience.

3 Directions for Future Research

Conducting research with the use of virtual environments and a distributed network of resources and stakeholders is still in its infancy and presents a fertile area for research to be conducted in order to better understand how research in the digital age can and will be different. This *chapter* is therefore dedicated to highlighting areas that require and are especially conducive to further research. According to Huff (2008), management research constitutes an ongoing discussion between scholars to help foster an understanding of relevant phenomena and to contribute to an advancement of knowledge. This dissertation is also part of a broader discussion: it has built on previous research by other scholars and the research gaps identified in their contributions to the discussion underlying this thesis. In the hope of furthering the discussion, this thesis concludes by pointing out research gaps that might help further the understanding of the phenomenon of *social research networking sites* and the enclosing areas of *research collaboration* and *social software*. Hence, this chapter presents directions for future research identified within this dissertation. These directions are presented in the following.

A systematic literature review of a total of 603 publications identified over a period of 17 years from 2000-2016 integrated widely scattered research in two focal areas: *research collaboration* (amounting to 92 publications included in the literature review) and *social software* (511 included papers). The analysis conducted on these 603 publications has revealed that the overall body of research in both areas is broken down and fragmented into separate streams with little interlinkages between some of the research streams. Regarding the phenomenon of *research collaboration,* this fragmentation is understandable, as the discussion takes place within several levels of analysis (macro, meso, micro, and a technological perspective) and the lenses employed in the analysis of the phenomenon are also stemming from different disciplines (Sonnenwald, 2007) as diverse as sociology, research policy, philosophy of science, as well as more practice-oriented disciplines like management research and information systems, that inform the perspective of this thesis. With *social software,* research is similarly broken down into silos, probably due to the newness of the research field and the rapid publication frequency, especially within conferences.

The systematic literature review identified research gaps in each of the four large categories dealing with the publications in the area of *research collaboration*, and in the seven overarching categories that structure the publications in the field of *social software*. In the following, some major research gaps for the two fields are listed in the following two tables below. For a more detailed discussion, the reader should refer to *part II* of this thesis.

Table 79: Research gaps identified in the systematic literature review regarding research collaboration

Category of research	Some important gaps identified for future research
Macro-level perspective	• Are the theories valid that explain the immense growth of international collaboration? • How can challenges associated with ensuring fairness and accountability within our networked scientific system be resolved? • How can changes our scientific system is currently undergoing be better understood and conceptualized?
Meso-level perspective	• What are the outcomes and impact of university-industry collaborations? • How can university research centers contribute to solving scientific problems and foster collaboration among researchers? • What are the long-term consequences of collaborations between multiple universities?
Micro-level perspective	• Further research should be conducted to shed more light on the phenomenon of *research productivity*, as it is only poorly understood • How can technological support increase research productivity? • How can interdisciplinary research management be organized to mitigate challenges associated with coordination?
Technological perspective	• How can institutional and social obstacles to sharing research tools, data, and results be overcome? • What are the specific collaborative practices of different scientific disciplines and how can they be supported by technology?

Table 80: Research gaps identified in the systematic literature review regarding social software

Category of research	Some important gaps identified for future research
Theoretical view	• What features are required to create the next generation of the Web, *Web 3.0*? • How can organizations make use of opportunities and mitigate threats inherent in the social web?
Social and behavioural view	• Which usage patterns of social media contribute to the formation of bridging and bonding social capital? • How do the properties of social media influence self-presentation and information disclosure?
Organizational view	• What is the impact of Enterprise 2.0 systems on employees? • What are the factors influencing the organizational adoption of social software?
Design view	• What are design principles that can provide guidance in the development of social software? • How can social software tools be best designed to facilitate collaboration?
Business view	• How can a firms' customer base be identified in social media? • What is the effect of implicit or explicit electronic word of mouth in social commerce? • How can corporate risk management frameworks be extended to deal with social media?
Political view	• What is the role of social media in political systems? • How can social media and social networking services be used to promote political discussions?
Academic use view	• How can educators leverage social software tools to enhance teaching and learning processes? • What are the features and affordances of the novel class of social networking services that have recently emerged, what use cases do they allow and what are the motivations of their providers?

Research conducted in *empirical study 1* presented an in-depth analysis of features and affordances of a sample of currently available and also now-defunct social research networking services. While the analysis of these features was straightforward on a superficial level, a cross-analysis of the cases, and taking into account the reaction of the academic community to these tools, many questions were raised that warrant future research in diverse areas. Some of the most important questions that require answers are:

- How can the contradiction and tension between the open-access philosophy promoted by the platforms and their lack of openness be resolved?
- As some of the platforms provide novel reputation tracking mechanisms, does the academic reputation system need an overhaul as a whole in the era of collaborative research and alternative forms of publication enabled by the Web 2.0?
- Is the academic reputation system as it is still valid and up-to-date nowadays?
- Is the much-criticized business model of academic publishing houses still valid today?

It is obvious that some of these questions reach deeply into our scientific system and will not be answered in a satisfactory manner in the near future. However, a discussion about our current academic reputation system and also the business model of academic publishing is inevitable, already going on since many years, and is probably being fueled further by the advent of the social research networking services discussed within this thesis, as they make existing shortfall within the system even more visible. Finally, findings from *empirical study 2* shed more light on these novel services by providing a thorough investigation into usage patterns and gratifications derived from their use by analyzing data from case studies with management researchers. By drawing upon a rich data set including in-depth interviews with researchers and an analysis of their profiles within these platforms, it allows for a more holistic understanding of the antecedents of adoption and use and complements the insights gained within *empirical study 1*. In general, the study has shown that uses and gratifications need to be taken more into account in order to explain why some platforms are more successful than others and platform providers should ingest these findings to further improve their offerings. In the field of *research collaboration*, further research should address what is the contribution of these social research networking services to solving challenges regarding the management of collaborative research projects and how these platforms can be further improved to be of more substantial value in supporting individual and collaborative research.

References

J.-H. Soeldner, *Understanding Social Research Networking Sites*,
Markt- und Unternehmensentwicklung Markets and Organisations,
https://doi.org/10.1007/978-3-658-31575-7

References

Abrahams, A. S., Jiao, J., Fan, W., Wang, G. A., & Zhang, Z. (2013). What's buzzing in the blizzard of buzz? Automotive component isolation in social media postings. *Decision Support Systems*, 55(4), 871-882.

Abramowicz, W., Fensel, D., & Frank, U. (2010). Semantik und Web 2.0 zur Unterstützung eines leistungsfähigen Geschäftsprozessmanagements. *Wirtschaftsinformatik*, 52(1), 1-2.

Ada, S., Rao, H. R., & Sharman, R. (2010). Online social networking site (SNS) use at the campus emergencies. *Proceedings of the 31st International Conference on Information Systems (ICIS)*, St. Louis, USA, paper 203.

Adamopoulos, P., & Todri, V. (2014). Social Media Analytics: The Effectiveness of Promotional Events on Brand User Base in Social Media. *Icis-Rp*, (Rubel 2006), 1–10.

Adams, C. (2011). Social networking and extending social capacity. *Proceedings of the 32nd International Conference on Information Systems (ICIS)*, Shanghai, China, paper 5.

Adams, J. D., Black, G. C., Clemmons, J. R., & Stephan, P. E. (2005). Scientific teams and institutional collaborations: evidence from U.S. universities, 1981-1999. *Research Policy*, 34(3), 259-285.

Aghakhani, N., & Karimi, J. (2013). Acceptance on implicit and explicit eWOM: a factor based study of social networking sites. *Proceedings of the 34th International Conference on Information Systems (ICIS)*, Milan, Italy.

Ahmed, A. (2011). Use of social media in disaster management. *Proceedings of the 32nd International Conference on Information Systems (ICIS)*, Shanghai, China.

Alalwan, J. A. (2014). Recruiters ' Intention to Adopt Social Information Systems. *Recruiters' Intention to Adopt Social Information Systems*, 1–10.

Alfaro, I., Bhattacharyya, S., Highlander, J., Sampath, S. M., & Watson-Manheim, M. B. (2012). Opening the social media black box – a feature-based approach. *Proceedings of the 20th European Conference on Information Systems (ECIS)*, Barcelona, Spain, paper 119.

Alfaro, I., Bhattacharyya, S., & Watson-Manheim, M. B. (2013). Organizational adoption of social media in the USA: a mixed method approach. *Proceedings of the 21st European Conference on Information Systems (ECIS)*, Utrecht, Netherlands, paper 201. [351]

Albert, C. S., & Salam, A. F. (2013). Critical discourse analysis: toward theories in social media. *Proceedings of the 19th Americas Conference on Information Systems (AMCIS)*, Chicago, USA.

Albors, J., Ramos, J. C., & Hervas, J. L. (2008). New learning network paradigms: communities of objectives, crowdsourcing, wikis and open source. *International Journal of Information Management, 28*, 194-202.

Al-Debei, M. M., Al-Lozi, E., & Papazafeiropoulou, A. (2013). Why people keep coming back to Facebook: explaining and predicting continuance participation from an extended theory of planned behaviour perspective. *Decision Support Systems*, 55(3), 43-54.

Ali-Hassan, H., & Nevo, D. (2009). Identifying social computing dimensions: a multidimensional scaling study. *Proceedings of the 30th International Conference on Information Systems (ICIS)*, Phoenix, USA, paper 148.

Ali-Hassan, H., Nevo, D., & Wade, M. (2015). Linking dimensions of social media use to job performance: The role of social capital. *The Journal of Strategic Information Systems*, 24(2), 65-89.

Allen, J. P., Rosenbaum, H., & Shachaf, P. (2007). Web 2.0: a social informatics perspective. *Proceedings of the 13th American Conference on Information Systems (AMCIS)*, Keystone, USA, paper 350.

Almeripour, A., Nicholson, B., & Newman, M. (2010). Conviviality of internet social networks: an exploratory study of internet campaigns in Iran. *Journal of Information Technology*, 25(2), 244-257.

Alqahtani, F. H., Watson, J., & Partridge, H. (2013). Employees' Adoption of Enterprise Web 2.0: The Role of Technological Attributes. *PACIS 2013 Proceedings*.

Alt, R., & Wittwer, M. (2014). Towards an ontology-based approach for social media analysis. In *ECIS 2014 Proceedings - 22nd European Conference on Information Systems*.

Amabile, T. M., Patterson, C., Mueller, J. S., Wojcik, T., Odomirok, P. W., Marsh, M., & Kramer, S. J. (2001). Academic-practitioner collaboration in management research: a case of cross-professional collaboration. *Academy of Management Journal*, 44(2), 418–431.

Amirtharajan, M., Radhika, L., & Rayappan, I. B. B. (2014). Is Facebook-A Global Library? *Information Technology Journal, 13*(12), 2027-2031.

Annabi, H., & McGann, S. T. (2013). Social media as the missing link: connecting communities of practice to business strategy. *Journal of Organizational Computing and Electronic Commerce, 23*(1-2), 56-83.

Aoun, C., Chew, E., & Vatanasakdakul, S. (2014). Beyond Speculation : A Holistic Investigation into Factors Affecting Social Media Utilisation in the Workplace. *Twentieth Americas Conference on Information Systems*, 1–12.

Appleford, S., Bottum, J. R., & Thatcher, J. B. (2014). Understanding the social web: towards defining an interdisciplinary research agenda for information systems. *Acm Sigmis Database, 45*(1), 29-37.

Arakji, R., Benbunan-Fich, R., & Koufaris, M. (2009). Exploring contributions of public resources in social bookmarking systems. *Decision Support Systems, 47*(3), 245-253.

Arazy, O., & Gellatly, I. R. (2012). Corporate wikis: the effects of owners' motivation and behavior on group members' engagement. *Journal of Management Information Systems, 29*(3), 87-116.

Argyris, Y. A., & Monu, K. (2015). Corporate use of social media: Technology affordance and external stakeholder relations. *Journal of Organizational Computing and Electronic Commerce, 25*(2), 140-168.

Arinze, B. (2012). E-Research Collaboration in Academia and Industry. *International Journal of E-Collaboration, 8*(2), 1–13.

Aron, D. (2009). Dynamic collaboration: a personal reflection. *Journal of Information Technology, 24*, 214-218.

Aronson, E., Timothy, D., & Akert, R. (2010). *Social psychology*. Upper Saddle River, NJ: Prentice Hall.

Ba, S., & Wang, L. (2013). Digital health communities: the effect of their motivation mechanisms. *Decision Support Systems, 55*(4), 941-947.

Bächle, M. (2007). Ökonomische Perspektiven des Web 2.0 – Open Innovation, Social Commerce und Enterprise 2.0. *Wirtschaftsinformatik, 50*(2), 129-132.

Bagozzi, R., & Dholakia, U. (2002). Intentional social action in virtual communities. *Journal of Interactive Marketing, 16*(2), 2–21.

Banal-Estañol, A., Jofre-Bonet, M., & Lawson, C. (2015). The double-edged sword of industry collaboration: Evidence from engineering academics in the UK. *Research Policy, 44*(6), 1160-1175.

Bao, H., Li, Q., Liao, S. S., Song, S., & Gao, H. (2013). A new temporal and social PMF-based method to predict users' interests in micro-blogging. *Decision Support Systems, 55*(3), 698-709.

Barham, B. L., Foltz, J. D., & Prager, D. L. (2014). Making time for science. *Research Policy, 43*(1), 21-31.

Barjak, F., Eccles, K., Meyer, E. T., Schroeder, R., & Robinson, S. (2013). The emerging governance of e-infrastructure. *Journal of Computer-Mediated Communication, 18*(2), 113-136.

Baruffaldi, S., Visentin, F., & Conti, A. (2016). The productivity of science & engineering PhD students hired from supervisors' networks. *Research Policy, 45*(4), 785-796.

Beaver, D., 2001. Reflections on scientific collaboration (and its study): past, present and future. *Scientometrics 52*, 365–377.

Beaver, D., Rosen, R., 1978. Studies in scientific collaboration. Part I. *Scientometrics 1*, 65–84.

Beaver, D., Rosen, R., 1979a. Studies in scientific collaboration. Part II. *Scientometrics 1*, 133–149.

Beaver, D., Rosen, R., 1979b. Studies in scientific collaboration. Part III. *Scientometrics 1*, 231–245.

Becker, J., Knackstedt, R., Lis, L., & Stein, A. (2010). Towards a maturity model for research portals. *Proceedings of the 18th European Conference on Information Systems (ECIS)*, Pretoria, South Africa, paper 38.

Beer, D. (2008). Social network(ing) sites…revisiting the story so far: a response to danah boyd & Nicole Ellison. *Journal of Computer-Mediated Communication, 13*(2), 516-529.

Beerkens, M. (2013). Facts and fads in academic research management: the effect of management practices on research productivity in Australia. *Research Policy, 42*(9), 1679-1693.

Behrendt, S., Klier, M., Klier, J., Richter, A., & Wiesneth, K. (2015). The Impact of Formal Hierarchies on Enterprise Social Networking Behavior. *Icis*, 1–19.

Benbasat, I., Goldstein, D., & Mead, M. (1987). The case research strategy in studies of information systems. *MIS Quarterly 11*(3), 369–386.

Benbasat, I., Barki, H. (2007). Quo vadis, TAM? *Journal of the Association of Information Systems, 8*(4), 211-218

Benlian, A., Hess, T. (2008). Supporting global software development with Web 2.0 technologies – insights from an empirical study. *Proceedings of the 14th Americas Conference on Information Systems (AMCIS)*, Toronto, Canada, paper 294.

Bente, S., Karla, J. (2009). Enterprise social network platforms as a management tool in complex technical systems. *Proceedings of the 15th Americas Conference on Information Systems (AMCIS)*, San Francisco, USA, paper 545.

Benthaus, J. (2014). Making the right impression for corporate reputation: Analyzing impression management of financial institutions in social media. *ECIS 2014 Proceedings*.

Benthaus, J., Risius, M., & Beck, R. (2016). Social media management strategies for organizational impression management and their effect on public perception. *The Journal of Strategic Information Systems, 25*(2), 127-139.

Bercovitz, J., & Feldman, M. (2011). The mechanisms of collaboration in inventive teams: Composition, social networks, and geography. *Research Policy, 40*(1), 81–93.

Berger, K., Klier, J., Klier, M., & Probst, F. (2014). A Review of information systems research on online social networks. *Communications of the Association for Information Systems 35*. 145–72.

Berger, K., Klier, J., Klier, M., & Richter, A. (2014). "Who is key...?" - Value adding users in enterprise social networks. In *22nd European Conference on Information Systems* (pp. 1–16)

Bernius, S. (2010). Speeding up the spiral: analysis of the effects of open access on scientific knowledge creation. *Proceedings of the 18th European Conference on Information Systems (ECIS)*, Pretoria, South Africa, paper 155.

Bertolotti, F., Mattarelli, E., Vignoli, M., & Macrì, D. M. (2015). Exploring the relationship between multiple team membership and team performance: The role of social networks and collaborative technology. *Research Policy, 44*(4), 911-924.

Bharati, P., Chaudhury, A., & Zhang, W. (2012). Building organizational knowledge quality: investigating the role of social media and social capital. *Proceedings of the 18th Americas Conference on Information Systems (AMCIS)*, Seattle, USA, paper 10.

Bibbo, D., Sprehe, E., Michelich, J., & Lee, Y. E. (2010). Employing wiki as a collaborative information repository in a media and entertainment company: the NBC universal case. *Proceedings of the 31st International Conference on Information Systems (ICIS)*, St. Louis, USA, paper 244.

Binder, J., Howes, A., & Sutcliffe, A. (2009). The problem of conflicting social spheres: effects of network structure on experienced tension in social network sites. *Proceedings of the SIGCHI Conference on Human Factors in Computing Systems*, 965-974.

Birnholtz, J. P., Horn, D. B. (2007). Shake, rattle and roles: lessons from experimental earthquake engineering for incorporating remote users in large-scale e-science experiments. *Journal of Computer-Mediated Communication, 12*(2), article 17.

Blinn, N., Lindermann, N., Faecks, K., & Nuettgens, M. (2009). Web 2.0 in SME networks – a design science approach considering multi-perspective requirements. *Proceedings of the 15th Americas Conference on Information Systems*, San Francisco, USA, paper 402.

Blinn, N., & Nüttgens, M. (2010). Web 2.0 in SME networks – a design science approach considering multi-perspective requirements. *Journal of Information Science and Technology, 7*(1), 3-21.

Blumler, J. G. (1979). The Role of Theory in Uses and Gratifications Studies. *Communication Research, 6*(1), 9–36.

Boardman, P. C. (2009). Government centrality to university – industry interactions: university research centers and the industry involvement of academic researchers. *Research Policy, 38*(10), 1505-1516.

Boardman, P. C., & Corley, E. A. (2008). University research centers and the composition of research collaborations. *Research Policy, 37*(5), 900-913.

Boateng, R., Malik, A., & Mbarika, V. (2009). Web 2.0 and organizational learning: conceptualizing the link. *Proceedings of the 15th Americas Conference on Information Systems*, San Francisco, USA, paper 546.

Borgman, C. L. (2006). What can studies of e-learning teach us about collaboration in e-research? Some findings from digital library studies. *Computer Supported Cooperative Work, 15*, 359-383.

Bos, N., Zimmerman, A., Olson, J., & Yew, J. (2007). From shared databases to communities of practice: a taxonomy of collaboratories. *Journal of Computer-Mediated Communication, 12*(2), article 16.

Bouman, W., de Bruin, B., Hoogenboom, T., Huizing, A., Jansen, R., & Schoondorp, M. (2007). The realm of sociality: notes on the design of social software. *Proceedings of the 28th Conference on Information Systems*, Montreal, Canada, paper 154.

Boyd, D. M., & Ellison, N. B. (2007). Social network sites: definition, history, and scholarship. *Journal of Computer-Mediated Communication, 13*(1), 210-230.

Bozeman, B., & Boardman, C. (2014). The outputs, outcomes and impacts of research collaboration (pp. 33-45). https://doi.org/10.1007/978-3-319-06468-0_4

Bozeman, B., & Corley, E. (2004). Scientists' collaboration strategies: implications for scientific and technical human capital. *Research Policy, 33*(4), 599-616.

Bozeman, B., & Gaughan, M. (2011). How do men and women differ in research collaborations? An analysis of the collaborative motives and strategies of academic researchers. *Research Policy, 40*(10), 1393-1402.

Brandzaeg, P. B. (2012). Social networking sites: their users and social implications – a longitudinal study. *Journal of Computer-Mediated Communication, 17*(4), 467-488.

Braun, V., Clarke, V. (2006). Using thematic analysis in psychology. *Qualitative Research in Psychology* 3(2): 77–101.

Braun, R., & Esswein, W. (2012). Corporate risks in social networks – towards a risk management framework. *Proceedings of the 18th Americas Conference on Information Systems (AMCIS)*, Seattle, USA, paper 9.

Brecht, F., Cudreasova, A., & Zhou, J. (2010). Corporate blogging today – usage and characteristics. *Proceedings of the 16th Americas Conference on Information Systems (AMCIS)*, Lima, Peru, paper 440.

Brecht, F., & Eckhardt, A. (2012). Employer branding via social network sites – a silver bullet to attract IT professionals? *Proceedings of the 20th European Conference on Information Systems (ECIS)*, Barcelona, Spain, paper 89.

Briggs, R. O., Kolfschoten, G., de Vreede, G. J., Albrecht, C., & Dean, D. R. (2009). A seven-layer model of collaboration: separation of concerns for designers of collaboration systems. *Proceedings of the 30th International Conference on Information Systems (ICIS)*, Phoenix, USA, paper 26.

Bruneel, J., D'Este, P., & Salter, A. (2010). Investigating the factors that diminish the barriers to university-industry collaboration. *Research Policy, 39*(7), 858-868.

Bruns, H. C. (2013). Working alone together: coordination in collaboration across domains of expertise. *Academy of Management Journal, 58*(1), 62-83.

Brunvand, S., & Duran, M. (2010). A taxonomy of e-research collaboration tools: Using Web 2.0 to connect, collaborate and create with research partners. In *E-research collaboration* (pp. 105-116). Springer Berlin Heidelberg.

Buckl, S., Matthes, F., Neubert, C., & Schweda, C. M. (2009). A wiki-based approach to enterprise architecture documentation and analysis. *Proceedings of the 17th European Conference on Information Systems*, Verona, Italy, paper 75.

Bukvova, H. (2010). Studying research collaboration: a literature review. *Working Papers on Information Systems, 10*(2010), https://doi.org/10.2307/3069464

Buhl, H. U., & Müller, G. (2010). Der „gläserne Bürger" im Web 2.0. *Wirtschaftsinformatik, 52*(4), 193-197.

Bullinger, A., Hallerstede, S., Renken, U., Söldner, J., & Möslein, K. (2010). Towards research collaboration – a taxonomy of social research network sites. *Proceedings of the 16th Americas Conference on Information Systems (AMCIS)*, Lima, Peru, paper 92.

Bullinger, A. C., Renken, U., & Möslein, K. M. (2011). Understanding online collaboration technology adoption by researchers – a model and empirical study. *Proceedings of the 32nd International Conference on Information Systems (ICIS)*, Shanghai, China, paper 2.

Burke, M., & Kraut, R. E. (2016). The relationship between Facebook use and well-being depends on communication type and tie strength. *Journal of Computer-Mediated Communication, 21*(4), 265-281.

Burke, M., Marlow, C., & Lento, T. (2009). Feed me: motivating newcomer distribution in social network sites. *Proceedings of the SIGCHI Conference on Human Factors in Computing Systems*, Boston, USA, 945-954.

Bush, G.P., Hattery, L.H., 1956. Teamwork and creativity in research. *Science Quarterly 1*, 361–362.

Callaert, J., Landoni, P., Van Looy, B., & Verganti, R. (2015). Scientific yield from collaboration with industry: The relevance of researchers' strategic approaches. *Research Policy, 44*(4), 990-998.

Cao, J., Basoglu, K. A., Sheng, H., & Lowry, P. B. (2015). A systematic review of social networks research in information systems: Building a foundation for exciting future research. *Communications of the Association for Information Systems, 36*, 727–758

Carlson, S., & Anderson, B. (2007). What *are* data? The many kinds of data and their implications for data re-use. *Journal of Computer-Mediated Communication, 12*(2), article 15.

Carroll, J. M. (2010). Beyond being social: prospects for transformative social computing. *Communication of the Association for Information Systems, 27,* article 34.

Chai, S., Das, S., & Rao, H. R. (2012). Factors affecting bloggers' knowledge sharing: an investigation across gender. *Journal of Management Information Systems, 27*(1), 145-173.

Chai, S., Joseph, P., & Mullins, P. (2010). The empirical investigation of a wiki based group systems in organizations. *Proceedings of the 16th Americas Conference on Information Systems (AMCIS),* Lima, Peru, paper 317.

Chai, S., Shih, W. (2016). Bridging science and technology through academic–industry partnerships. *Research Policy, 45*(1), 148-158.

Chakraborty, R., Vishik, C., & Rao, H. R. (2013). Privacy preserving actions of older adults on social media: exploring the behavior of opting out of information sharing. *Decision Support System, 55*(4), 948-956.

Chang, I., Liu, C. C., & Chen, K. (2014). The push, pull and mooring effects in virtual migration for social networking sites. *Information Systems Journal, 24*(4), 323-346.

Chau, M. (2010). Friend suggestion and friend browsing in Web 2.0 applications. *Proceedings of the 16th Americas Conference on Information Systems (AMCIS),* Lima, Peru, paper 309.

Chau, M., & Xu, J. (2012). Business intelligence in blogs: understanding consumer interactions and communities. *MIS Quarterly, 36*(4), 1189-1216.

Chaves, M., & Gomes, R., & Pedron, C. (2012). Decision-making based on Web 2.0 data: the small and medium hotels management. *Proceedings of the 20th European Conference on Information Systems (ECIS),* Barcelona, Spain, paper 65.

Chen, C., & Mitchell, A. (2010). Improving the trust of users on social networking sites via self-construal traits. *Proceedings of the 16th Americas Conference on Information Systems (AMCIS),* Lima, Peru, paper 5.

Chen, J. V., Su, B. C., & Widjaja, A. E. (2016). Facebook C2C social commerce: A study of online impulse buying. *Decision Support Systems, 83,* 57-69.

Chen, J., Liu, J. (2014). Introduction: Social Computing and Social Networks. *Journal of Organizational Computing and Electronic Commerce, 24*(2-3), 119-121.

Chen, H., Papazafeiropoulou, A., Chen, T. K., & Hsiu-Wen, L. (2012). Commercial exploitation of Facebook: how companies adopt Facebook as a marketing tool. *Proceedings of the 20th European Conference on Information Systems (ECIS)*, Barcelona, Spain, paper 7.

Chen, J., Geyer, W., Dugan, C., Muller, M., & Guy, I. (2009). Make new friends, but keep the old – recommending people on social networking sites. *Proceedings of the SIGCHI Conference on Human Factors in Computing Systems*, 201-210.

Chen, Q., Clifford, S. J., & Wells, W. D. (2002). Attitude toward the site II: New information. *Journal of Advertising Research, 42*, 33–46.

Chen, R. (2013a). Member use of social networking sites – an empirical examination. *Decision Support Systems, 54*(3), 1219-1227

Chen, R. (2013b). Living a private life in public social networks: an exploration of member self-disclosure. *Decision Support Systems, 55*(3), 661-668.

Chen, X., Davison, R., & Huang, Q. (2015). The Impact of Technology Support for Contextualization and Media System Dependency on Enterprise Social Media Use

Cheng, J., Sun, A., Hu, D., & Zeng, D. (2011). An information diffusion-based recommendation framework for micro-blogging. *Journal of the Association for Information Systems, 12*(7), 463-486.

Cheung, C., Lee, M. (2009). Understanding the sustainability of a virtual community: model development and empirical test. *Journal of Information Science, 35*(3), 279–298.

Cheung, C., Lee, M. (2010). A theoretical model of intentional social action in online social networks. *Decision Support Systems, 49*(1), 24-30.

Cheung, C., Chiu, P.-Y., & Lee, M. (2011). Online social networks: why do students use Facebook? *Computers in Human Behavior, 27*(4), 1337–1343.

Cheung, C., Lee, Z., & Lee, M. (2013). Understanding compulsive use of Facebook through the reinforcement process. *Proceedings of the 21st European Conference on Information Systems (ECIS)*, Utrecht, Netherlands, paper 22.

Cheung, C., Zheng, X., & Lee, M. (2012). Consumer engagement behaviors in brand communities of social networking sites. *Proceedings of the 18th Americas Conference on Information Systems (AMCIS)*, Seattle, USA, paper 20.

Chin, G., Lansing, C. S. (2004). Capturing and supporting contexts for scientific data sharing via the biological sciences collaboratory. *Proceedings of the 2004 ACM conference on Computer supported cooperative work*, Chicago, USA, 409-148.

Chin, C. P. Y., Evans, N., & Choo, K. K. R. (2015). Exploring factors influencing the use of enterprise social networks in multinational professional service firms. *Journal of Organizational Computing and Electronic Commerce, 25*(3), 289-315.

Chin, C. P., & Choo, K. R. (2015). Enterprise Social Networks : A Successful Implementation within a Telecommunication Company Full Paper. *Twenty-First Americas Conference on Information Systems*, (November), 1–11.

Chinnov, A., Kerschke, P., & Meske, C. (2015). An Overview of Topic Discovery in Twitter Communication through Social Media Analytics Full Paper. *In Twenty-first Americas Conference on Information Systems* (pp. 1–10).

Chiu, C., Cheng, H., Huang, H., & Chen, C. (2013). Exploring individuals' subjective well-being and loyalty towards social network sites from the perspective of network externalities: the Facebook case. *International Journal of Information Management, 33*, 539–552.

Cho, V. (2017). A study of negative emotional disclosure behavior in social network media: Will an unexpected negative event and personality matter? *Computers in Human Behavior, 73*, 172–180.

Choi, C. F., & Jiang, Z. (2013a). Trading friendship for value: an investigation of collective privacy concerns in social application usage. *Proceedings of the 34th International Conference on Information Systems (ICIS)*, Milan, Italy.

Choi, C.F., & Jiang, Z. (2013b). Responses to social predicament on online social networks. *Proceedings of the 19th Americas Conference on Information Systems (AMCIS)*, Chicago, USA.

Chompalov, I., Genuth, J., & Shrum, W. (2002). The organization of scientific collaborations. *Research Policy, 31*(5), 749-767.

Choudrie, J., & Zamani, E. D. (2016). Understanding individual user resistance and workarounds of enterprise social networks: the case of Service Ltd. *Journal of Information Technology, 31*(2), 130-151.

Chung, N., & Koo, C. (2012). Knowledge sharing in social networking sites for e-collaboration: identity and bond theory perspective. *Proceedings of the 18th Americas Conference on Information Systems (AMCIS)*, Seattle, USA, paper 5.

Chung, S., Animesh, A., Han, K., & Pinsonneault, A. (2014). Firm's social media efforts, consumer behavior, and firm performance. In *International Conference on Information Systems.*

Church, E. M., Zhao, X., & Iyer, L. (2013). Pin it to win it: a study of marketing success in "curation-based" online social networks. *Proceedings of the 34th International Conference on Information Systems (ICIS),* Milan, Italy.

Church, M., & Salam, A. F. (2010). Facebook, the spice of life? *Proceedings of the 32nd International Conference on Information Systems (ICIS),* Shanghai, China, paper 212.

Clarke, B.L., 1967. Communication patterns of biomedical scientists. *Federation Proceedings 26,* 1288–1292.

Clemons, E. K. (2009). The complex problem of monetizing virtual electronic social networks. *Decision Support Systems, 48*(1), 46-56.

Cleveland, S., & Ellis, T. J. (2013). Determining microblogging effectiveness for capturing quality knowledge. *Proceedings of the 19th Americas Conference on Information Systems (AMCIS),* Chicago, USA.

Clifford, N., Cope, M., Gillespie, T., & French, S. (2016). *Key methods in geography,* Third edition, Sage, London.

Collins, R., Dwyer, C., Hiltz, S., & Shrivastav, H. (2012). Do I know what you can see? Social networking sites and privacy management. *Proceedings of the 18th Americas Conference on Information Systems (AMCIS),* Seattle, USA, paper 3

Connolly, A., & Jones, J. (2012a). Volunteering 2.0: how can volunteer organizations employ online social networks? *Proceedings of the 18th Americas Conference on Information Systems (AMCIS),* Seattle, USA, paper 16.

Connolly, A. J., & Jones, J. L. (2012b). Volunteering 2.0: how online social networks motivate volunteer retention. *Proceedings of the 33rd International Conference on Information Systems (ICIS),* Orlando, USA.

Conti, A., & Liu, C. C. (2015). Bringing the lab back in: Personnel composition and scientific output at the MIT Department of Biology. *Research Policy, 44*(9), 1633-1644.

Coursaris, C. K., Van Osch, W., & Balogh, B. A. (2013). A social media marketing typology: classifying brand Facebook page messages for strategic consumer engagement. *Proceedings of the 21st European Conference on Information Systems (ECIS),* Utrecht, Netherlands, paper 46.

Cragin, M. H., & Shankar, K. (2006). Scientific data collections and distributed collective practice. *Computer Supported Cooperative Work, 15*, 185-204.

Cronin, B. (2005). *The hand of science: Academic writing and its rewards*. Scarecrow Press.

Cummings, J., & Dennis, A. (2014). Do SNS impressions matter? Virtual Team and impression formation in the era of social technologies. In *Twentieth Americas Conference on Information Systems* (pp. 1–9).

Cummings, J. N., & Kiesler, S. (2005). Collaborative research across disciplinary and organizational boundaries. *Social Studies of Science, 35*(5), 703–722.

Cummings, J. N., & Kiesler, S. (2007). Coordination costs and project outcomes in multi-university collaborations. *Research Policy, 36*(10), 1620-1634.

Cummings, J. N., & Kiesler, S. (2008). Who collaborates successfully? Prior experience reduces collaboration barriers in distributed interdisciplinary research. *Proceedings of the 2008 ACM Conference on Computer Supported Cooperative Work*, San Diego, USA, 437-446.

Cummings, J., & Reinicke, B. A. (2014). Enterprise SNS Use and Profile Perceptions: A Comparison of Cultures. *Proceedings of the Americas Conference on Information Systems (AMCIS)*, (1), 1–10.

Cunliffe, D., Morris, D., & Prys, C. (2013). Young bilinguals' language behavior in social networking sites: the use of Welsh on Facebook. *Journal of Computer-Mediated Communication, 18*(3), 339-361.

Dahlander, L., & McFarland, D. A. (2013). Ties that last: tie formation and persistence in research collaborations over time. *Administrative Science Quarterly, 58*(1), 69-110.

Danis, C., & Singer, D. (2008). A wiki instance in the enterprise: opportunities, concerns and reality. *Proceedings of the 2008 ACM Conference on Computer Supported Cooperative Work*, San Diego, USA, 495-504.

Dantu, R., Wang, J., & Mahapatra, R. (2014). Social media use in physician-patient interaction - A fit perspective. In *20th Americas Conference on Information Systems, AMCIS 2014* (pp. 1–10).

Davidson, E., Lamb, R. (2000). Examining socio-technical networks in scientific academia/industry collaborations. *Proceedings of the 6th Americas Conference on Information Systems (AMCIS)*, Long Beach, USA, paper 202.

Davison, C., Singh, M., & Cerotti, P. R. (2010). Social technologies: a six dimensions review of genre. *Proceedings of the 16th Americas Conference on Information Systems (AMCIS)*, Lima, Peru, paper 201.

Defazio, D., Lockett, A., & Wright, M. (2009). Funding incentives, collaborative dynamics and scientific productivity: evidence from the EU framework program. *Research Policy, 38*(2), 293-305.

de Oliveira, G. H., & Watson-Manheim, M. B. (2013). Use of social media in the workplace: contradictions and unintended consequences. *Proceedings of the 19th Americas Conference on Information Systems (AMCIS)*, Chicago, USA.

De Meo, P., Ferrara, E., Fiumara, G., & Provetti, A. (2014). On Facebook, most ties are weak. *Communications of the ACM, 57*(11), 78-84.

Demetz, L., Heinrich, B., & Klier, M. (2011). Analyzing the impact of new features on users' communication activities in online social networks. *Proceedings of the 19th European Conference on Information Systems (ECIS)*, Helsinki, Finland, paper 269.

Den Besten, M., David, P. A., & Schroeder, R. (2009). Research in e-science and open access to data and information. In *International Handbook of Internet Research* (pp. 65-96). Springer Netherlands.

Dennis, A. R., Fuller, R. M., & Valacich, J. S. (2008). Media, Tasks, and Communication Processes: A Theory of Media Synchronicity. *MIS Quarterly, 32*(3), 575–600.

Dennis, A. R., Minas, R. K., & Lockwood, N. S. (2016). Mapping the corporate blogosphere: linking audience, content, and management to blog visibility. *Journal of the Association for Information Systems, 17*(3), 162.

Deuker, A. (2012). Friend-to-friend privacy protection on social networking sites: a grounded theory study. *Proceedings of the 18th Americas Conference on Information Systems (AMCIS)*, Seattle, USA, paper 5.

De Wever, B., Mechant, P., Veevaete, P., & Hauttekeete, L. (2007). E-Learning 2.0: Social software, for educational use. In *Proceedings ISM Workshops 2007 9th IEEE International Symposium on Multimedia - Workshops* (pp. 511–516). https://doi.org/10.1109/ISMW.2007.4476020

Dhillon, G., & Chowdhuri, R. (2013). Individual values for protecting identity in social networks. *Proceedings of the 34th International Conference on Information Systems (ICIS)*, Milan, Italy.

Dholakia, U., Bagozzi, R., & Pearo, L. (2004). A social influence model of consumer participation in network- and small- group-based virtual communities. *International Journal of Research in Marketing, 21*, 241–263.

DiMicco, J., Millen, D. R., Geyer, W., Dugan, C., Brownholtz, B., & Muller, M. (2008). Motivations for social networking at work. *Proceedings of the 2008 ACM Conference on Computer Supported Cooperative Work*, San Diego, USA, 711-720.

Ding, G., Liu, H., Wei, S., & Gu, J. (2015). Leveraging Work-Related Stressors for Employee Innovation : The Moderating Role of Enterprise Social Networking Use. *Icis*, 1–16.

Dinter, B., Lorenz, A. (2012). Social business intelligence: a literature review and research agenda. *Proceedings of the 33rd International Conference on Information Systems (ICIS)*, Orlando, USA.

Dolan, R., Conduit, J., Fahy, J., & Goodman, S. (2015). Social media engagement behavior: a uses and gratifications perspective. *Journal of Strategic Marketing*, DOI: 10.1080/0965254X.2015.1095222

Dong, J. Q., & Wu, W. (2015). Business value of social media technologies: Evidence from online user innovation communities. *The Journal of Strategic Information Systems, 24*(2), 113-127.

Drakos, N., Sussin, J. (2015, July 27). *Hype Cycle for Social Software, 2015* (ID: G00277657). Retrieved from Gartner database.

Drucker, P. F. (2012). *Innovation and Entrepreneurship* (Rev. ed.). Abingdon: Routledge

Dubé, L., Paré, G. (2003). Rigor in information systems positivist case research: current practices, trends, and recommendations. *MIS Quarterly* 27(4), 597–636.

Duffy, A. (2010). Shifting the research grant collaboration paradigm with research 2.0. In *e-Research Collaboration* (pp. 219-232). Springer Berlin Heidelberg.

Dugan, C., Geyer, W., Muller, M., DiMicco, J., Brownholtz, B., & Millen, D. R. (2008). It's all 'about you' – diversity in online profiles. *Proceedings of the 2008 ACM Conference on Computer Supported Cooperative Work*, San Diego, USA, 703-706.

Dunne, A., Lawlor, M., & Rowley, J. (2010). Young people's use of online social networking sites - a uses and gratifications perspective. *Journal of Research in Interactive Marketing*, 4(1), 46-58.

Dutton, W. H. (2011). The politics of next generation research: democratizing research-centred computational networks. *Journal of Information Technology, 26*, 109-119.

Dwivedi, Y., Williams, M., Ramdani, B., Niranjan, S., & Weerakkody, V. (2011). Understanding factors for successful adoption of Web 2.0 applications. *Proceedings of the 19th European Conference on Information Systems (ECIS)*, Helsinki, Finland, paper 263.

Dwyer, C. (2007). Task technology fit, the social technical gap and social networking sites. *Proceedings of the 13th American Conference on Information Systems (AMCIS)*, Keystone, USA, paper 374.

Dwyer, C., Hiltz, S., & Passerini, K. (2007). Trust and privacy concern within social networking sites: a comparison of Facebook and MySpace. *Proceedings of the 13th American Conference on Information Systems (AMCIS)*, Keystone, USA, paper 339.

Dyrby, S., Jensen, T. B., & Avital, M. (2014). Enterprise social media at work: weaving the social fabric of collaboration. In *The 35th International Conference on Information Systems. ICIS 2014.*

Ebermann, J., Stanoevska-Slabeva, K., & Wozniak, T. (2011). Influential factors of recommendation behaviour in social network sites – an empirical analysis. *Proceedings of the 19th European Conference on Information Systems (ECIS)*, Helsinki, Finland, paper 259.

Edmondson, A., McManus, S. (2007). Methodological fit in management field research. *Academy of Management Review, 32*(4), 1155–1179.

Effing, R., & Spil, T. A. (2016). The social strategy cone: Towards a framework for evaluating social media strategies. *International journal of information management, 36*(1), 1-8.

Eighmey, J., & McCord, L. (1998). Adding value in the information age: Uses and gratifications of sites on the world wide web. *Journal of Business Research, 41*, 187–194.

Eisend, M., & Schmidt, S. (2013). The influence of knowledge-based resources and business scholars' internationalization strategies on research performance. *Research Policy, 43*(1), 48-59.

Eisenhardt, K. (1989). Building theories from case study research, *Academy of Management Review, 14*(4), 532–550.

Eisenhardt, K., Graebner, M. (2007). Theory building from cases. Opportunities and challenges. *Academy of Management Journal, 50*(1), 25–32.

Ellis, T. J. (2015). The Role of Microblogging Capacities in Knowledge Sharing and Collaboration in Virtual Teams. In *Twenty First Americas Conference on Information Systems* (pp. 1–9). Puerto Rico.

Ernst, C. P. H., Pfeiffer, J., & Rothlauf, F. (2013). The influence of perceived belonging on social network site adoption. *Proceedings of the 19th Americas Conference on Information Systems (AMCIS)*, Chicago, USA.

Evans, M. P. (2009). The aggregator blog model: how a blog leverages long tail economics. *Journal of Information Science and Technology, 6*(2), 3-21.

Fan, W., & Gordon, M. D. (2014). The power of social media analytics. *Communications of the ACM, 57*(6), 74-81.

Ferro, E., Loukis, E., Charalabidis, Y., & Osella, M. (2013). Evaluating advanced forms of social media use in government. *Proceedings of the 19th Americas Conference on Information Systems (AMCIS)*, Chicago, USA.

Ford, D. P., & Mason, R. M. (2013a). Knowledge management and social media: the challenges and benefits. *Journal of Organizational Computing and Electronic Commerce, 23*(1-2), 1-6.

Ford, D. P., & Mason, R. M. (2013b). A multilevel perspective of tensions between knowledge management and social media. *Journal of Organizational Computing and Electronic Commerce, 23*(1-2), 7-33.

Forman, C. (2010). From wires to partners: how the internet has fostered R&D collaborations among firms. *Proceedings of the 31st International Conference on Information Systems (ICIS)*, St. Louis, USA, paper 95.

Fox, M. F., Mohapatra, S. (2007). Social-organizational characteristics of work and publication productivity among academic scientists in doctoral-granting departments. *The Journal of Higher Education, 78*(5), 542–571.

Franck, G. (1999). Scientific communication--A vanity fair?. *Science, 286*(5437), 53-55.

Franzoni, C., Sauermann, H. (2014). Crowd science: the organization of scientific research in open collaborative projects. *Research Policy*, 43(1), 1-20.

Fraser, M., Hindmarsh, J., Best, K., Heath, C., Biegel, G., Greenhalgh, C., & Reeves, S. (2006). Remote collaboration over video data: towards real-time e-social science. *Computer Supported Cooperative Work, 15*, 257-279.

Freeman, M. B., Halliwell, M., & Freeman, A. (2013). Social media influence on viewer engagement. *Proceedings of the 34th International Conference on Information Systems (ICIS)*, Milan, Italy, 3489-3504.

Friedrich, T. (2015). Analyzing the Factors that Influence Consumers' Adoption of Social Commerce–A Literature Review.

Fu, W. T. (2008). The microstructures of social tagging: a rational model. *Proceedings of the 2008 AMC Conference on Computer Supported Cooperative Work*, San Diego, USA, 229-238.

Füller, J. (2006). Why consumers engage in virtual new product developments initiated by producers. *Advances in Consumer research, 33*, 639–646.

Ganesh, J., & Padmanabhuni, S. (2007). Web 2.0: conceptual framework and research directions. *Proceedings of the 13th American Conference on Information Systems (AMCIS)*, Keystone, USA, paper 332.

Ganesh, J., & Sethi, P. (2013). Reputation and trust in social networks: empirical results from a Facebook reputation system. *Proceedings of the 19th Americas Conference on Information Systems (AMCIS)*, Chicago, USA.

Ganley, D., & Lampe, C. (2009). The ties that bind: social network principles in online communities. *Decision Support Systems, 47*(3), 266-274.

García-Crespo, A., Colomo-Palacios, R., Gómez-Berbís, J. M., & Ruiz-Mezcua, B. (2010). SEMO: a framework for customer social networks analysis based on semantics. *Journal of Information Technology, 25*(2), 178-188.

Garg, R., Smith, M. D., & Telang, R. (2011). Measuring information diffusion in an online community. *Journal of Management Information Systems*, 28(2), 11-37.

Garg, R., & Telang, R. (2012). Role of online social networks in job search by unemployed individuals. *Proceedings of the 33rd International Conference on Information Systems (ICIS)*, Orlando, USA, 509-523.

Gerlach, J., Widjaja, T., & Buxmann, P. (2015). Handle with care: How online social network providers' privacy policies impact users' information sharing behavior. *The Journal of Strategic Information Systems*, 24(1), 33-43.

Germonprez, M., & Hovorka, D. S. (2013). Member engagement within digitally enabled social network communities: new methodological considerations. *Information Systems Journal*, 23(6), 525-549.

Ghose, A., Ipeirotis, P. G., & Li, B. (2012). Search less, find more? Examining limited consumer search with social media and product search engines. *Proceedings of the 33rd International Conference on Information Systems (ICIS)*, Orlando, USA.

Gibbons, M., Limoges, C., Nowotny, H., Schwartzman, S., Scott, P., & Trow, M. (1994). *The new production of knowledge: The dynamics of science and research in contemporary societies*. Sage.

Gibson, J. 1977. "The theory of affordances", in R. E. S. J. Bransford (Ed.). *Perceiving, acting, and knowing: Toward an ecological psychology*. Hillsdale, NJ: Lawrence Erlbaum, pp. 67-82.

Gill, A. Q., Alam, S. L., & Eustace, J. Using Social Architecture to Analyzing Online Social Network Use in Emergency Management.

Glänzel, W., Schubert, A. (2004). Analysing scientific networks through co-authorship. *Handbook of quantitative science and technology research, 11*, 257-279.

Godinho de Matos, M., Ferreira, P. A., & Krackhardt, D. (2011). Peer influence in a very large social network: the diffusion of the iPhone handset. *Proceedings of the 32nd International Conference on Information Systems (ICIS)*, Shanghai, China.

Goldenberg, J., Oestreicher-Singer, G., & Reichman, S. (2010). The quest for content: the integration of product networks and social networks in online content exploration. *Proceedings of the 31st International Conference on Information Systems (ICIS)*, St. Louis, USA, paper 90.

Gonzales, E. S., Leidner, D. E., Riemenschneider, C., & Koch, H. (2013). The impact of internal social media usage on organizational socialization and commitment. *Proceedings of the 34th International Conference on Information Systems (ICIS)*, Milan, Italy.

Gonzales-Brambila, C. N., Veloso, F. M., & Krackhardt, D. (2013). The impact of network embeddedness on research output. *Research Policy*, 42(9), 1555-1567.

Gonzalez-Bailon, S., Kaltenbrunner, A., & Banchs, R. E. (2010). The structure of political discussion networks: a model for the analysis of online deliberation. *Journal of Information Technology*, 25(2), 230-243.

Gorbacheva, E., Stein, A., Schmiedel, T., & Müller, O. (2015). A gender perspective on business process management competences offered on professional online social networks. *In 23rd European Conference on Information Systems, ECIS 2015* (Vol. 2015–May).

Goswami, S., Köbler, F., Leimeister, J. M., & Krcmar, H. (2010). Using online social networking to enhance social connectedness and social support for the elderly. *Proceedings of the 32nd International Conference on Information Systems (ICIS)*, Shanghai, China, paper 109.

Gotta, M., Drakos, N., & Mann, J. (2015, October 26). *Magic quadrant for social software in the workplace* (ID: G00270286). Retrieved from Gartner database.

Grange, C., & Benbasat, I. (2013). The value of social shopping networks for product search and the moderating role of network scope. *Proceedings of the 34th International Conference on Information Systems (ICIS)*, Milan, Italy.

Gray, P. H., Parise, S., & Iyer, B. (2010). Innovation impacts of using social bookmarking systems. *MIS Quarterly, 35*(3), 629-643.

Graziano, A. M., & Raulin, M. L. (2007). *Research methods: A process of inquiry, 6th Edition*. Allyn and Bacon, Boston.

Green, D., Pearson, J. (2005). Social software and cyber networks: Ties that bind or weak associations within the political organization? In *Proceedings of the 38th Annual Hawaii International Conference on System Sciences*. IEEE.

Greenhow, C., & Robelia, B. (2009). Old communication, new literacies: social network sites as social learning resources. *Journal of Computer-Mediated Communication, 14*(4), 1130-1161.

Grudin, J. (1988). Why Cscw Applications Fail : Problems in the Design and Evaluation of Organizational Interfaces. *Proceedings of the 1988 ACM Conference on Computersupported Cooperative Work CSCW 88, 4*, 85–93.

Gunarathne, P., Rui, H., & Seidmann, A. (2015, January). Customer Service on Social Media: The Effect of Customer Popularity and Sentiment on Airline Response. In *System Sciences (HICSS), 2015 48th Hawaii International Conference on System Sciences* (pp. 3288-3297). IEEE.

Gupta, H., Nicholson, B., & Newman, M. (2013). Assimilation of social media: researching challenges to adoption. *Proceedings of the 19th Americas Conference on Information Systems (AMCIS)*, Chicago, USA.

Haeussler, C. (2011). Information-sharing in academia and the industry: a comparative study. *Research Policy, 40*(1), 105-122.

Haeussler, C., & Sauermann, H. (2013). Credit where credit is due? The impact of project contributions and social factors on authorship and inventorship. *Research Policy, 42*(3), 688-703.

Haeussler, C., Jiang, L., Thursby, J., & Thursby, M. (2014). Specific and general information sharing among competing academic researchers. *Research policy, 43*(3), 465-475.

Haider, A. (2009). Continuance usage intention in microblogging services: the case of twitter. *Proceedings of the 17th European Conference on Information Systems (ECIS)*, Verona, Italy, paper 28.

Hammersley, M. (2012). *What is Qualitative Research?, The 'what is?' research methods series*, Bloomsbury Publishing, London.

Hara, N., Solomon, P. Kim, S.-L., Sonnenwald, D. H. (2003). An emerging view of scientific collaboration: Scientists' perspectives on collaboration and factors that impact collaboration. *Journal of the American Society for Information Science and Technology, 54*(10), 952–965.

Harden, G. (2010). Satisfaction with social networking sites: effect of playfulness and change in use. *Proceedings of the 16th Americas Conference on Information Systems (AMCIS)*, Lima, Peru, paper 101.

Harden, G., Al Beayeyz, A., & Visinescu, L. (2012). Concerning SNS use: How do issues of privacy and trust concern users? *Proceedings of the 18th Americas Conference on Information Systems (AMCIS)*, Seattle, USA, paper 4.

Hasani-Mavriqi, I., Leitner, H., Helic, D., & Maurer, H. (2011). Implementation of a wiki-based information and communication system for Academia Europaea. *Journal of Computing and Information Technology, 19*(4), 231-238.

Hassell, M. D., & Sukalich, M. F. (2016). A deeper look into the complex relationship between social media use and academic outcomes and attitudes. *Information Research, 21*(4).

He, Z. L., Geng, X. S., & Campbell-Hunt, C. (2009). Research collaboration and research output: a longitudinal study of 65 biomedical scientists in a New Zealand university. *Research Policy, 38*(2), 306-317.

He, D., Jeng, W. (2016). Scholarly Collaboration on the Academic Social Web. *Synthesis Lectures on Information Concepts, Retrieval, and Services, 8*(1), 1-106.

He, S., Rui, H., & Whinston, A. B. (2015). Social Media Strategies in Product Harm Crises. In *Thirty Sixth International Conference on Information Systems* (pp. 1–18). Fort Worth.

Heath, D., & Singh, R. (2012). Strategic social media engagement. *Proceedings of the 18th Americas Conference on Information Systems (AMCIS)*, Seattle, USA, paper 12.

Heidemann, J., Klier, M., & Probst, F. (2010). Identifying key users in online social networks: a PageRank based approach. *Proceedings of the 31st International Conference on Information Systems (ICIS)*, St. Louis, USA, paper 10.

Heimeriks, G., van den Besselaar, P., & Frenken, K. (2008). Digital disciplinary differences: an analysis of computer-mediated science and 'Mode 2' knowledge production. *Research Policy, 37*(2), 1602-1615.

Heinze, T., & Kuhlmann, S. (2008). Across institutional boundaries? Research collaboration in German public sector nanoscience. *Research Policy, 37*(5), 888-899.

Heinze, T., Shapira, P., Rogers, J. D., & Senker, J. M. (2009). Organizational and institutional influences on creativity in scientific research. *Research Policy, 38*(4), 610-623.

Hekkala, R., Väyrynen, K., & Wiander, T. (2012). Information security challenges of social media for companies. *Proceedings of the 20th European Conference on Information Systems (ECIS)*, Barcelona, Spain, paper 56.

Helms, R. W., Booij, E., & Spruit, M. R. (2012). Reaching out: involving users in innovation tasks through social media. *Proceedings of the 20th European Conference on Information Systems (ECIS)*, Barcelona, Spain, paper 193.

Hemsley, J., & Mason, R. M. (2013). Knowledge and knowledge management in the social media age. *Journal of Organizational Computing and Electronic Commerce*, 23(1-2), 138-167.

Hennig-Thurau, T., Gwinner, K., Walsh, G., & Gremler, D. (2004). Electronic word-of mouth via consumer-opinion platforms: What motivates consumers to articulate themselves on the Internet? *Journal of Interactive Marketing, 18*, 38–52.

Herzog, H. (1944). What do we really know about daytime serial listeners? In P. F. Lazarsfeld & F. N. Stanton (Eds.), *Radio research*, 1942–1943, (pp. 3–33). New York: Duell, Sloan & Pearce.

Herzog, C., Richter, A., Steinhüser, M., Hoppe, U., & Koch, M. (2013). Methods and metrics for measuring the success of enterprise social software – what we can learn from practice and vice versa. *Proceedings of the 21st European Conference on Information Systems (ECIS)*, Utrecht, Netherlands, paper 132.

Herzog, C., Richter, A., & Steinhüser, M. (2015). Towards a framework for the evaluation design of enterprise social software. *In 2015 International Conference on Information Systems: Exploring the Information Frontier, ICIS 2015*. University of Osnabrück, Osnabrück, Germany: Association for Information Systems.

Hessels, L. K., Van Lente, H. (2008). Re-thinking new knowledge production: a literature review and a research agenda. *Research Policy, 37*(4), 740-760.

Hewitt-Dundas, N. (2012). Research intensity and knowledge transfer activity in UK universities. *Research Policy, 41*(2), 262-275.

Hillmann, R., & Trier, M. (2012). Sentiment polarization and balance among users in online social networks. *Proceedings of the 18th Americas Conference on Information Systems (AMCIS)*, Seattle, USA, paper 10.

Hillmann, R., & Trier, M. (2013). Influence and dissemination of sentiments in social network communication patterns. *Proceedings of the 21st European Conference on Information Systems (ECIS)*, Utrecht, Netherlands, paper 52.

Hoekman, J., Frenken, K., & Tijssen, R. J. W. (2010). Research collaboration at a distance: changing spatial patterns of scientific collaboration within Europe. *Research Policy, 39*(5), 662-673.

Hofmann, S. (2014). Just Because We Can - Governments' Rationale for Using Social Media. *ECIS*, 1–16.

Hollenbaugh, E. E., & Everett, M. K. (2013). The effects of anonymity on self-disclosure in blogs: an application of the online disinhibition effect. *Journal of Computer-Mediated Communication, 18*(3), 283-302.

Holsapple, C., Hsiao, S., & Pakath, R. (2014). Business Social Media Analytics: Definition, Benefits, and Challenges. *Business Social Media Analytics*, (2010), 1–12.

Hou, H., Kretschmer, H., & Liu, Z. (2007). The structure of scientific collaboration networks in Scientometrics. *Scientometrics, 75*(2), 189-202.

Howe, J. (2006). The Rise of Crowdsourcing. *Wired, 06*(6), 176-183.

Hu, C., & Racherla, P. (2008). Visual representation of knowledge networks: A social network analysis of hospitality research domain. *International Journal of Hospitality Management, 27*(2), 302–312.

Hu, M., & Schlagwein, D. (2013). Why firms use social media: an absorptive capacity perspective. *Proceedings of the 21st European Conference on Information Systems (ECIS)*, Utrecht, Netherlands, paper 108.

Hu, T., & Kettinger, W. J. (2008). Why people continue to use social networking services: developing a comprehensive model. *Proceedings of the 29th International Conference on Information Systems (ICIS)*, Paris, France, paper 89.

Hu, T., Poston, R. S., & Kettinger, W. J. (2011). Nonadopters of online social network services: is it easy to have fun yet? *Communications of the Association for Information Systems, 29*, article 25.

Huang, K. Y., Chai, N., & Horowitz, L. (2010). Web 2.0 use and organizational innovation: a knowledge transfer enabling perspective. *Proceedings of the 16th Americas Conference on Information Systems (AMCIS)*, Lima, Peru, paper 189.

Huang, K. Y., & Güney, S. (2012). Toward a framework of Web 2.0-driven organizational learning. *Communications of the Association for Information Systems, 31*, article 6.

Huber, J., Landherr, A., Probst, F., & Reisser, C. (2012). Stimulating user activity on company fan pages in online social networks. *Proceedings of the 20th European Conference on Information Systems (ECIS)*, Barcelona, Spain, paper 188.

Huberman, B. A., Romero, D. M., & Wu, F. (2009). Crowdsourcing, attention and productivity. *Journal of Information Science, 35*(6), 758-765.

Huff, A. S. (2008). *Designing Research for Publication*. SAGE. Los Angeles, California: SAGE.

Ifinedo, P. (2016). Applying uses and gratifications theory and social influence processes to understand students' pervasive adoption of social networking sites: Perspectives from the Americas. *International Journal of Information Management, 36*. 192-206.

Ip, R. (2007). Use of social software in personal and organizational settings. *Proceedings of the 13th American Conference on Information Systems (AMCIS)*, Keystone, USA, paper 483.

Irvine, J., & Martin, B. R. (1984). CERN: Past performance and future prospects: II. The scientific performance of the CERN accelerators. *Research Policy, 13*(5), 247-284.

Islam, A. K. M., & Mäntymäki, M. (2011). Continuance of professional social networking sites: a decomposed expectation-confirmation approach. *Proceedings of the 32nd International Conference on Information Systems (ICIS)*, Shanghai, China.

Islam, N., & Mäntymäki, M. (2014). Relationship attachment and subjective vitality as outcomes of social networking site use. *Twentieth Americas Conference on Information Systems, Savannah*, 1–10.

Ivens, S., & Schaarschmidt, M. (2015). Does Reputable Employee Behaviour in Social Networks Affect Customers ' Trust and Word of Mouth ? An Experimental Study. *Ecis*, (May), 1–16.

Jacks, T., & Salam, A. F. (2009). Computer-mediated friendship networks. *Proceedings of the 30th International Conference on Information Systems (ICIS)*, Phoenix, USA, paper 115.

Jacobs, A., & Nakata, K. (2012). Organizational semiotics methods to assess organizational readiness for internal use of social media. *Proceedings of the 18th Americas Conference on Information Systems (AMCIS)*, Seattle, USA, paper 24

Jarrahi, M. H., & Sawyer, S. (2013). Social technologies, informal knowledge practices, and the enterprise. *Journal of Organizational Computing and Electronic Commerce, 23*(1-2), 110-137.

Jassawalla, A. R., Sashittal, H. C. (1998). An examination of collaboration in hightechnology new product development processes. *Journal of Product Innovation Management, 15*(3), 237-254.

Javadi, E., & Gebauer, J. (2009). Modeling user behavior in web 2.0 collaborative knowledge creation application. *Proceedings of the 15th Americas Conference on Information Systems (AMCIS)*, San Francisco, USA, paper 200.

Jensen, M. L., Dunbar, N. E., Connelly, M. S., Taylor, W., Adame, B., Rozzell, B., & Hughes, M. (2013). Social media on violent ideological group websites. *Proceedings of the 19th Americas Conference on Information Systems (AMCIS)*, Chicago, USA.

Jensen, T. B., & Dyrby, S. (2013). Exploring affordances of Facebook as a social media plattform in political campaigning. *Proceedings of the 21st European Conference on Information Systems (ECIS)*, Utrecht, Netherlands, paper 40.

Jha, Y., & Welch, E. W. (2010). Relational mechanisms governing multifaceted collaborative behavior of academic scientists in six fields of science and engineering. *Research Policy, 39*(9), 1174-1184.

Jiang, T., & Wang, X. (2009). How do bloggers comment: an empirical analysis of the commenting network of a blogging community. *Proceedings of the 30th International Conference on Information Systems (ICIS)*, Phoenix, USA, paper 99.

Jirotka, M., Procter, R., Rodden, T., & Bowker, G. C. (2006). Special issue: collaboration in e-research. *Computer Supported Cooperative Work, 15*(4), 251-255.

Jirotka, M., Lee, C. P., & Olson, G. M. (2013). Supporting scientific collaboration: methods, tools and concepts. *Computer Supported Cooperative Work, 22*(4), 667-715.

Johannessen, M. R., & Bjørn, E. M. (2012). Defining the IT artefact in social media for eparticipation: an ensemble view. *Proceedings of the 20th European Conference on Information Systems (ECIS)*, Barcelona, Spain, paper 2012.

Johannessen, M. R., & Følstad, A. (2014). Political Social Media Sites as Public Sphere: A Case Study of the Norwegian Labour Party. *CAIS, 34*, 56.

John, S. P. (2013). Antecedents and effects of computer self-efficacy on social networking adoption among Asian online users. *Proceedings of the 19th Americas Conference on Information Systems (AMCIS)*, Chicago, USA.

Johnson. V. (2012). Member retention in social networking sites. *Proceedings of the 18th Americas Conference on Information Systems (AMCIS)*, Seattle, USA, paper 14.

Johnson, T. J., & Kaye, B. K. (2014). Credibility of social network sites for political information among politically interested Internet users. *Journal of Computer-Mediated Communication, 19*(4), 957-974.

Joinson, A. N. (2008). 'Looking at', 'looking up' or 'keeping up with' people? Motives and uses of Facebook. *Proceedings of the SIGCHI Conference on Human Factors in Computing Systems*, Florence, Italy, 1027-1036.

Jong, S., & Slavova, K. (2014). When publications lead to products: The open science conundrum in new product development. *Research Policy, 43*(4), 645-654.

Jordan, Katy (2017). *Understanding the structure and role of academics' ego-networks on social networking sites*. PhD thesis The Open University.

Jung, E. J., Lankton, N., McKnight, H., & Jung, E. (2012). Three processes that form online social networking post-adoptive use intention. *Proceedings of the 18th Americas Conference on Information Systems (AMCIS)*, Seattle, USA, paper 3.

Kabo, F. W., Cotton-Nessler, N., Hwang, Y., Levenstein, M. C., & Owen-Smith, J. (2014). Proximity effects on the dynamics and outcomes of scientific collaborations. *Research Policy, 43*(9), 1469-1485.

Kafouros, M., Wang, C., Piperopoulos, P., & Zhang, M. (2015). Academic collaborations and firm innovation performance in China: The role of region-specific institutions. *Research Policy, 44*(3), 803-817.

Kahl, C. (2012). Create attention to attract attention – viral marketing of digital music in social networks. *Proceedings of the 18th Americas Conference on Information Systems (AMCIS)*, Seattle, USA, paper 9.

Kalb, H., Pirkkalainen, H., Pawlowski, J., & Schoop, E. (2011). Social networking services as facilitator for scientists' sharing activities. *Proceedings of the 19th European Conference on Information Systems (ECIS)*, Helsinki, Finland, paper 267.

Kam, H. J., & Katerattanakul, P. (2010). Collaborative learning with Web 2.0 technology: synchronicity dimension. *Proceedings of the 16th Americas Conference on Information Systems (AMCIS)*, Lima, Peru, paper 132.

Kane, G. C. (2013). Psychological stages of symbolic action in social media. *Proceedings of the 34th International Conference on Information Systems (ICIS)*, Milan, Italy.

Kane, G., & Fichman, R.. (2009). The shoemaker's children: Using wikis for information systems teaching, research, and publication. *MIS Quarterly, 33*(1), 1-17.

Kane, G. C., Fichman, R. G., Gallaugher, J., & Glaser, J. (2009). Community Relations 2.0. *Harvard Business Review, 87*(11), 45-50.

Kane, G.C., & Ransbotham, S. (2012). Codification and collaboration: information quality in social media. *Proceedings of the 33rd International Conference on Information Systems (ICIS)*, Orlando, USA.

Kane, G. C., Alavi, M., Labianca, G. J., & Borgatti, S. P. (2014). What's different about social media networks? A framework and research agenda. *MIS Quarterly, 38*(1), 275-304.

Kang, Y. S., Min, J., Kim, J.; & Lee, H. (2013). Roles of alternative and self-oriented perspectives in the context of the continued use of social network sites. *International Journal of Information Management, 33*, 496-511.

Karakayali, N., & Kilic, A. (2013). More network conscious than ever? Challenges, strategies, and analytic labor of users in the Facebook environment. *Journal of Computer-Mediated Communication, 18*(2), 61-79.

Karla, J. (2010). Digitales Vergessen im Web 2.0. *Wirtschaftsinformatik, 52*(2), 105-108.

Karoui, M., Dudezert, A., & Leidner, D. E. (2015). Strategies and symbolism in the adoption of organizational social networking systems. *The Journal of Strategic Information Systems, 24*(1), 15-32.

Kasemvilas, S., & Olfman, L. (2009). Design alternatives for a MediaWiki to support collaborative writing. *Journal of Information, Information Technology, and Organizations, 4*, 45-64.

Katz, E., Blumler, J. G., & Gurevitch, M. (1974). Utilization of mass communication by the individual. *Critical Readings Media and Audiences, 5578 LNCS(May 1973)*, 19–31.

Katz, E., & Foulkes, D. (1962). On the use of the mass media as 'escape': Clarification of a concept. *The Public Opinion Quarterly, 26*(3), 377–388. https://doi.org/10.1086/267111

Katz, J. S., & Martin, B. R. (1997). What is research collaboration? *Research Policy, 26*(1), 1-18.

Kaufhold, M. A., & Reuter, C. (2015). Konzept und Evaluation einer Facebook-Applikation zur crossmedialen Selbstorganisation freiwilliger Helfer. In *Wirtschaftsinformatik* (pp. 1844-1858).

Kaye, B. (1998). Uses and gratifications of the World Wide Web: From couch potato to Web potato. *The New Jersey Journal of Communication, 6*(1), 21-40.

Kefi, H., Mlaiki, A., & Kalika, M. (2010). Shy people and Facebook continuance of usage: does gender matter? *Proceedings of the 16th Americas Conference on Information Systems (AMCIS)*, Lima, Peru, paper 27.

Kefi, H., Mlaiki, A., & Kalika, M. (2015). Social Networking Continuance: When Habit leads to information overload. *ECIS 2015 Proceedings*, 1–13.

Kelman, H. (1958). Compliance, identification, and internalization: three processes of attitude change. *Journal of Conflict Resolution, 1*, 51–60.

Kelman, H. (1974). Social influence and linkages between the individual and the social system: further thoughts on the processes of compliance, identification, and internalization. In J. T. Tedeschi (Ed.), *Perspectives on social power* (pp.125–171). Chicago, IL: Aldine.

Kenix, L. J. (2009). Blogs as alternative. *Journal of Computer-Mediated Communication, 14*(4), 790-822.

Khan, Z., & Jarvenpaa, S. L. (2010). Exploring temporal coordination of events with Facebook.com. *Journal of Information Technology, 25*(2), 137-151.

Kietzmann, J. H., Hermkens, K., McCarthy, I. P., & Silvestre, B. S. (2011). Social media? Get serious! Understanding the functional building blocks of social media. *Business horizons, 54*(3), 241-251.

Kim, D. (2012). Interacting is believing? Examining bottom-up credibility of blogs among politically interested internet users. *Journal of Computer-Mediated Communication, 17*(4), 422-435.

Kim, E., Lee, D., & Ahn, J. (2009). An empirical study on media characteristics and knowledge sharing in Web 2.0 environment, *Proceedings of the 15th Americas Conference on Information Systems (AMCIS)*, San Francisco, USA, paper 380.

Kim, I. (2012). Social media in a social phenomenon: social media in the entrainment of contention to innovation. *Proceedings of the 33rd International Conference on Information Systems (ICIS)*, Orlando, USA. [217]

Kim, I., Miranda, S. (2013). How do social media increase firm performance? Entrainment of innovation to contention. *Proceedings of the 19th Americas Conference on Information Systems (AMCIS)*, Chicago, USA.

Kim, Y., Natali, F., Zhu, F., & Lim, E. (2016). Investigating the influence of offline friendship on twitter networking behaviors. In *Proceedings of the Annual Hawaii International Conference on System Sciences* (Vol. 2016–March, pp. 736–745). IEEE Computer Society.

Kisyovska, Y., Krönung, J., & Eckhardt, A. (2015). Peer Influence, Family Dysfunction or Conditioning?-An Empirical Analysis of Facebook Addiction Predispositions. In *Wirtschaftsinformatik* (pp. 1874-1889).

Kling, R., McKim, G., Fortuna, J., & King, A. (2000). Scientific collaboration as socio-technical interaction networks: a theoretical approach. *Proceedings of the 6th American Conference on Information Systems (AMCIS)*, Long Beach, USA.

Ko, H., Cho, C.-H., & Roberts, M. S. (2005). Internet uses and gratifications: A structural equation model of interactive advertising. *Journal of Advertising, 34*, 57–70.

Koch, H., Leidner, D. E., & Gonzales, E. S. (2013). Digitally enabling social networks: resolving IT-culture conflict. *Information Systems Journal*, 23(6), 501-523.

Koch, M., Richter, A. (2009). *Enterprise 2.0: Planung, Einführung und erfolgreicher Einsatz von Social Software in Unternehmen*. Oldenbourg Verlag.

Koch, M., Richter, A., & Schlosser, A. (2007). Produkte zum IT-gestützten Social Networking in Unternehmen. *Wirtschaftsinformatik*, 49(6), 448-455.

Köbler, F., & Riedl, C. (2010). Social connectedness on Facebook – an explorative study on status message use. *Proceedings of the 16th Americas Conference on Information Systems (AMCIS)*, Lima, Peru, paper 247.

König, B., Diehl, K., Tscherning, K., & Helming, K. (2013). A framework for structuring interdisciplinary research management. *Research Policy*, 42(1), 261-272.

Köster, A., Matt, C., & Hess, T. (2015). The Role of Communication Types on Referral Acceptance in Social Networks. In *Proceedings of Americas Conference on Information Systems* (pp. 1–11).

Kopton, I. M., Sommer, J., Winkelmann, A., Riedl, R., & Kenning, P. (2013). Users' trust building processes during their initial connecting behavior in social networks: behavioral and neural evidence. *Proceedings of the 34th International Conference on Information Systems (ICIS)*, Milan, Italy.

Kordzadeh, N., & Young, D. (2015). Understanding how hospitals use social media: An exploratory study of Facebook posts.

Koroleva, K., Krasnova, H., & Günther, O. (2010). 'Stop spamming me!' – Exploring information overload on Facebook. *Proceedings of the 16th Americas Conference on Information Systems (AMCIS)*, Lima, Peru, paper 447.

Koroleva, K., Krasnova, H., Veltri, N., & Günther, O. (2011). It's all about networking! Empirical investigation of social capacity formation on social network sites. *Proceedings of the 32nd International Conference on Information Systems (ICIS)*, Shanghai, China.

Koroleva, K., Stimac, V. (2012). Tie strength vs. network overlap: why information from lovers is more valuable than from close friends on social network sites? *Proceedings of the 33rd International Conference on Information Systems (ICIS)*, Orlando, USA.

Koroleva, K., Stimac, V., Krasnova, H., & Kunze, D. (2011). I like it because I('m) like you – measuring user attitudes towards information on Facebook. *Proceedings of the 32nd International Conference on Information Systems (ICIS)*, Shanghai, China.

Kosalge, P., & Tole, O. (2010). Web 2.0 and business: early results on perceptions of Web 2.0 and factors influencing its adoption. *Proceedings of the 16th Americas Conference on Information Systems (AMCIS)*, Lima, Peru, paper 208.

Koschmider, A., Song, M., & Reijers, H. A. (2010). Social software for business process modeling. *Journal of Information Technology*, 25(3), 308-322.

Kotha, R., George, G., & Sirkanth, K. (2013). Bridging the mutual knowledge gap: coordination and the commercialization of university science. *Academy of Management Journal*, 56(2), 498-524.

Krasnova, H., Eling, N., Schneider, O., & Wenninger, H. (2013). Does this app ask for too much data? The role of privacy perceptions in user behavior towards Facebook applications and permission dialogs. *ECIS 2013 Proceedings*, paper 179.

Krasnova, H., Hildebrand, T., & Günther, O. (2009). Investigating the value of privacy in online social networks: conjoint analysis. *Proceedings of the 30th International Conference on Information Systems (ICIS)*, Phoenix, USA, paper 173.

Krasnova, H., Kolesnikova, E., & Guenther, O. (2010). Leveraging trust and privacy concerns in online social networks: an empirical study. *Proceedings of the 18th European Conference on Information Systems (ECIS)*, Pretoria, South Africa, paper 160.

Krasnova, H., Kolesnikova, E., & Günther, O. (2011). One size fits all? Managing trust and privacy on social networking sites in Russia and Germany. *Proceedings of the 19th European Conference on Information Systems (ECIS)*, Helsinki, Finland, paper 71.

Krasnova, H., Korolova, K., & Veltri, N. F. (2010). Investigation of the network construction behavior on social networking sites. *Proceedings of the 31st International Conference on Information Systems (ICIS)*, St. Louis, USA, paper 182.

Krasnova, H., Spiekermann, S., Koroleva, K., & Hildebrand, T. (2010). Online social networks: why we disclose. *Journal of Information Technology, 25*(2), 109-125.

Krasnova, H., Veltri, N. F., & Günther, O. (2012). Die Rolle der Kultur in der Selbstoffenbarung und Privatsphäre in sozialen Onlinenetzwerken. *Wirtschaftsinformatik, 54*(3), 123-133.[72]

Kraut, R., & Burke, M. (2015). Internet use and psychological well-being: Effects of activity and audience. *Communications of the ACM, 58*(12), 94-100.

Krishen, A. S., Trembath, L., & Muthaly, S. (2015). From liking to loyalty: The impact of network affinity in the social media digital space. *ACM SIGMIS Database: the DATABASE for Advances in Information Systems, 46*(2), 30-42.

Krüger, N., Brockmann, T., & Stieglitz, S. (2013). A framework for enterprise social media guidelines. *Proceedings of the 19th Americas Conference on Information Systems (AMCIS)*, Chicago, USA.

Ku, Y.-C., Chen, R., Zhang, H. (2013). Why do users continue using social networking sites? An exploratory study of members in the United States and Taiwan. *Information & Management, 50*, 571-581.

Kügler, M., Smolnik, S., & Raeth, P. (2012). Why don't you use it? Assessing the determinants of enterprise social software usage: a conceptual model integrating innovation infusion and social capital theories. *Proceedings of the 33rd International Conference on Information Systems (ICIS)*, Orlando, USA.

Kügler, M., Lübbert, C., & Smolnik, S. (2015). Organizational Climate's Role in Enterprise Social Software Usage: An Empirical Assessment. In *Wirtschaftsinformatik* (pp. 811-826).

Kuegler, M., Smolnik, S., & Kane, G. (2015). What's in IT for employees? Understanding the relationship between use and performance in enterprise social software. *The Journal of Strategic Information Systems, 24*(2), 90-112.

Kügler, M., & Smolnik, S. (2014). Uncovering the Phenomenon of Employees ´ Enterprise Social Software Use in the Post- Acceptance Stage - Proposing a Use Typology. *Ecis*, 0–18.

Kühne, M., Blinn, N., Rosenkranz, C., & Nüttgens, M. (2011). Diffusion of Web 2.0 in healthcare: a complete inventory count in the German health insurance landscape. *Proceedings of the 19th European Conference on Information Systems (ECIS)*, Helsinki, Finland, paper 270.

Küpper, T., Lehmkuhl, T., Jung, R., & Wieneke, A. (2014). Features for social CRM technology - An organizational perspective. In *20th Americas Conference on Information Systems, AMCIS 2014*. Savannah, GA: Association for Information Systems.

Kulathuramaiyer, N., & Maurer, H. (2015). A survey of communications and collaborative web technologies. *Journal of Computing and Information Technology*, 23(1), 1–18.

Kumar, V., Loonam, J., Allen, J. P., & Sawyer, S. (2016). Exploring enterprise social systems & organisational change: implementation in a digital age. *Journal of Information Technology*, *31*(2), 97-100.

Lampe, C., Ellison, N., & Steinfield, C. (2006). A Face(book) in the crowd: social searching vs. social browsing. *Proceedings of the 2006 ACM Conference on Computer Supported Cooperative Work*, San Diego, USA, 167-170.

Lampe, C., Ellison, N., & Steinfield, C. (2008). Changes in use and perception of Facebook. In Proceedings of the 2008 ACM conference on Computer supported cooperative work, 721-730.

Landherr, A. (2010). Eine kritische Analyse von Vernetzungsmaßen in sozialen Netzwerken. *Wirtschaftsinformatik*, 52(6), 367-382.

Lane, J. I., Owen-Smith, J., Rosen, R. F., & Weinberg, B. A. (2015). New linked data on research investments: Scientific workforce, productivity, and public value. *Research policy*, 44(9), 1659-1671.

Larosiliere, G. D., & Leidner, D. E. (2012). The effects of social network usage on organizational identification. *Proceedings of the 33rd International Conference on Information Systems (ICIS)*, Orlando, USA.

Larson, K., & Watson, R. T. (2011). The value of social media: toward measuring social media strategies. *Proceedings of the 32nd International Conference on Information Systems (ICIS)*, Shanghai, China, paper 10.

Laudel, G., 2002. What do we measure by co-authorships? *Research Evaluation 11*(1), 3–15.

Lawrence, K. A. (2006). Walking the tightrope: the balancing acts of a large e-research project. *Computer Supported Cooperative Work*, 15, 385-411.

Lee, S., Bozeman, B. (2005). The impact of research collaboration on scientific productivity. *Social Studies of Science*, 35(5), 673–702.

Lee, C. P., Dourish, P., & Mark, G. (2006). The human infrastructure of cyberinfrastructure. *Proceedings of the 2006 ACM Conference on Computer Supported Cooperative work*, Banff, USA.

Lee, H., Connelly, R., Li, K., Hales, K., & LaRose, R. (2013). Impacts of social media connection demands: a study of Irish college students. *Proceedings of the 19th Americas Conference on Information Systems (AMCIS)*, Chicago, USA.

Lee, Y. N., Walsh, J. P., & Wang, J. (2015). Creativity in scientific teams: Unpacking novelty and impact. *Research Policy*, 44(3), 684-697.

Lee, K. J. (2006). What goes around comes around: an analysis of del.icio.us as social space. *Proceedings of the 2008 ACM Conference on Computer Supported Cooperative work*, San Diego, USA, 191-194.

Lee, S., & Jahng, J. (2013). Tense moods make you use habitually Facebook: a new framework for habitual IT use based on the mechanisms of mood regulation. *Proceedings of the 19th Americas Conference on Information Systems (AMCIS)*, Chicago, USA.

Lee, K., Lee, B., & Oh, W. (2015). Thumbs up, sales up? The contingent effect of Facebook likes on sales performance in social commerce. *Journal of Management Information Systems*, 32(4), 109-143.

Lemarchand, G. A. (2012). The long-term dynamics of co-authorship scientific networks: Iberoamerican countries (1973-2010). *Research Policy*, 41(2), 291-305.

Leonardi, P. M. (2015). Ambient Awareness and Knowledge Acquisition: Using Social Media to Learn" Who Knows What" and" Who Knows Whom". *Mis Quarterly*, 39(4).

Leong, C. M. L., Pan, S. L., Ractham, P., & Kaewkitipong, L. (2015). ICT-enabled community empowerment in crisis response: Social media in Thailand flooding 2011. *Journal of the Association for Information Systems*, 16(3), 174.

Levina, O., & Vilnai-Yavetz, I. (2013). Use of social software in e-business: a cross-sectional, cross-country study. *Proceedings of the 19th Americas Conference on Information Systems (AMCIS)*, Chicago, USA.

Levy, Y., Ellis, T. (2006). A systems approach to conduct an effective literature review in support of information systems research. *Informing Science: International Journal of an Emerging Transdiscipline, 9*, 181–212.

Leung, L. (2009). User-generated content on the internet: An examination of gratifications, civic engagement and psychological empowerment. *New Media & Society, 11*, 1327–1347.

Li, E. Y., Liao, C. H., & Yen, H. R. (2013). Co-authorship networks and research impact: a social capital perspective. *Research Policy*, 42(9), 1515-1530.

Li, F., Miao, Y., & Yang, C. (2015). How do alumni faculty behave in research collaboration? An analysis of Chang Jiang Scholars in China. *Research Policy*, 44(2), 438-450.

Li, L., Goethals, F., Giangreco, A., & Baesens, B. (2013). Using social network data to predict technology acceptance. *Proceedings of the 34th International Conference on Information Systems (ICIS)*, Milan, Italy.

Li, X., & Wang, M. (2012). A multi-theoretical framework for social network-based recommendation. *Proceedings of the 33rd International Conference on Information Systems (ICIS)*, Orlando, USA.

Li, Y., & Joshi, K. D. (2012). The state of social computing research: a literature review and synthesis using the latent semantic analysis approach. *Proceedings of the 18th Americas Conference on Information Systems (AMCIS)*, Seattle, USA, paper 13.

Li, Y. M., & Li, T. Y. (2013). Deriving market intelligence from microblogs. *Decision Support Systems*, 55(1), 206-217.

Li, Y. M., & Shiu, Y. L. (2012). A diffusion mechanism for social advertising over microblogs. *Decision Support Systems*, 54(1), 9-22.

Li, Y. M., Wu, C. T., & Lai, C. Y. (2013). A social recommender mechanism for e-commerce: combining similarity, trust, and relationship. *Decision Support Systems*, 55(4), 740-752.

Liao, Q., & Li, Q. (2008). NetWORK patterns: designing effective user interfaces for connections management at work. *Proceedings of the 2008 ACM Conference on Computer Supported Cooperative Work*, San Diego, USA, 707-710.

Limaj, E., & Bernroider, E. W. N. (2013). Understanding the different priorities of Web 2.0 technologies for knowledge acquisition and assimilation for developing an organization's potential absorptive capacity. *Proceedings of the 19th Americas Conference on Information Systems (AMCIS)*, Chicago, USA.

Liu, X., Guo, Z., Lin, Z., & Ma, J. (2013). A local social network approach for research management. *Decision Support Systems, 56*, 427-438.

Liu, Y., Venkatanathan, J., Goncalves, J., Karapanos, E., & Kostakos, V. (2014). Modeling what friendship patterns on Facebook reveal about personality and social capital. *ACM Transactions on Computer-Human Interaction (TOCHI), 21*(3), 17.

Livingston, S., Ólafsson, K., & Staksrud, E. (2013). Risky social networking practices among "underage" users: lessons for evidence-based policy. *Journal of Computer-Mediated Communication, 18*(3), 303-320.

Lo, J., & Riemenschneider, C. (2010). An examination of privacy concerns and trust entities in determining willingness to disclose personal information on a social networking site. *Proceedings of the 16th Americas Conference on Information Systems (AMCIS)*, Lima, Peru, paper 46.

Loiacono, E., Carey, D., Misch, A., Spencer, A., Sperenza, R. (2012). Personality impacts on self-disclosure behavior on social networking sites. *Proceedings of the 18th Americas Conference on Information Systems (AMCIS)*, Seattle, USA, paper 6.

Loiacono, E. T. (2015). Self-disclosure behavior on social networking web sites. *International Journal of Electronic Commerce, 19*(2), 66-94.

Lovejoy, K., & Saxton, G. D. (2012). Information, community, and action: how nonprofit organizations use social media. *Journal of Computer-Mediated Communication, 17*(3), 337-353.

Lu, B., Guo, X., Luo, N., & Chen, G. (2015). Corporate Blogging and Job Performance: Effects of Work-related and Nonwork-related Participation. *Journal of Management Information Systems, 32*(4), 285-314.

Luarn, P., Yang, J. C., & Chiu, Y. P. (2015). Why people check in to social network sites. *International Journal of Electronic Commerce, 19*(4), 21-46.

Lucas Júnior, D., & Ornellas, R. (2012). Using social networking sites (SNS) for environmental scanning: an analysis of content monitoring tools. *Proceedings of the 18th Americas Conference on Information Systems (AMCIS)*, Seattle, USA, paper 15.

Ludwig, T., Reuter, C., & Pipek, V. (2015). Social haystack: Dynamic quality assessment of citizen-generated content during emergencies. *ACM Transactions on Computer-Human Interaction (TOCHI), 22*(4), 17.

Luo, M. M., Chea, S., & Chen, J. S. (2011). Web-based information service adoption: a comparison of the motivational model and the uses and gratifications theory. *Decision Support Systems, 51*(1), 21–30.

Luo, X., & Zhang, J. (2013). How do consumer buzz and traffic in social media marketing predict the value of the firm? *Journal of Management Information Systems, 30*(2), 213-238.

Lux, T., Schufft, K., & Lorenz, A. (2013). Evaluating the potential of social networking services for hospital recruitment. *Proceedings of the 21st European Conference on Information Systems (ECIS)*, Utrecht, Netherlands, paper 67.

Maddox, K. (1998). E-commerce becoming reality. *Advertising Age, 69*, S1–S2.

Maghrabi, R. O., & Salam, A. F. (2011). Social media, social movement, and political change: the case of 2011 Cairo revolt. *Proceedings of the 32nd International Conference on Information Systems (ICIS)*, Shanghai, China, paper 8.

Magnusson, M., Bellström, P., & Thoren, C. (2012). Facebook usage in government – a case study of information content. *Proceedings of the 18th Americas Conference on Information Systems (AMCIS)*, Seattle, USA, paper 11.

Magro, M., Ryan, K., Ryan, S., & Sharp, J. (2012). Facebook's use in higher education. *Proceedings of the 18th Americas Conference on Information Systems (AMCIS)*, Seattle, USA, paper 10.

Maier, C., Laumer, S., Eckhardt, A., & Weitzel, T. (2012a). Online social networks as a source and symbol of stress: an empirical analysis. *Proceedings of the 33rd International Conference on Information Systems (ICIS)*, Orlando, USA, paper 10.

Maier, C., Laumer, S., Eckhardt, A., & Weitzel, T. (2012b). When social networking turns to social overload: explaining the stress, emotional exhaustion, and quitting behavior from social network sites' users. *Proceedings of the 20th European Conference on Information Systems (ECIS)*, Barcelona, Spain, paper 71.

Maier, C., Laumer, S., & Weinert, C. (2013a). The negative side of ICT-enabled communication: the case of social interaction overload in online social networks. *Proceedings of the 21st European Conference on Information Systems (ECIS)*, Utrecht, Netherlands, paper 86.

Maier, C., Laumer, S., Weinert, C., & Weitzel, T. (2015). The effects of technostress and switching stress on discontinued use of social networking services: a study of Facebook use. *Information Systems Journal, 25*(3), 275-308.

Maier, C., Laumer, S., & Weitzel, T. (2013b). Although I am stressed, I still use IT! Theorizing the decisive impact of strain and addiction of social network site users in post-acceptance theory. *Proceedings of the 34th International Conference on Information Systems (ICIS)*, Milan, Italy.

Maietta, O. W. (2015). Determinants of university–firm R&D collaboration and its impact on innovation: A perspective from a low-tech industry. *Research Policy, 44*(7), 1341-1359.

Majchrzak, A. (2009). Where is the theory in wikis? *MIS Quarterly, 33*(1), 18-20.

Majchrzak, A., Wagner, C., & Yates, D. (2013). The impact of shaping on knowledge reuse for organizational improvement with wikis. *MIS Quarterly, 37*(2), 455-469.

Majumdar, A., & Krishna, S. (2012). Empirical analysis of Web 2.0 implications on collaborative tool usage and team interactions in virtual teams. *Proceedings of the 18th Americas Conference on Information Systems (AMCIS)*, Seattle, USA, paper 9.

Majumdar, A., Krishna, S., & Bjorn, P. (2013). Manager's perceptions of social software use in the workplace: identifying the benefits of social software and emerging patterns of use. *Proceedings of the 19th Americas Conference on Information Systems (AMCIS)*, Chicago, USA.

Makkonen, P. (2010). Combining wikis and screen capture videos as a part of information systems science course. *Proceedings of the 16th Americas Conference on Information Systems (AMCIS)*, Lima, Peru, paper 25.

Malhotra, Y., Galletta, D. (1999). Extending the technology acceptance model to account for social influence: theoretical bases and empirical validation. *Proceedings of the 32nd Hawaii international conference on system sciences*, 1–11.

Malsbender, A., Becker, J., Kohlborn, T., & Beverungen, D., & Tanwer, S. (2013). Much ado about nothing? Tracing the progress of innovations borne on enterprise social network sites. *Proceedings of the 34th International Conference on Information Systems (ICIS)*, Milan, Italy.

Mamonov, S. (2013). The antecedents and consequences of sense of community on social networking sites. *Proceedings of the 19th Americas Conference on Information Systems (AMCIS)*, Chicago, USA.

Mann, J., Drakos, N., & Gotta, M. (2014, December 18). *Critical capabilities for social software in the workplace* (ID: G00262775). Retrieved from Gartner database.

Manour, O., Askenäs, L., & Ghazawneh, A. (2013). Social media and organizing – an empirical analysis of the role of wiki affordances in organizing practices. *Proceedings of the 34th International Conference on Information Systems (ICIS)*, Milan, Italy.

Marcolin, B. L., & Saunders, W. C. (2015). A Strategic Roadmap for Navigating Academic-Industry Collaborations in Information Systems Research: Avoiding Rigor Mortis. *ACM SIGMIS Database, 46*(3), 23-51.

Marshall, M. (1996). Sampling for qualitative research., *Family Practice 13*(6):522.

Matook, S., Cummings, J., & Bala, H. (2015). Are you feeling lonely? The impact of relationship characteristics and online social network features on loneliness. *Journal of Management Information Systems, 31*(4), 278-310.

Mattessich, P. W., & Monsey, B. R. (1992). *Collaboration: what makes it work. A review of research literature on factors influencing successful collaboration*. Amherst H. Wilder Foundation, 919 Lafond, St. Paul, MN 55104..

Mayer, A. (2009). Online social networks in economics. *Decision Support Systems, 47*(3), 169-184.

Mayer, P., & Dibbern, J. (2010). An exploratory study about microblogging acceptance at work. *Proceedings of the 16th Americas Conference on Information Systems (AMCIS)*, Lima, Peru, paper 449.

Mayring, P. (2002). *Einführung in die qualitative Sozialforschung: Eine Anleitung zu qualitativem Denken, 5th edition*, Beltz Verlag, Düsseldorf.

McAfee, A. P. (2009). Shattering the myths about Enterprise 2.0. *Harvard Business Review, 87*(11), 1-6.

McDowell, J. M., Singell, L. D., & Stater, M. (2006). Two to tango? Gender differences in the decisions to publish and coauthor. *Economic Inquiry, 44*(1), 153–168.

McLure Wasko, M., Teigland, R., & Faraj, S. (2009). The provision of online public goods: examining social structure in an electronic network of practice. *Decision Support Systems, 47*(3), 254-265.

McQuail, D. (1983). *Mass communication theory*. London: Sage.

Melin, G. (2000). Pragmatism and self-organization: research collaboration on the individual level. *Research Policy, 29*(1), 31-40.

Melin, G., Persson, O. (1996). Studying research collaboration using coauthorships. *Scientometrics, 36*(3), 363-377.

Meishar-Tal, H., Pieterse, E. (2017). Why do academics use academic social networking sites? *International Review of Research in Open and Distributed Learning, 18*(1): 1–22.

Menchen-Trevino, E., Jha, S., Pathak, M., Sangareddy, S. R. P., Seo, D. B., & Ye, C. (2009). Wikis in the classroom: an agenda for studying collaborative writing in information system research. *Proceedings of the 15th Americas Conference on Information Systems (AMCIS)*, San Francisco, USA, paper 732.

Meraz, S. (2009). Is there an elite hold? Traditional media to social media agenda setting influence in blog networks. *Journal of Computer-Mediated Communication, 14*(3), 682-707.

Merz, A., Seeber, I., & Maier, R. (2015). Social Meets Structure: Revealing Team Collaboration Activities and Effects in Enterprise Social Networks. *ECIS*, (2015), 1–16.

Messinger, P. R., Stroulia, E., Lyons, K., Bone, M., Niu, R. H., Smirnov, K., & Perelgut, S. (2009). Virtual worlds – past, present, and future: new directions in social computing. *Decision Support Systems*, 47(3), 204-228.

Mettler, T., & Winter, R. (2016). Are business users social? A design experiment exploring information sharing in enterprise social systems. *Journal of Information Technology, 31*(2), 101-114.

Michel, F., Gil, Y., Ratnakar, V., & Hauder, M. (2015). A Virtual Crowdsourcing Community for Open Collaboration in Science Processes. In *Twenty-First Americas Conference on Information Systems, Puerto Rico* (pp. 1–14). Puerto Rico.

Miles, M. B., & Huberman, A. M. (1994). *Qualitative data analysis: An expanded sourcebook*. Sage.

Millar, M. M. (2013). Interdisciplinary research and the early career: the effect of interdisciplinary dissertation research on career placement and publication productivity of doctoral graduates in the sciences. *Research Policy*, 42(5), 1152-1164.

Millen, D. R., Feinberg, J., & Kerr, B. (2006). Dogear: social bookmarking in the enterprise. *Proceedings of the SIGCHI Conference on Human Factors in Computing Systems*, Montreal, Canada, 111-120.

Millen, D. R., Yang, M., Whittaker, S., & Feinberg, J. (2008). Social bookmarking and exploratory research. *Proceedings of the 2008 European Conference on Computer Supported Cooperative Work*, San Diego, USA, 21-40.

Mirabeau, L., Mignerat, M., & Grangé, C. (2013). The utility of using social media networks for data collection in survey research. *Proceedings of the 34th International Conference on Information Systems (ICIS)*, Milan, Italy.

Mlaiki, A., Walsh, I., & Kalika, M. (2013). Computer mediated social ties as predictors of SNS usage continuance. *Proceedings of the 34th International Conference on Information Systems (ICIS)*, Milan, Italy.

Mochalova, A., & Nanopoulos, A., (2013). On the role of centrality in information diffusion in social networks. *Proceedings of the 21st European Conference on Information Systems (ECIS)*, Utrecht, Netherlands, paper 101.

Mochalova, A., & Nanopoulos, A. (2014). Restricting the Spread of Firestorms in Social Networks. *Proceedings of the 22nd European Conference on Information Systems (ECIS)*.

Möslein, K. (1999). Medientheorien: Perspektiven der Medienwahl und Medienwirkung im Überblick. Arbeitsberichte des Lehrstuhls für Allgemeine und Industrielle Betriebswirtschaftslehre (Band 10). München, Germany: Technische Universität München.

Möslein, K. (2005). *Der Markt für Managementwissen*. Wiesbaden, Germany: Gabler.

Möslein, K., Bullinger, A., & Söldner, J. (2009). Open collaborative development: Trends, tools, and tactics. In *Lecture Notes in Computer Science (including subseries Lecture Notes in Artificial Intelligence and Lecture Notes in Bioinformatics)* (Vol. 5610 LNCS, pp. 874–881).

Moser, C., Ganley, D., & Groenewegen, P. (2013). Communicative genres as organising structures in the online communities – of team players and storytellers. *Information Systems Journal, 23*(6), 551-567.

Muller, M. J., Freyne, J., Dugan, C., Millen, D. R., & Thom-Santelli, J. (2009). Return on contribution (ROC): a metric for enterprise social software. *Proceedings of the 2009 European Conference on Computer Supported Cooperative Work*, Vienna, Austria, 143-150.

Munkvold, B. E., & Zigurs, I. (2005). Integration of E-Collaboration Technologies: Research Opportunities and Challenges. *International Journal of e-Collaboration, 1*(2), 1-24

Muntinga, D., Moorman, M., & Smit, E. (2011). Introducting COBRAs: Exploring motivations for brand-related social media use. *International Journal of Advertising, 30*, 13–46.

Murayama, K., Nirei, M., & Shimizu, H. (2015). Management of science, serendipity, and research performance: Evidence from a survey of scientists in Japan and the US. *Research Policy, 44*(4), 862-873.

Murray, M. (2014). *Analysis of a scholarly social networking site: The case of the dormant user*. DigitalCommons@ Kennesaw State University.

Musembwa, S., & Paul, S. (2012). Social networks: cultural diversity, trust, reciprocity and social capital. *Proceedings of the 18th Americas Conference on Information Systems (AMCIS)*, Seattle, USA, paper 18.

Narin, F., Stevens, K., & Whitlow, E. (1991). Scientific co-operation in Europe and the citation of multinationally authored papers. *Scientometrics, 21*(3), 313-323.

Nath, A. K., Singh, R., & Iyer, L. S. (2009). Web 2.0: capabilities, business value and strategic practice. *Proceedings of the 15th Americas Conference on Information Systems (AMCIS)*, San Francisco, USA, paper 451.

Nath, A.K., Singh, R., & Iyer, L. S. (2010). Web 2.0: capabilities, business value and strategic practice. *Journal of Information Science and Technology, 7*(1), 22-39.

Neben, T., & Lips, D. (2013). Breaking the norm – on the determinants of informational nonconformity in online social networks. *Proceedings of the 19th Americas Conference on Information Systems (AMCIS)*, Chicago, USA.

Nedeva, M. (2013). Between the global and the national: organizing European science. *Research Policy, 42*(1), 220-230.

Nentwich, M. (2003). *Cyberscience: Research in the Age of the Internet*. Vienna: Austrian Academy of Sciences Press.

Nentwich, M., & König, R. (2012). *Cyberscience 2.0: Research in the age of digital social networks* (Vol. 11). Campus Verlag.

Newman, R., Chang, V., Walters, R. J., & Wills, G. B. (2016). Web 2.0—The past and the future. *International Journal of Information Management, 36*(4), 591-598.

Ng, C. S. P., & Wang, W. Y. C. (2013). Best practices in managing social media for business. *Proceedings of the 34th International Conference on Information Systems (ICIS)*, Milan, Italy.

Nguyen, Q., & Sidorova, A. (2016). Responding to Negative Social Media Content: an Organizational Identification Perspective.

Niehaves, B., & Tavakoli, A. (2012). When routine work becomes social: how virtual social facilitation increases performance on simple IT-based tasks. *Proceedings of the 18th Americas Conference on Information Systems (AMCIS)*, Seattle, USA, paper 1.

Nissen, M. E., & Bergin, R. D. (2013). Knowledge work through social media applications: team performance implications of immersive virtual worlds. *Journal of Organizational Computing and Electronic Commerce, 23*(1-2), 84-109.

Nov, O., & Wattal, S. (2009). Social computing privacy concerns: antecedents & effects. *Proceedings of the SIGCHI Conference on Human Factors in Computing Systems*, Boston, USA, 333-336.

Nzabandora, W., Kamdjoug, K., Robert, J., & Wamba, F. (2016). Factors adoption of Facebook in the workplace Cameroon.

Oakley, R. L., & Salam, A. F. (2011). Computer-mediated social networks and environmental behavior. *Proceedings of the 32nd International Conference on Information Systems (ICIS)*, Shanghai, China.

Oehlhorn, C., Maier, C., Wirth, J., Laumer, S., & Dürr, S. (2016). The impact of curiosity on user acceptance A Temptation to Stalk: The Impact of Curiosity on User Acceptance of Social Networking Sites. In *Americas Conference on Information Systems* (pp. 1–10). San Diego.

Oinas-Kukkonen, H., Lyytinen, K., & Yoo, Y. (2010). Social networks and information systems: ongoing and future research streams. *Journal of the Association for Information Systems, 11*, 61-68.

O'Leary, D. E. (2011). Blog mining-review and extensions: "From each according to his opinion". *Decision Support Systems, 51*(4), 821-830.

Oostervink, N., Agterberg, M., & Huysman, M. (2016). Knowledge sharing on enterprise social media: Practices to cope with institutional complexity. *Journal of Computer-Mediated Communication, 21*(2), 156-176.

Ortbach, K., & Recker, J. C. (2014). Do good things and talk about them: a theory of academics' usage of enterprise social networks for impression management tactics. In *Proceedings of the 35th International Conference on Information Systems.* Association For Information Systems.

O'Reilly, T. (2005). What Is Web 2.0: Design Patterns and Business Models for the Next Generation of Software. Retrieved from http://www.oreillynet.com/pub/a/oreilly/tim/news/2005/09/30/what-is-web-20.html

O'Riordan, S., Feller, J., & Nagle, T. (2012). Exploring the affordances of social network sites: an analysis of three networks. *Proceedings of the 20th European Conference on Information Systems (ECIS), Barcelona, Spain*, paper 177.

Ortega, J. (2016). *Social network sites for scientists: a quantitative survey*. Chandos Publishing.

Osatuyi, B. (2012). Information seeking on social media sites: an exploratory study. *Proceedings of the 18th Americas Conference on Information Systems (AMCIS)*, Seattle, USA, paper 15.

Paluch, S., Egbert, D., & Blut, M. (2015). Acceptance of Social Media By Organizational Users – Testing the Impact of System Design Features. In *ICIS 2015 Proceedings*, 1–20.

Parameswaran, M., & Whinston, A. B. (2007). Research issues in social computing. *Journal of the Association for Information Systems, 8*(6), 336-350.

Park, H. W. (2010). Mapping the e-science landscape in South Korea using the webometrics method. *Journal of Computer-Mediated Communication, 15*(2), 211-229.

Park, J.-H. (2014). The effects of personalization on user continuance in social networking sites. *Information Processing and Management, 50*, 462-475

Park, N., Kee, K., & Valenzuela, S. (2009). Being immersed in social networking environment: Facebook groups, uses and gratifications, and social outcomes. *CyberPsychology & Behavior, 12*, 729–733.

Park, S., Lee, J. K., & Lee, M. (2013). Sustaining Web 2.0 services: a survival analysis of a live crowd-casting service. *Decision Support Systems, 54*(3), 1256-1268.

Patten, K. P., & Keane, L. B. (2010). Enterprise 2.0 management and social issues. *Proceedings of the 16th Americas Conference on Information Systems (AMCIS)*, Lima, Peru, paper 395.

Pawlowski, J. (2014). Soziale Wissensumgebungen. *Wirtschaftsinformatik, 56*(2), 91-100.

Perkmann, M., & Schildt, H. (2015). Open data partnerships between firms and universities: The role of boundary organizations. *Research Policy, 44*(5), 1133-1143.

Perkmann, M., Tartari, V., McKelvey, M., Autio, E., Broström, A., D'Este, P., Fini, R., Geuna, A., Grimaldi, R., Hughes, A., Krabel, S., Kitson, M., Llerena, P., Lissoni, F., Salter, A., & Sobrero, M. (2013). Academic engagement and commercialization: a review of the literature on university-industry relations. *Research Policy*, 42(2), 423-442.

Peters, A., & Salazar, D. (2010). Globalization in marketing: an empirical analysis of business adoption and use of social network sites. *Proceedings of the 16th Americas Conference on Information Systems (AMCIS)*, Lima, Peru, paper 570.

Pike, J., Bateman, P., & Butler, B. (2012). You saw THAT?: social networking sites, self-presentation, and impression formation in the hiring process. *Proceedings of the 18th Americas Conference on Information Systems (AMCIS)*, Seattle, USA, paper 8.

Pillet, J. C., & Carillo, K. D. A. (2016). Email-free collaboration: An exploratory study on the formation of new work habits among knowledge workers. *International Journal of Information Management*, 36(1), 113-125.

Pilson, C., & Foster, C. (2006). Life within the "empire" a framework for using the internet as a research collaboration space. *Proceedings of the 12th American Conference on Information Systems (AMCIS)*, Acapulco, Mexico, paper 436.

Ping, J. W., Goh, K. Y., Lin, Z., & Goh, A. C. G. (2012). Does social media brand community translate to real sales? A critical evaluation of purchase behavior by fans and non-fans of a Facebook fan page. *Proceedings of the 20th European Conference on Information Systems (ECIS)*, Barcelona, Spain, paper 155.

Pishdad, A., & Haider, A. (2012). Technological and non-technological aspects of Web 2.0 institutionalisation. *Proceedings of the 18th Americas Conference on Information Systems (AMCIS)*, Seattle, USA, paper 27.

Pittaway, L., Robertson, M., Munir, K., Denyer, D., & Neely, A. (2004). Networking and innovation: a systematic review of the evidence. *International journal of management reviews*, 5(3-4), 137-168.

Ploderer, B., Howard, S., & Thomas, P. (2008). Being online, living offline: the influence of social ties over the appropriation of social network sites. *Proceedings of the 2008 ACM Conference on Computer Supported Cooperative Work*, San Diego, USA, 333-342.

Ploderer, B., Howard, S., & Thomas, P. (2010). Collaboration on social network sites: amateurs, professionals and celebrities. *Computer Supported Cooperative Work*, 19, 419-455.

Plotnick, L., White, C., & Plummer, M. M. (2009). The design of an online social network site for emergency management: a one stop shop. *Proceedings of the 15th Americas Conference on Information Systems (AMCIS)*, San Francisco, USA, paper 420.

Ponomariov, B. L., & Boardman, P. C. (2010). Influencing scientists' collaboration and productivity patterns through new institutions: university research centers and scientific and technical human capital. *Research Policy, 39*(5), 613-624.

Price, D.J. de Solla, 1963. *Little Science, Big Science.* Columbia University Press, New York.

Probst, F. (2013). Who will lead and who will follow: Identifikation einflussreicher Nutzer in Online Social Networks. *Wirtschaftsinformatik, 55*(3), 175-192.

Probst, F., & Görz, Q. (2013). Data quality goes social: what drives data currency in online social networks? *Proceedings of the 21st European Conference on Information Systems (ECIS)*, Utrecht, Netherlands, paper 193.

Pu, W., Li, S., & Thatcher, J. B. (2016). Self-disclosure and SNS Platforms: The Impact of SNS Transparency and Culture. *Self*, 12, 11-2016.

Qiu, J., & Lin, Z. (2011). A framework for exploring organizational structure in dynamic social networks. *Decision Support Systems, 51*(4), 760-771.

Quan-Haase, A., Young, A. (2010). Uses and gratifications of social media: A comparison of Facebook and instant messaging. *Bulletin of Science, Technology & Society, 30*(5), 350-361.

Quinio, B., & Marciniak, R. (2013). Virtual social network characterization: a reference framework for a comparative analysis. *Proceedings of the 34th International Conference on Information Systems (ICIS)*, Milan, Italy.

Raasch, C., Lee, V., Spaeth, S., & Herstatt, C. (2013). The rise and fall of interdisciplinary research: the case of open source innovation. *Research Policy, 42*(5), 1138-1151.

Ractham, P., Kaewkitipong, L., & Firpo, D. (2010). MIS 2.0: designing the next generations MIS course using social networking technology. *Proceedings of the 16th Americas Conference on Information Systems (AMCIS)*, Lima, Peru, paper 199.

Rader, E., & Rick, W. (2008). Influences on tag choices in del.icio.us. *Proceedings of the 2008 ACM Conference on Computer Supported Cooperative Work*, San Diego, USA, 239-248.

Raeth, P., Kügler, M., & Smolnik, S. (2011). Measuring the impact of organizational social web site usage on work performance: a multilevel model. *Proceedings of the 32nd International Conference on Information Systems (ICIS)*, Shanghai, China, paper 15.

Raeth, P., Smolnik, S., Urbach, N., & Zimmer, C. (2009). Towards assessing the success of social software in corporate environments. *Proceedings of the 15th Americas Conference on Information Systems (AMCIS)*, San Francisco, USA, paper 662.

Raeth, P., Urbach, N., Smolnik, S., Butler, B. S., & Königs, P. (2010). The adoption of Web 2.0 in corporations: a process perspective. *Proceedings of the 16th Americas Conference on Information Systems (AMCIS)*, Lima, Peru, paper 405.

Rafols, I., Leydesdorff, L., O'Hare, A., Nightingale, P., & Stirling, A. (2012). How journal rankings can suppress interdisciplinary research: A comparison between innovation studies and business & management. *Research Policy, 41*(7), 1262-1282.

Ramotar, M., & Baptista, J. (2013). Legitimating user participation in mature organizations – exploring social media adoption in a financial services organization. *ICIS 2013 Proceedings*.

Raney, A. A., & Janicke, S. H. (2013). How we enjoy and why we seek out morally complex characters in media entertainment. In Tamborini, R. (Ed.), *Media and the moral mind* (pp. 152–170). London: Routledge.

Razmerita, L., Kirchner, K., & Nabeth, T. (2014). Social media in organizations: leveraging personal and collective knowledge processes. *Journal of Organizational Computing and Electronic Commerce, 24*(1), 74-93.

Recine, M., Prichard, J. J., & Chaudhury, A. (2013). Social Media and Evolving Marketing Communication Using IT. *CAIS, 33*, 8.

Recker, J., & Lekse, D. (2016). A field study of spatial preferences in enterprise microblogging. *Journal of Information Technology, 31*(2), 115-129.

Renken, U., Soeldner, J.-H., Bullinger, A., & Möslein, K. (2010). Wer mit wem und vor allem warum? Soziale Netzwerke für Forscher. In K. Meissner & M. Engelien (Eds.), *Proceedings of GeNeMe 2010, Dresden* (pp. 141–152).

Renken, U. B. (2012). *To Use Or Not to Use?*: Examining the Adoption of Social Research Network Sites (Doctoral dissertation).

Rhoten, D., Pfirman, S. (2007). Women in interdisciplinary science: Exploring preferences and consequences. *Research Policy, 36*(1), 56–75.

Richter, D., & Riemer, K. (2013). The contextual nature of enterprise social networking: a multi case study comparison. *Proceedings of the 34th International Conference on Information Systems (ICIS)*, Milan, Italy, paper 94.

Richter, D., Riemer, K., & vom Brocke, J. (2011). Internet Social Networking – Stand der Forschung und Konsequenzen für Enterprise 2.0. *Wirtschaftsinformatik*, 53(2), 89-108.

Richter, A., Söldner, J.-H., Bullinger, A. C., & Koch, M. (2009). Ein Ordnungsrahmen für Social Networking Services. In *Proceedings of the 12th Workshop Gemeinschaften in Neuen Medien: Virtuelle Organisation und Neue Medien (GeNeMe 2009)* (pp. 2–6). Dresden. https://doi.org/10.1007/BF01950826

Riemer, K., Altenhofen, A., & Richter, A. (2011). What are you doing? – Enterprise microblogging as context building. *Proceedings of the 19th European Conference on Information Systems (ECIS)*, Helsinki, Finland, paper 252.

Riemer, K., Finke, J., & Hovorka, D. S. (2015). Bridging or Bonding : Do Individuals gain Social Capital from Participation in Enterprise Social Networks ? *Thirty Sixth International Conference on Information Systems*, 1–20.

Riemer, K., vom Brocke, J., Richter, D., & Große Böckmann, S. (2008). Cooperation systems in research networks – case evidence of network (mis)fit and adoption challenges. *Proceedings of the 16th European Conference on Information Systems (ECIS)*, Galway, Ireland, paper 213. [030]

Riemer, K., Overfeld, P., Scifleet, P., & Richter, A. (2012). Eliciting the anatomy of technology appropriation process: a case study in enterprise social media. *Proceedings of the 20th European Conference on Information Systems (ECIS)*, Barcelona, Spain, paper 134.

Riemer, K., Richter, A., & Bohringer, M. (2010a). Enterprise microblogging. *Wirtschaftsinformatik*, 52(6), 387-390.

Riemer, K., Richter, A., & Seltsikas, P. (2010b). Enterprise microblogging: procrastination or productive use? *Proceedings of the 16th Americas Conference on Information Systems (AMCIS)*, Lima, Peru, paper 506.

Rigby, J., & Edler, J. (2005). Peering inside research networks: some observations on the effect of the intensity of collaboration on the variability of research quality. *Research Policy*, 34(6), 784-194.

Risius, M. (2014). Is It Really About Facts? the Positive Side of "Meforming" for Turning Self-Disclosure Into Social Capital in Enterprise Social Media. *ECIS*, 1–16.

Risius, M., & Akolk, F. (2015). Differentiated sentiment analysis of corporate social media accounts. In 2015 *Americas Conference on Information Systems, AMCIS 2015*. Fajardo, Puerto Rico.

Rizk, R., Gürses, S., & Guenther, O. (2010). SNS and 3rd party applications private policies and their construction of privacy concerns. *Proceedings of the 18th European Conference on Information Systems (ECIS)*, Pretoria, South Africa, paper 143.

Rode, H. (2016). To share or not to share: the effects of extrinsic and intrinsic motivations on knowledge-sharing in enterprise social media platforms. *Journal of Information Technology, 31*(2), 152-165.

Rogers, D. L., & Whetten, D. 1982. *Interorganizational Coordination: Theory, Research, and Implementation*. Ames, Iowa: Iowa State University Press

Rohmann, S., Heuschneider, S., & Schumann, M. (2014). Social software in new product development - State of research and future research directions. In *20th Americas Conference on Information Systems, AMCIS 2014*.

Rohmann, S., Heuschneider, S., & Schumann, M. (2015). Social Software for Product Development-Explorative Study on Influencing Factors and related Challenges. *The 2015 Americas Conference on Information Systems (AMCIS2015)*, 1–13.

Rosen, P., & Kluemper, D. (2008). The impact of the big five personality traits on the acceptance of social networking website. *Proceedings of the 14th Americas Conference on Information Systems (AMCIS)*, Toronto, Canada, paper 274.

Rosen, P., & Sherman, P. (2006). Hedonic information systems: acceptance of social networking websites. *Proceedings of the 12th American Conference on Information Systems (AMCIS)*, Acapulco, Mexico, paper 162.

Rui, H., Liu, Y., & Whinston, A. (2013). Whose and what chatter matters? The effect of tweets on movie sales. *Decision Support Systems, 55*(4), 863-870.

Ryan, J. C., & Hurley, J. (2007). An empirical examination of the relationship between scientists' work environment and research performance. *R&D Management, 37*(4), 345-354.

Ryan, T., Chester, A., Reece, J., & Xenos, S. (2014). The uses and abuses of Facebook: a review of Facebook addiction. *Journal of Behavioral Addictions, 3*(3), 133-148.

Sabharwal, M., & Hu, Q. (2013). Participation in university-based research centers: is it helping or hurting researchers? *Research Policy, 42*(6-7), 1301-1311.

Saldanha, T. J. V., & Krishnan, M. S. (2010). Organizational adoption of Web 2.0 technologies: an empirical analysis. *Proceedings of the 16th Americas Conference on Information Systems (AMCIS)*, Lima, Peru, paper 103.

Saldanha, T. J. V., & Krishnan, M. S. (2012). Organizational adoption of Web 2.0 technologies: an empirical analysis. *Journal of Organizational Computing and Electronic Commerce, 22*(4), 301-333.

Salehan, M., Mousavizadeh Kashipaz, S. M., & Xu, C. (2013). Information sharing on social networking websites: antecedents and consequences of trust. *Proceedings of the 19th Americas Conference on Information Systems (AMCIS)*, Chicago, USA.

Salustri, F. A., & Weerasinghe, J. S. (2010). Wikis in Design Engineering Research. In *e-Research Collaboration* (pp. 201-217). Springer Berlin Heidelberg.

Scellato, G., Franzoni, C., & Stephan, P. (2015). Migrant scientists and international networks. *Research Policy, 44*(1), 108-120.

Schaefer, C. (2008). Motivations and usage patterns on social network sites. *Proceedings of the 16th European Conference on Information Systems (ECIS)*, Galway, Ireland, paper 143.

Schall, D. (2014). A multi-criteria ranking framework for partner selection in scientific collaboration environments. *Decision Support Systems, 59*, 1-14.

Schlagwein, D., Schoder, D., & Fischbach, K. (2011). Social information systems: review, framework, and research agenda. *Proceedings of the 32nd International Conference on Information Systems (ICIS)*, Shanghai, China, paper 33.

Schlagwein, D., & Prasarnphanich, P. (2014). Social media around the GLOBE. *Journal of Organizational Computing and Electronic Commerce, 24*(February), 122–137

Schniederjans, D., Cao, E. S., & Schniederjans, M. (2013). Enhancing financial performance with social media: an impression management perspective. *Decision Support Systems, 55*(4), 911-918.

Schöndienst, V., & Dang-Xuan, L. (2012). '… a friend indeed?' – An empirical analysis of interactions on Facebook. *Proceedings of the 20th European Conference on Information Systems (ECIS)*, Barcelona, Spain, paper 234.

Scholtz, J., & Steves, M. P. (2004). A Framework for Real-World Software System Evaluations. *CSCW '04: Proceedings of the 2004 ACM Conference on Computer Supported Cooperative Work*, 600–603.

Schrage, M. (1995). *No more teams: mastering the dynamics of creative collaboration.* Currency and Doubleday, New York.

Schröder, A., Minocha, S., & Schneider, C. (2010). Social software in higher education: the diversity of applications and their contributions to students' learning experiences. *Communications of the Association for Information Systems, 26*, article 25.

Schwämmlein, E., & Wodzicki, K. (2012). What to tell about me? Self-Presentation in online communities. *Journal of Computer-Mediated Communication, 17*(4), 387-407.

Seawright, J., Gerring, J. (2008). Case selection techniques in case study research: A menu of qualitative and quantitative options. *Political Research Quarterly, 61*(2), 294-308.

Seebach, C., Beck, R., & Denisova, O. (2012). Sensing social media for corporate reputation management: a business agility perspective. *Proceedings of the 20th European Conference on Information Systems (ECIS)*, Barcelona, Spain, paper 140.

Seebach, C., Beck, R., & Pahlke, I. (2011). Situation awareness through social collaboration platforms in distributed work environments. *Proceedings of the 32nd International Conference on Information Systems (ICIS)*, Shanghai, China, paper 2.

Seo, D., & Rietsema, A. (2010). A way to become Enterprise 2.0: beyond Web 2.0 tools. *Proceedings of the 33rd International Conference on Information Systems (ICIS)*, Orlando, USA, paper 140.

Seo, M., Kim, J., & Yang, H. (2016). Frequent Interaction and Fast Feedback Predict Perceived Social Support: Using Crawled and Self-Reported Data of Facebook Users. *Journal of Computer-Mediated Communication, 21*(4), 282-297.

Shah, V., Subramanian, S., Rouis, S., & Limayem, M. (2012). A study on the impact of Facebook usage on student's social capital and academic performance. *AMCIS 2012 Proceedings*, paper 27.

Shao, G. (2009). Understanding the appeal of user-generated media: A uses and gratification perspective. *Internet Research, 19*(1), 7-25.

Sharma, S. (2016). High Engagement , Psychosocial Well-being and Fear of Missing Out in Online Social Network. In *Twenty-Second Americas Conference on Information Systems* (pp. 1–7).

Shen, A. X. L., Lee, M. K. O., Cheung, C. M. K., & Chen, H. (2010). Gender differences in intentional social action: we-intention to engage in social network-facilitated team collaboration. *Journal of Information Technology, 25*(2), 152-169.

Shim, S., & Lee, B. (2009). Internet portals' strategic utilization of UCC and Web 2.0 ecology. *Decision Support Systems, 47*(4), 415-423.

Shim, J. P., Dekleva, S., French, A. M., & Guo, C. (2013). Social Networking and Social Media in the United States, South Korea, and China. *CAIS, 33*(28), 485-496.

Shi, N., Lee, M. K. O., Cheung, C., Chen, H. (2010). The continuance of online social networks: how to keep people using Facebook? *Proceedings of the 43rd Hawaii International Conference on System Sciences*, Honolulu, USA, 1–10.

Shi, Z., Rui, H., & Whinston, A. B. (2014). Content sharing in a social broadcasting environment: Evidence from Twitter. *MIS Quarterly: Management Information Systems, 38*(1), 123-142.

Shin, S. I., & Hall, D. J. (2012). How do social networking site users become loyal? A social exchange perspective. *Proceedings of the 33rd International Conference on Information Systems (ICIS)*, Orlando, USA.

Shin, S. I., & Hall, D. J. (2013). Does trustworthy social networking sites draw user's persistency behaviors? Examining role of trust in social networking sites continuance usage. *Proceedings of the 19th Americas Conference on Information Systems (AMCIS)*, Chicago, *USA*.

Shrivastav, H., Collins, R., Hiltz, S., & Dwyer, C. (2012). Facebook news feed: relevance or noise? *Proceedings of the 19th Americas Conference on Information Systems (AMCIS)*, Chicago, USA, paper 18.

Siedlok, F., Hibbert, P., & Sillince, J. (2015). From practice to collaborative community in interdisciplinary research contexts. *Research Policy, 44*(1), 96-107.

Siggelkow, N. (2007). Persuasion with case studies. *Academy of Management Journal, 50*(1), 20-24

Siles, I. (2012). Web technologies of the self: the arising of the "blogger" identity. *Journal of Computer-Mediated Communication, 17*(4), 408-421.

Silva, L., Goel, L., & Mousavidin, E. (2008). Exploring the dynamics of blog communities: the case of MetaFilter. *Information Systems Journal, 19*(1), 55-81.

Silva, T., Guo, Z., Ma, J., Jiang, H., & Chen, H. (2013). A social network-empowered research analytical framework for project selection. *Decision Support Systems, 55*(4), 957-968.

Silverman, D. (2013). *Doing qualitative research: A practical handbook.* Sage Publications.

Simeth, M., & Raffo, J. D. (2013). What makes companies pursue an Open Science strategy? *Research Policy, 42*(9), 1531-1543.

Simon, T., Goldberg, A., & Adini, B. (2015). Socializing in emergencies—A review of the use of social media in emergency situations. *International Journal of Information Management, 35*(5), 609-619.

Singh, M., Davison, C., & Wickramasinghe, N. (2010). Organizational use of Web 2.0 technologies: an Australian perspective. *Proceedings of the 16th Americas Conference on Information Systems (AMCIS)*, Lima, Peru, paper 198.

Sivan, L., Libai, B., & Oestreicher-Singer, G. (2012). Predicting participation in social media sites by analyzing user participation patterns. *Proceedings of the 33rd International Conference on Information Systems (ICIS)*, Orlando, USA.

Skageby, J. (2010). Gift-giving as a conceptual framework: framing social behavior in online networks. *Journal of Information Technology, 25*(2), 170-177.

Sledgianowski, D., & Kulviwat, S. (2008). Social network sites: antecedents of user adoption and usage. *Proceedings of the 14th Americas Conference on Information Systems (AMCIS)*, Toronto, Canada, paper 83.

Smailhodzic, E., Boonstra, A., & Langley, D. (2015). Social Media Enabled Interactions in Healthcare : Towards a Typology. *ECIS*, (2015), 1–16.

Smith, M., 1958. The trend toward multiple authorship in psychology. *American Psychologist 13*, 596–599.

Smith, H. A., & McKeen, J. D. (2011). Enabling collaboration with IT. *Communications of the Association for Information Systems, 28*, article 16. [379] [076]

Smykla, E., Zippel, K. (2010). Literature review: Gender and international research collaboration. *Report prepared with funding from NSF, OISE, 936970.*

Söldner, J.-H., Bullinger, A., & Möslein, K. (2010). Social Software for Research Collaboration A Systematic Literature Review. In *EURAM Annual Conference 2010 Rome* (Vol. 2010, pp. 1–39). https://doi.org/10.1002/qua.21736

Söldner, J., Haller, J., Bullinger, A., & Möslein, K. (2009). Supporting research collaboration - on the needs of virtual research teams. In H. R. Hansen, D. Karagiannis, & H. G. Fill (Eds.). *Business services: Konzepte, Technologien, Anwendungen*, 9. Internationale Tagung Wirtschaftsinformatik (Vol. 1). Wien, Austria: Österreichische Computer Gesellschaft. Available from http://www.dke.univie.ac.at/wi2009/Tagungsband 8f9643f/Band1.pdf

Soliman, M.A., & Beaudry, A. (2010). Understanding individual adoption and use of social computing: a user-system fit model and empirical study. *Proceedings of the*

31st International Conference on Information Systems (ICIS), St. Louis, USA, paper 22.

Sonnenwald, D. H. (2007). Scientific Collaboration. *Annual Review of Information Science and Technology (ARIST), 41*, 643–681.

Sonnenwald, D. H., Whitton, M. C., Maglaughlin, K. L. (2003). Evaluating a scientific collaboratory: results of a controlled experiment. *ACM Transactions of Computer-Human Interaction, 10*(2), 150-176.

Sooryamoorthy, R., & Shrum, W. (2007). Does the internet promote collaboration and productivity? Evidence from the scientific community in South Africa. *Journal of Computer-Mediated Communication, 12*(2), article 20.

Sopha, M., & Raghu, T. S. (2012). It's not all about the music: user preferences for musicians on Facebook. *Proceedings of the 18th Americas Conference on Information Systems (AMCIS)*, Seattle, USA, paper 19.

Spagnoletti, P., Resca, A., & Sæbø, Ø. (2015). Design for social media engagement: insights from elderly care assistance. *The Journal of Strategic Information Systems, 24*(2), 128-145.

Stafford, T., Stafford, M., & Schkade, L. (2004). Determining uses and gratifications for the Internet. *Decision Sciences, 35*(2), 259-288.

Stavrositu, C., & Sundar, S. S. (2012). Does blogging empower women? Exploring the role of agency and community. *Journal of Computer-Mediated Communication, 17*(4), 369-386.

Steininger, D. M., Huntgeburth, J., & Veit, D. (2011). A systemizing research framework for Web 2.0. *Proceedings of the 19th European Conference on Information Systems (ECIS)*, Helsinki, Finland, paper 255.

Steininger, D. M., Wunderlich, P., & Pohl, F. (2013). Exploring competitive advantages of social networking sites: a business model perspective. *Proceedings of the 21st European Conference on Information Systems (ECIS)*, Utrecht, Netherlands, paper 214.

Stenmark, D. (2008). Web 2.0 in the business environment: the new intranet or a passing hype? *Proceedings of the 16th European Conference on Information Systems (ECIS)*, Galway, Ireland, paper 35.

Stenmark, D., & Zaffar, F. O. (2014). Consultant strategies and technological affordances: Managing organisational social media. *In 20th Americas Conference on Information Systems, AMCIS 2014*. Association for Information Systems.

Stieglitz, S., & Dang-Xuan, L. (2013). Emotions and information diffusion in social media – sentiment of microblogs and sharing behavior. *Journal of Management Information Systems, 29*(4), 217-247.

Stieglitz, S., Bruns, A., & Krüger, N. (2015). Enterprise-related crisis communication on Twitter. *Proceedings der 12. Internationalen Tagung Wirtschaftsinformatik (WI 2015)*, 917-932.

Stocker, A., Richter, A., Hoefler, P., & Tochtermann, K. (2012). Exploring appropriation of enterprise wikis: a multiple-case study. *Computer Supported Cooperative Work, 21*, 317-356.

Stojmenovic, M., & Lindgaard, G. (2014). Social network analysis and communication in emergency response simulations. *Journal of Organizational Computing and Electronic Commerce, 24*(2-3), 236-256.

Su, X. (2014). Academic scientists' affiliation with university research centers: Selection dynamics. *Research Policy, 43*(2), 382-390.

Summers, J. D., & Young, A. G. (2016). Gamification and brand engagement on facebook: An exploratory case study. *Proceedings of the 22nd Americas Conference on Information Systems (AMCIS)*, 1–10.

Takahashi, M. (2012). R&D Network – case study and social network analysis. *Proceedings of the 33rd International Conference on Information Systems (ICIS)*, Orlando, USA.

Talaei-Khoei, A., & Daniel, J. (2016). Peer Tutoring on Facebook to Engage Students with Flipped Classes: A Correlational Experiment on Learning Outcomes

Tan, W. K., Nguyen, T. H. D., Tha, K. K. O., & Yu, X. (2009). Designing groupware that fosters social capital creation: can Facebook support global virtual team? *Proceedings of the 15th Americas Conference on Information Systems (AMCIS)*, San Francisco, USA, paper 525.

Tan, S. S. (2015). Health 2. 0 Enabled Collaborative Healthcare Maintenance. In *ICIS-RP* (pp. 1–12).

Tanbeer, S. K., Leung, C. K., & Cameron, J. J. (2014). Interactive mining of strong friends from social networks and its applications in e-commerce. *Journal of Organizational Computing and Electronic Commerce, 24*(2-3), 157-173.

Tartari, V., Salter, A. (2015). The engagement gap: Exploring gender differences in University–Industry collaboration activities. *Research Policy, 44*(6), 1176-1191.

Tashakkori, A., Teddlie, C. (2010). *Sage handbook of mixed methods in social & behavioral research.* Sage publications.

Taylor, D., Lewin, J., & Strutton, D. (2011). Friends, fans, and followers: Do ads work on social networks? How gender and age shape receptivity. *Journal of Advertising Research, 51*, 258–275.

Te'eni, D. (2009). Comment: The wiki way in a hurry – the ICIS anecdote. *MIS Quarterly, 33*(1), 20-22.

Teten, D., & Allen, S. (2005). *The virtual handshake: opening doors and closing deals online.* AMACOM Div American Mgmt Assn.

Thadani, D. R., & Cheung, C. M. K. (2011). Exploring the role of online social network dependency in habit formation. *Proceedings of the 32nd International Conference on Information Systems (ICIS)*, Shanghai, China, paper 34.

Thambusamy, R., Church, M., Nemati, H., & Barrick, J. (2010). Socially exchanging privacy for pleasure: hedonic use of computer-mediated social networks. *Proceedings of the 31st International Conference on Information Systems (ICIS)*, St. Louis, USA, paper 253.

Thambusamy, R., & Nemati, H. R. (2011). A sociomateriality practice perspective of online social networking. *Proceedings of the 32nd International Conference on Information Systems (ICIS)*, Shanghai, China.

Thom-Santelli, J., Muller, M. J., & Millen, D. R. (2008). Social tagging roles: publishers, evangelists, leaders. *Proceedings of the SIGCHI Conference on Human Factors in Computing Systems*, 1041-1044.

Tow, W. N. H., Dell, P., & Venable, J. (2010). Understanding information disclosure behavior in Australian Facebook users. *Journal of Information Technology, 25*(2), 126-136.

Tranfield, D., Denyer, D., & Smart, P. (2003). Towards a methodology for developing evidence-informed management knowledge by means of systematic review. *British journal of management, 14*(3), 207-222.

Trier, M., & Richter, A. (2015). The deep structure of organizational online networking–an actor-oriented case study. *Information Systems Journal, 25*(5), 465-488.

Tschersich, M., & Botha, R. A. (2013). Understanding the impact of default policy settings on self-disclosure in social network services. *Proceedings of the 19th Americas Conference on Information Systems (AMCIS)*, Chicago, USA.

Turban, E., Bolloju, N., & Liang, T. P. (2013). Enterprise Social Networking: opportunities, adoption, and risk mitigation. *Journal of Organizational Computing and Electronic Commerce, 21*(3), 202-220.

Turban, E., Liang, T. P., and Wu, S. P. J. (2011). A Framework for Adopting Collaboration 2.0 Tools for Virtual Group Decision Making. *Group Decision and Negotiation, 20*(2), 137-154.

Ubfal, D., & Maffioli, A. (2011). The impact of funding on research collaboration: evidence from a developing country. *Research Policy, 40*(9), 1269-1279.

Ulmer, G., & Pallud, J. (2014). Understanding Usages and Affordances of Enterprise Social Networks: A Sociomaterial Perspective. *Twentieth Americas Conference on Information Systems*, 1–14.

Urquhart, C., & Vaast, E. (2012). Building social media theory from case studies: a new frontier for IS research. *Proceedings of the 33rd International Conference on Information Systems (ICIS)*, Orlando, USA.

Utz, S. (2009). The (potential) benefits of campaigning via social network sites. *Journal of Computer-Mediated Communication, 14*(2), 221-243. [137]

Utz, S. (2010). Show me your friends and I will tell you what type of person you are: how one's profile, number of friends, and type of friends influence impression formation on social network sites. *Journal of Computer-Mediated Communication, 15*(2), 314-335.

Utz, S., & Beukeboom, C. J. (2011). The role of social network sites in romantic relationships: effects on jealousy and relationship happiness. *Journal of Computer-Mediated Communication, 16*(4), 511-527.

Vaast, E., Lapointe, L., Negoita, B., & Safadi, H. (2012). Stakeholders' use of microblogging to engage in emotion strategies during a crisis. *Proceedings of the 33rd International Conference on Information Systems (ICIS)*, Orlando, USA.

Vaezi, R., Torkzadesh, G., & Chang, J. C. J. (2011). Understanding the influence of blog on the development of social capital. *The DATA BASE for Advances in Information Systems, 42*(3), 34-45.

Väyrynen, K., Hekkala, R., & Liias, T. (2013). Knowledge protection challenges of social media encountered by organizations. *Journal of Organizational Computing and Electronic Commerce, 23*(1-2), 34-55.

Valenzuela, S., Park, N., & Kee, K. F. (2009). Is There Social Capital in a Social Network Site?: Facebook Use and College Students' Life Satisfaction, Trust, and Participation. *Journal of Computer-Mediated Communication, 14*(4), 875–901.

Vanderhaeghen, D., Fettke, P., & Loos, P. (2010). Organisations- und Technologieoptionen des Geschäftsprozessmanagements aus der Perspektive des Web 2.0. *Wirtschaftsinformatik, 52*(1), 17-32.

Van Dam, J. W., & van de Velden, M. (2015). Online profiling and clustering of Facebook users. *Decision Support Systems, 70*, 60-72.

Van de Ven, A.H. (1986). Central problems in the management of innovation. *Management Science, 32(5)*, 590-607

Van Gorp, A., Pogrebnyakov, N., & Maldonado, E. (2015). Just Keep Tweeting: Emergency Responder's Social Media Use Before and During Emergencies. *Proceedings of the 23rd European Conference on Information Systems (ECIS 2015)*, 1–15.

Vannoy, S. A., & Medlin, B. D. (2013). Exploring the factors that influence social computing intentions. *Proceedings of the 19th Americas Conference on Information Systems (AMCIS)*, Chicago, USA.

Van Osch, W., & Steinfield, C. W. (2013). Boundary spanning through enterprise social software: an external stakeholder perspective. *Proceedings of the 34th International Conference on Information Systems (ICIS)*, Milan, Italy, 604-621.

Van Osch, W., & Steinfield, C. W. (2016). Team boundary spanning: strategic implications for the implementation and use of enterprise social media. *Journal of Information Technology, 31*(2), 207-225.

Van Rijnsoever, F. J., & Hessels, L. K. (2011). Factors associated with disciplinary and interdisciplinary research collaboration. *Research Policy, 40*(3), 463-472.

Van Rijnsoever, F. J., Hessels, L. K., & Vandeberg, R. L. J. (2008). A resource-based view on the interactions of university researchers. *Research Policy, 37*(8), 1255-1266.

Vasileiadou, E., & Vliegenthart, R. (2009). Research productivity in the era of the internet revisited. *Research Policy, 38*(8), 1260-1268.

Velamuri, V. (2013). *Hybrid value creation*. Springer Fachmedien Wiesbaden. https://doi.org/10.1007/978-3-8349-3961-6

Velenzuala, S., Park, N., & Kee, K. F. (2009). Is there social capital in a social network site?: Facebook use and college students' life satisfaction, trust, and participation. *Journal of Computer-Mediated Communication, 14*(4), 875-901.

Vergeer, M., & Hermans, L. (2013). Campaigning on twitter: microblogging and online social networking as campaign tools in the 2010 general elections in the Netherlands. *Journal of Computer-Mediated Communication, 18*(3), 399-419.

Vishwanath, A. (2015). Habitual Facebook use and its impact on getting deceived on social media. *Journal of Computer-Mediated Communication, 20*(1), 83-98.

Von Hippel, E., Franke, N., & Prügl, R. (2009). Pyramiding: Efficient search for rare subjects. *Research Policy, 38*(9), 1397-1406.

Von Krogh, G. (2012). How does social software change knowledge management? Toward a strategic research agenda. *Journal of Strategic Information Systems, 21*, 154-164.

Vrandečić, D., & Krötzsch, M. (2014). Wikidata: A Free Collaborative Knowledgebase. *Communications of the ACM, 57*(10), 78–85.

Vyas, A., & Choudrie, J. (2013). Online social networking in older individuals: a study of Hertfordshire. *Proceedings of the 21st European Conference on Information Systems (ECIS)*, Utrecht, Netherlands, paper 93.

Wagner, C. S., Brahmakulam, I., Jackson, B., Wong, A., & Yoda, T. (2001). *Science and technology collaboration: Building capacity in developing countries?* (Vol. MR-1357.0-WB). Santa Monica, CA: RAND. Available from http://www.rand.org/pubs/monograph reports/2005/MR1357.0.pdf

Wagner, C., & Leydesdorff, L. (2005). Network structure, self-organization, and the growth of international collaboration in science. *Research Policy, 34*(10), 1608-1618.

Wagner, C., & Majchrzak, A. (2006). Enabling customer-centricity using wikis and the wiki way. *Journal of Management Information Systems, 23*(3), 17-43.

Wagner, C.S., Park, H.W., & Leydesdorff, L. (2015). The continuing growth of global cooperation networks in research: A conundrum for national governments. *PLoS ONE, 10*(7).

Wagner, D., Richter, A., Trier, M., & Wagner, H.-T. (2014). Toward a conceptualization of online community health. *35th International Conference on Information Systems: Building a Better World Through Information Systems, ICIS 2014*.

Wakefield, R., & Wakefield, K. (2016). Social media network behavior: A study of user passion and affect. *The Journal of Strategic Information Systems, 25*(2), 140-156.

Walsh, J. P., Huang, H. (2014). Local context, academic entrepreneurship and open science: Publication secrecy and commercial activity among Japanese and US scientists. *Research Policy, 43*(2), 245-260.

Walsh, J. P., Maloney, N. G. (2007). Collaboration structure, communication media, and problems in scientific work teams. *Journal of Computer-Mediated Communication, 12*(2), article 19.

Walsh, J. P., Lee, Y. N. (2015). The bureaucratization of science. *Research Policy, 44*(8), 1584-1600.

Walther, J. B., Liang, Y., Gangster, T., Wohn, D. Y., & Emington, J. (2012). Online reviews, helpfulness ratings, and consumer attitudes: an extension of congruity theory to multiple sources in Web 2.0. *Journal of Computer-Mediated Communication, 18*(1), 97-112.

Wang, C. Y., Chou, S. T., & Chang, H. C. (2009). The moderating role of utilitarian/hedonic user motivation on user behavior towards Web 2.0 applications. *Proceedings of the 17th European Conference on Information Systems (ECIS)*, Verona, Italy, paper 154.

Wang, G. (2013). Understanding positive and negative outcomes of SNSs usage from a social network analysis aspect. *Proceedings of the 19th Americas Conference on Information Systems (AMCIS)*, Chicago, USA.

Wang, Y., & Li, D. (2013). Testing the moderating effects of toolkits and user communities in personalization: the case of social networking service. *Decision Support Systems, 55*(1), 31-42.

Wang, C., Lee, M. K., & Hua, Z. (2015). A theory of social media dependence: Evidence from microblog users. *Decision Support Systems*, 69, 40-49.

Wang, J. (2016). Knowledge creation in collaboration networks: Effects of tie configuration. *Research Policy, 45*(1), 68-80.

Wattal, S. (2010). Web 2.0 and politics: the 2008 U.S. presidential election and an e-politics research agenda. *MIS Quarterly, 34*(4), 669-688.

Wattal, S., Racherla, P., & Mandviwalla, M. (2010). Network externalities and technology use: a quantitative analysis of intraorganizational blogs. *Journal of Management Information Systems*, 27(1), 145-173.

Webster, J., Watson, R. (2002). Analyzing the Past to Prepare for the Future: Writing a Literature Review. *MIS Quarterly, 26*(2), 13-23.

Wei, L. (2009). Filter blogs vs. personal journals: understanding the knowledge production gap on the internet. *Journal of Computer-Mediated Communication, 14*(3), 532-558.

Weinert, C., Maier, C., & Laumer, S. (2012). The shady side of Facebook: the influence of perceived information and network characteristics on the attitude towards information overload. *Proceedings of the 18th Americas Conference on Information Systems (AMCIS)*, Seattle, USA, paper 14.

Wenninger, H., Krasnova, H., & Buxmann, P. (2014). Activity Matters: Investigating the influence of Facebook on life satisfaction of teenage users. *Twenty Second European Conference on Information Systems*, 1–18.

West, R., Turner, L. (2007). *Introducing communication theory (analysis and application.* 4th edn). New York: McGraw-Hill.

Wigand, R. T., Wood, J. R., & Mande, D. M. (2010). Taming the social network jungle: from Web 2.0 to social media. *Proceedings of the 16th Americas Conference on Information Systems (AMCIS)*, Lima, Peru, paper 416.

Willard, M., & Leffingwell, D. (2010). Blogging to Accelerate Peer Review of Doctoral Dissertations. In *e-Research Collaboration* (pp. 117-131). Springer Berlin Heidelberg.

Wilson, D. W., Proudfoot, J. G., & Valacich, J. S. (2014). Saving Face on Facebook : Privacy Concerns , Social Benefits , and Impression Management. *Proceedings of the 35th International Conference on Information Systems*, 1–18.

Winter, S., & Krämer, N. C. (2012). Selecting science information in Web 2.0: how source cues, message sidedness, and need for cognition influence users' exposure to blog posts. *Journal of Computer-Mediated Communication*, 18(1), 80-96.

Wisniewski, P. J., Najmul Islam, A. K. M., Lipford, H. R., & Wilso, D. C. (2016). Framing and Measuring Multi-dimensional Interpersonal Privacy Preferences of Social Networking Site Users. *Communications of the Association for information systems, 38*(1).

Wöhner, T., Köhler, S., & Peters, R. (2015). Good Authors= Good Articles?-How Wikis Work. In *Wirtschaftsinformatik* (pp. 872-886).

Wray, K., 2006. Scientific authorship in the age of collaborative research. *Studies In History and Philosophy of Science Part A* 37(3), 505–514.

Wu, H. L. (2009a). Utilitarian and hedonic values of social network services. *Proceedings of the 15th Americas Conference on Information Systems (AMCIS)*, San Francisco, USA, paper 289.

Wu, H. L. (2009b). An integrated framework of SNS users' motivations. *Proceedings of the 15th Americas Conference on Information Systems (AMCIS)*, San Francisco, USA, paper 379.

Wu, H., & Gordon, M. D. (2009). From social tagging to social hierarchies: sharing deeper structural knowledge in Web 2.0. *Communications of the Association for Information Systems, 24*, article 45.

Wu, J., & Srite, M. (2014). How Envy Influences SNS Intentions to Use. *Twentieth Americas Conference on Information Systems, Savannah*, 1–13.

Wu, Y. L., & Tseng, K. H. (2012). Exploring antecedents of habit on social network service. *Proceedings of the 18th Americas Conference on Information Systems (AMCIS)*, Seattle, USA, paper 14.

Wyatt, J., Djamasbi, S., & Traietti, M. (2016). User Experience of Enterprise Social Networks and Collaboration.

Xie, K., & Lee, Y. (2014). Quantifying the Impact of Earned and Owned Social Media Exposures in a Two-stage Decision Making Model of Brand Purchase. *Icis, 1222*(December), 1–17.

Xu, C., Ryan, S., Magro, M., & Wen, C. (2012). Why do people stick with a specific social networking site? An integrated relationship and uses gratification perspective. *Proceedings of the 18th Americas Conference on Information Systems (AMCIS)*, Seattle, USA, paper 24.

Xu, H., Parks, R., Chu, C. H., & Zhang, X. (2010). Information disclosure and online social networks: from the case of Facebook News Feed controversy to a theoretical understanding. *Proceedings of the 16th Americas Conference on Information Systems (AMCIS)*, Lima, Peru, paper 503.

Xu, H., Phan, T. Q., & Tan, B. C. Y. (2013). How does online social network change my mood? An empirical study of depression contagion on social network sites using text-mining. *Proceedings of the 34th International Conference on Information Systems (ICIS)*, Milan, Italy.

Xu, K., Li, J., Lau, R. Y. K., Liao, S. S., & Fang, B. (2011). An effective method of discovering target groups on social networking sites. *Proceedings of the 32nd International Conference on Information Systems (ICIS)*, Shanghai, China, paper 11.

Xu, Y., Guo, X., Hao, J., Ma, J., Lau, R. Y. K., & Xu, W. (2012). Combining social network and semantic concept analysis for personalized academic researcher recommendation. *Decision Support Systems, 54*(1), 564-573.

Xu, Y., Lu, X., Goh, K. Y., Jiang, Z., & Zhu, X. (2009). The impact of online social network on customer loyalty: an empirical study of an online dining community. *Proceedings of the 30th International Conference on Information Systems (ICIS)*, Phoenix, USA, paper 17.

Yang, J., Wen, Z., Adamic, L. A., Ackerman, M. S., & Lin, C. Y. (2011). Collaborating globally: culture and organizational computer-animated communication. *Proceedings of the 32nd International Conference on Information Systems (ICIS)*, Shanghai, China.

Yao, J. T. (2006). Supporting Research with Weblogs: A study on web-based research support systems. *The 3rd international workshop on web-based research support systems, HongKong, China*, 161-164.

Yao, J. T., & Yao, Y. Y. (2003). Web-based Information Retrieval Support Systems: Building research tools for scientists in the new information age, Proceedings of the IEEE/WIC International Conference on Web Intelligence, Halifax, Canada, 570-573.

Yao, Y. Y. (2003). A framework for web-based research support systems. *Proceedings of the 27th Annual International Computer Software and Applications Conference, Dallas, USA: IEEE Computer Society*. 601-606.

Yardi, S., Golder, S. A., & Brzozowski, M. J. (2009). Blogging at work and the corporate attention economy. *Proceedings of the SIGCHI Conference on Human Factors in Computing Systems*, 2071-2080.

Yates, D., & Paquette, S. (2016). The Impact of Key Words on Knowledge Reuse in Emergency Management Social Media. *AMCIS 2016 Proceedings*.

Yeh, N. C., Lin, J., & Lu, H. P. (2012). Exploring users' behavioral model in Web 2.0 applications – the moderating effects of hedonic versus utilitarian motivations. *Proceedings of the 18th Americas Conference on Information Systems (AMCIS)*, Seattle, USA, paper 3.

Yin, R. (2013). *Case study research: Design and methods*. Sage publications.

Yin, G., Cheng, X., & Zhu, L. (2011). Understanding continuance usage of social networking services: a theoretical model and empirical study of the Chinese context. *Proceedings of the 32nd International Conference on Information Systems (ICIS)*, Shanghai, China.

Ynalvez, M. A., & Shrum, W. M. (2011). Professional networks, scientific collaboration, and publication productivity in resource-restrained institutions in a developing country. *Research Policy, 40*(2), 204-216.

Yu, A. Y., & Tian, S. W. (2010). Embedded social learning in online social networking. *Proceedings of the 31st International Conference on Information Systems (ICIS)*, St. Louis, USA, paper 100.

Yu, J., Hu, P. J. H., & Cheng, T. H. (2015). Role of affect in self-disclosure on social network websites: A test of two competing models. *Journal of Management Information Systems, 32*(2), 239-277.

Zafeiropoulou, S., Sarker, S., & Carlsson, S. A. (2015). What's trending in social media analytics area? A retrospective. In *21st Americas Conference on Information Systems, AMCIS 2015*. Department of Informatics, Lund University, School of Economics and Management, Sweden: Americas Conference on Information Systems.

Zaman, M. (2010). Doctoral programs in the age of research 2.0. In *e-Research Collaboration* (pp. 233-246). Springer Berlin Heidelberg.

Zhang, B., Krackhardt, D., Krishnan, R., & Doreian, P. (2011). An effective and efficient subpopulation extraction method in large social networks. *Proceedings of the 32nd International Conference on Information Systems (ICIS)*, Shanghai, China, 447-493.

Zhang, K. Z. K., Lee, M. K. O., Cheung, C. M. K., & Chen, H. (2009). Understanding the role of gender in bloggers' switching behavior. *Decision Support Systems, 47*(4), 540-546.

Zhang, N., Wang, C., & Xu, Y. (2011). Privacy on online social networks. *Proceedings of the 32nd International Conference on Information Systems (ICIS)*, Shanghai, China, 2252-2272.

Zhang, X., & Olfman, L. (2010). Using blogs to support constructivist and social learning – a case study in a university setting. *Proceedings of the 16th Americas Conference on Information Systems (AMCIS)*, Lima, Peru, paper 564.

Zhang, X., Qu, Y., Giles, C. L., & Song, P. (2008). CiteSense: supporting sensemaking of research literature. *Proceedings of the SIGCHI Conference on Human Factors in Computing Systems*, Florence, Italy.

Zhang, Y., Fang, Y., & He, W. (2011). Wiki-induced cognitive elaboration in project teams: an empirical study. *Proceedings of the 32nd International Conference on Information Systems (ICIS)*, Shanghai, China, paper 8.

Zhang, S., Yu, L., Wakefield, R. L., & Leidner, D. E. (2016). Friend or Foe: Cyberbullying in Social Network Sites. *ACM SIGMIS Database, 47*(1), 51-71.

Zhang, K. Z., & Benyoucef, M. (2016). Consumer behavior in social commerce: A literature review. *Decision Support Systems, 86*, 95-108.

Zhao, Y., & Srite, M. (2013). Modeling online social network use: incorporating espoused national cultural values into an extended unified theory of acceptance and use of technology. *Proceedings of the 34th International Conference on Information Systems (ICIS)*, Milan, Italy.

Zheng, Y., & Yu, A. (2014). Social media, institutional innovation and affordances: The case of free lunch for children in China. *Icis*, 1–15.

Zhou, Y. (2009). Are you finding the right person? A name translation system towards Web 2.0. *Proceedings of the 30th International Conference on Information Systems (ICIS)*, Phoenix, USA, paper 18.

Zhou, M. J., Qiao, Z., Zhang, X., Du, Q., Wang, A. G., & Fan, W. (Patrick). (2015). Do Facebook Activities Increase Sales ? In *Americas Conference on Information Systems* (pp. 1–8).

Zhu, B., Watts, S., & Chen, H. (2010). Visualizing social networks concepts. *Decision Support Systems*, 49(2), 151-161.

Zimbra, D., & Fu, T. (2009). Assessing public opinions through Web 2.0: a case study on Wal-Mart. *Proceedings of the 30th International Conference on Information Systems (ICIS)*, Phoenix, USA, paper 67.

Appendix

J.-H. Soeldner, *Understanding Social Research Networking Sites*,
Markt- und Unternehmensentwicklung Markets and Organisations,
https://doi.org/10.1007/978-3-658-31575-7

1 Appendix A: Interview Guideline for Part III

Friedrich-Alexander-Universität
Erlangen-Nürnberg

Lehrstuhl für Betriebswirtschaftslehre,
insbes. industrielle Informationssysteme

Lange Gasse 20 · 90403 Nürnberg · Germany
Phone: +49 911 5302 262
Fax: +49 911 5302 155
Mail: jens.soeldner@wiso.uni-erlangen.de

Social Research Network Sites

Interview Guide

1. **General Information**

Interviewee	Company	Site
- First and last name - Education background - Professional experience (researcher? academic career?) - Position in the company (since when?, history, department) - Responsibilities/ role during the product development process	- Name - Industry/vertial (only relevant, if there are further products) - Product and service portfolio - number of employees - Turnover and profit (if possible) - Legal status of company (limited etc.)	- Background - Actors and motives - Functionalities - Target group / audience - Date of launch - Fees / costs for usage

2. **Questions about the site**

Our intention and objective is to generate a better understanding of previously understudied field of social research network sites (SRNS). As SRNS we understand web services supporting the collaboration and networking processes of researchers.

Topic	Questions
Vision: Initial idea	- What prompted you to develop your SRNS? - What was your goal with the SRNS? What did you want to achieve?
Initiative: process and organization of SRNS development	- Who were the main drivers / initators of the SRNS? - What motives and goals played a role in that process? - What were the objectives? Have the objectives changed? - What was the perceived gap in the market you wanted to close?
Target Group / Audience	- Who is the intended audience of the SRNS and why (specific disciplines, geographical background, language, age, career level)? - What target groups / audiences and stakeholders have been identified? (e.g. different users, administrators) a. Current usage statistics / status quo (how many researchers are using the platform, how many inactive users, how many single visits?

Figure 45: Interview Guideline for part III, page 1

	b. Acceptance of functionalities (differentiate between: ex ante survey, ex ante determination WITHOUT survey) c. Intended disciplinary audiences (exclusive/ broad range) d. Career level of users (student, undergraduate, graduate students, postdoc, professor; public vs. private researchers (researchers from government/industry/academia); gender structure; age structure; regional distribution; different cultural backgrounds) - What were expectations regarding IT and web affinity of the users (familiarity with web 2.0 applications etc.)?
Environment: Market of SRNS	- What is the structure of your market like? Which market players and main competitors do you see? - What differences do you see between the market players? - What developments do you expect in the near future? - What do you see as your own USP?
Sales and Marketing: Mncreasing acceptance and diffusion of the SRNS	- What forms of marketing are being used? - Were certain target groups already being addressed during the development? - Are the registered users actually identical with the intended audience?
Functionality:	- What functionalities do you offer? - Do you offer functionalities that support users in their research processes (e.g. during idea generation, literature search, data analysis etc.)? What are the most important functionalites?
Intermediaries: Development of the SRNS	- What were distinct steps you had to go through in the development process between ideation and completion of the platform? - Did you use support from third parties for design and development of the SRNS? If yes, why and how?
Development Process: Determination of functionalities and implementation of the idea	- Requirements analysis of functionalities: What were your expectations regarding users' expectations of functionalities? - How did you determine those (e.g. experience-based, surveys, etc.)? Did you first conduct a requirements analysis among (potential) users? - How were requirement catalogues developed? What methods were used during their development (e.g. interviews with stakeholders, online survey of users, etc.)? - Were members of the target audience involved in the development of the SRNS? If yes, how did you involve these members (= what methodologies, e.g. interviews, observations what users are doing; when were users involved – e.g. during requirement analysis, evaluation, iteratively?) Why was the target audience involved, what did you expect by the involvement (e.g. higher productivity, higher acceptance, less errors during development)? How many members per target audience were involved? - Development guide: How were the final functionalities selected? - How did you select the the requirements which were finally included (e.g. survey more important than theoretical analysis)?
Feedback: Managing the user feedback process	- How is the continuous development of the SRNS implemented (selection of new and deactivation of old functionalities)?

Figure 46: Interview Guideline for part III, page 2

	- How are functionalities rated (e.g. tracking)? - Does user feedback play a significant role? - If yes, how is it collected and used?
Problems: Challenges and barriers in the continuous development of the SRNS	- Were there any surprises after the launch of the platform (negative/positive)? - Dooes the number of users and the features that are actually used match the expectations? - Were there law-related questions and problems (e.g. privacy concerns)? - How is the current market situation?
Future: Expectations and plans	- Are you content with the state of your SRNS and could you fulfill your expectations / goals? - What are your immediate plans? Can you tell us about your next milestones? - What steps do you plan to take next? What features are currently under development? - Are you going to address broader target audiences or rather a more radical specialization? - How do you expect your product to be at the end of 2010? - What would you do in a different way?
Users	- Could you imagine to conduct a user survey regarding functionalities and usage patterns together with us?

Figure 47: Interview Guideline for part III, page 3

2 Appendix B: Interview Guideline for Part IV

2.1 General information

- First and last name
- Education background
- Academic position (PhD student, PostDoc, Professor)
- Academic experience (since when active in academia? history?)
- SRNS Platforms used, since when
- What other research-related platforms are known
- Are other platforms used (non-SRNS) for research-related activities

2.2 Usage Patterns, Uses and Gratifications

- Per platform mentioned in 2.1, usage patterns as well as uses and gratifications are explored
    - Since when do you use the platform?
    - What prompted you to join or use the platform?
    - How often is the platform used?
    - What exactly is done within the platform?
    - What functionalities do you use?
    - What do you like or dislike about the platform? What could be better?
    - Is the platform used for collaboration?
    - Was collaboration ever initiated within the platform?
    - What drives the platform usage (exploration of uses and gratifications along the lines of the UGT theory and SI processes framework)
    - Do you have any concerns about the platforms, e.g. openness or lack thereof, privacy, information security?
    - If the platform use has been discontinued, why has it been discontinued?
- Other information that might be helpful for the goals of the study (explained at the beginning of the interview)

The manufacturer's authorised representative in the EU is Springer Nature Customer Service Centre GmbH, Europaplatz 3, 69115 Heidelberg, Germany. If you have any concerns regarding our products, please contact ProductSafety@springernature.com

Printed and bound by CPI Group (UK) Ltd, Croydon, CR0 4YY
30/09/2026
02225659-0002